Evidence: Law and Practice

Evidence:
Law and Practice

Third Edition

Eric Cowsill

Solicitor

John Clegg

Solicitor
Senior Lecturer at The College of Law

LONGMAN

© Longman Group UK Ltd 1990

Reprinted 1991

ISBN 0 85121 674 9

Published by
Longman Law, Tax and Finance
Longman Group UK Ltd
21–27 Lamb's Conduit Street, London WC1N 3NJ

Associated offices
Australia, Hong Kong, Malaysia, Singapore, USA

A CIP catalogue record for this book is available from
the British Library.

Printed and bound in Great Britain by
Biddles Ltd, Guildford and King's Lynn

Contents

Part III: Case Studies

Part IV: Evidence in the Police Station

Preface

The law of evidence is inextricably bound up with the rules which regulate the conduct of proceedings in the courts. We hope that this book will have achieved its object of discussing the law of evidence in a practical context. It is our belief that this is the approach which will most assist the busy practitioner in his endeavours to come to terms with this difficult subject.

The book is divided into three parts. The first part of the book deals with the general problems of determining what has to be proved at the trial, who has to prove a matter which is in issue between the parties, and the means by which such matters may be proved.

In the second part of the book we turn our attention to questions of admissibility. The problem now is whether an item of evidence may be introduced at the trial and, if so, what the court is entitled to deduce from it.

Throughout these first two parts there are numerous examples, some taken from the facts of decided cases, others wholly fictitious, which we hope will serve to illustrate the points made in the text.

The third part of the book presents three case studies. These show evidential points arising in a practical context. Annotations to the case studies refer the reader to those sections in the text in which he will find discussion of the evidential points raised by the case studies. The implementation of the Police and Criminal Evidence Act 1984 has resulted in an almost nationwide twenty-four hour duty solicitor scheme to advise suspects held in police custody. We have therefore included a self-contained section dealing with the evidential implications of such advice.

In this third edition we have resisted, where possible, the temptation to expand the subject matter, preferring to keep in mind our original aim, namely to produce a work dealing with the general principles of evidence in practice.

Areas of the law of evidence which have been affected by recent developments include the treatment of the evidence of children and the admissibility of documentary evidence in criminal cases (Criminal Justice Act 1988). There has been a considerable volume of case law on the exercise of the court's discretion to exclude evidence under the Police and Criminal Evidence Act 1984 s 78 particularly in cases in which the accused has been denied rights under the Act (eg right of access to a solicitor) or the Codes of Practice have not been properly adhered to (eg with regard to identification procedures). The operation of the Police and Criminal Evidence Act 1984, s 74, has fallen to be considered in a number of cases and the principles of admissibility are now emerging. These developments are amongst those covered in this new edition.

We have endeavoured to state the law as at 1 February 1990

February 1990   *JC*
                                                                   EJC

Table of Cases

xiii

Table of Statutes

Table of Statutory Instruments

Part 1

Preliminary Points of Evidence

Chapter 1

Burdens and Standards of Proof

Burdens of Proof

The rules of evidence and procedure regulate the manner in which the parties to any proceedings may seek to prove or disprove any matter which is in dispute between them. Before considering those rules there is an important preliminary question to be answered: on which party does the burden of proof rest?

Example
Alan is charged with handling stolen goods. The facts are that a quantity of video recorders have been stolen from a local warehouse and the police find them in Alan's garage. Alan's defence is that someone must have put the goods in his garage without his knowledge when he was out for the day.

Must Alan prove his innocence or is it for the prosecution to prove his guilt? Can Alan be required to give an explanation?

Example
Bill is involved in a road accident and as a result is sued by Joe for damages for negligence.

Must Joe prove that Bill was negligent or is Bill required to explain the accident and prove that he was not?

Questions concerned with the incidence of the burden of proof are determined by substantive law, rather than by rules of evidence. Whilst there are practical and procedural consequences which may follow from the answer given, the question becomes crucial in cases where the court is unable to decide whether one or more of the issues of fact has been proved to the required standard. Whilst it is the function of the tribunal of fact to resolve those issues, it is inevitable that there will be occasions when it cannot. For example, it may be unable to choose between the conflicting evidence adduced by the parties to a civil action.

The proceedings cannot remain inconclusive. The parties are entitled to a decision. In such circumstances, it is said that the party bearing the burden of proof of that issue has failed to discharge that burden to the requisite standard and the issue is therefore decided against him, often with the result that his case fails in its entirety.

Whilst the incidence of the burden of proof must be determined by reference to substantive law, some general points may be made and these are considered in the following sections. It will be seen in particular that the rules differ between civil and criminal cases.

1.1 Criminal cases

(a) The legal burden of proof

The general rule is that the legal burden of proof is on the prosecution (*Woolmington* v *DPP* [1935] AC 462). This means that they are required to prove every fact in issue in the case if they are to secure a conviction.

Thus in Alan's case, discussed above, the prosecution are required to prove all of the elements of the offence of handling to the satisfaction of the jury or justices. If they fail to do this then Alan is entitled to be acquitted. Therefore, the prosecution will have to adduce evidence to satisfy the court that:

(1) The goods are stolen. This they could do, for example, by proving the conviction of the thief (see the Police and Criminal Evidence Act 1984, s 74(1) and **7.6**).

(2) Alan handled the goods in one of the ways specified by the Theft Act 1968, s 22. This they could do, for example, by calling the police officer who found the goods on Alan's premises or by calling the thief who allegedly passed them on to Alan.

(3) Alan acted dishonestly and knowing or believing that the goods were stolen. Again this could come from evidence from the thief.

(b) Exceptions to the general rule

Having established the general rule, there are a number of exceptions to be considered. These are the common law defence of insanity and those cases where statute places the legal burden of proof on the accused.

If an accused wishes to allege that he is not guilty of an offence by reason of insanity then the defence have the legal burden of proving the fact of insanity (see *M'Naghten's Case* (1843) 10 Cl & F 200). This is not a situation that is encountered very often for the obvious reason that if accepted by the court, it will be followed by an indefinite period of 'hospitalisation'.

Some statutes specifically provide that the defence have the legal burden of proving a fact, an example being the Homicide Act 1957, s 2(2), relating to diminished responsibility. Again, if a statute makes it a criminal offence to do a specified act unless it is done by a person with a particular qualification or with the licence or permission of a particular authority, a defendant relying on such an exemption has the legal burden of proving it. The authority for this is derived from the Magistrates' Courts Act 1980, s 101 in summary proceedings and from *R* v *Edwards* [1975] QB 27 in the Crown Court.

Example
The Road Traffic Act 1972, s 84, makes it an offence for a person to drive a motor vehicle if he is not the holder of a licence to do so. This is an offence where the prosecution have the legal burden of proving that the accused drove a vehicle and the accused then has the legal burden of proving that he held a licence to do so.

Example
The Licensing Act 1964, s 160(1), makes it an offence to sell intoxicating liquor without a justices' licence. Again the statute prohibits a certain act unless it is done by a person licensed by a particular authority. The prosecution, therefore, have the legal burden of proving that alcohol was sold and the accused has the legal burden of proving that he held a licence. (*R* v *Edwards*)

Example
Fred is charged with careless driving. The offence includes a person driving a motor vehicle without due care and attention. This is an offence where the legal burden of proof is solely on the prosecution; it is not for Fred to prove that he drove with due care and attention. In this case statute does not make it an offence to drive a vehicle unless it is by a person using due care and attention. It makes it an offence to drive a motor vehicle in a particular manner.

The test to be applied if the prosecution are seeking to rely on this exception to the general rule is to look at the statute creating the offence. If the statute makes it an offence to do a particular act and then goes on to give certain qualifications that will excuse liability then it is likely that the defence will have a legal burden of proof.

(c) *The evidential burden*

Imagine that the horizontal line below represents the progress of a criminal trial in the Crown Court where the judge determines questions of law and the jury questions of fact. Subject to the exceptional cases just discussed it has been established that the legal burden of proof stays with the prosecution throughout the case.

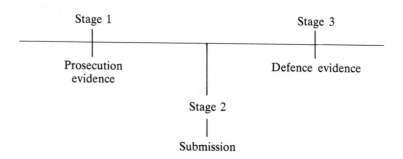

As the prosecution have the legal burden of proof they will begin the case (stage 1) by calling their evidence. When the prosecution case has been completed the defence have a number of options open to them. They can, if appropriate, contend that the prosecution have failed to adduce sufficient evidence to justify a finding in the prosecution's favour by the jury. If the defence feel that this is the appropriate course of action to take they are submitting that the prosecution have failed to satisfy what is sometimes called the evidential burden. In practice this is known as submitting no case to answer (stage 2). The trial judge will decide whether the submission is to succeed. If he agrees with the defence then he will not allow the prosecution evidence to go to the jury. The prosecution have failed to satisfy the evidential burden and therefore have failed to discharge the legal burden of proof.

This principle can be illustrated by returning to Alan's case of handling stolen goods. To satisfy the evidential burden the prosecution are required to adduce sufficient evidence to justify the jury in finding that Alan did handle stolen goods. Imagine that the prosecution fail to adduce any evidence to prove that the video recorders were stolen. The defence will obviously submit that the prosecution have not satisfied their evidential burden. If this contention is upheld by the judge then the accused will be acquitted. In failing to satisfy the evidential burden the prosecution must inevitably fail to satisfy the legal burden of proof.

Of course in the majority of cases the prosecution will be able to satisfy the evidential burden. However, and this is the point that must be grasped, this does not mean that the legal burden of proof has also been satisfied. All that it means is that the judge is prepared to let the evidence go before the jury when they come to decide at the end of the case whether or not the legal burden of proof is satisfied. The jury may decide at the end of the case that they do not believe the evidence and thus the legal burden of proof is not discharged. (This introduces one of the most important practical considerations of evidence—namely that evidence even if admissible is worthless if the court are not going to believe it (see further Chapter 4).)

Example
Bill is charged with assaulting George thereby causing actual bodily harm contrary to the Offences Against the Person Act 1861, s 47. The legal burden of proof is on the prosecution. At stage 1 of the trial they also have the evidential burden. Their evidence consists of oral testimony from George and a supporting witness who tell the court how Bill, during the course of an argument with George, punched George in the face and gave him a black eye.

In adducing this evidence, normally the prosecution will have satisfied the evidential burden (as to the exceptional case when it may be contested that they have not, see head (*d*) below). Remember they have not yet satisfied the legal burden of proof. The evidential burden will then move to Bill (stage 3). This does not mean that Bill must adduce any evidence. He can simply hope that the jury will not believe the prosecution evidence and acquit him. However, normally this is a very dangerous course for an accused to follow and evidence will be called in his defence. Having heard all of the evidence the jury must decide whether the prosecution have satisfied the legal burden of proof. This will depend on whose evidence they believe. If there is a certain degree of doubt as to which evidence to accept, then Bill is entitled to be acquitted.

The examples given show that the legal burden of proof normally does not move. It stays with the prosecution throughout. The evidential burden, however, can move from prosecution to defence. The prosecution must satisfy the evidential burden if they are to have any chance of success. If they do satisfy the evidential burden it moves to the defence. The defence are not obliged to adduce any evidence but the prospects of an acquittal will be considerably enhanced if they do so.

Having established the difference between a legal burden and an evidential burden, it is necessary to develop the concept of the defence's evidential burden. It has been established that when the evidential burden moves to the defence, it is up to them whether to call any evidence. There are, however, two situations when the evidential burden has moved to the defence that virtually demand defence evidence if there is going to be any chance of an acquittal. These are when the accused wishes to rely on certain specific defences to a charge or where there is a presumption or inference raised against him.

If an accused wishes to rely on a *specific defence* to a charge as opposed to a general denial then, if he wants the jury to take this defence into account when deciding whether the legal burden of proof has been satisfied, he must adduce some evidence in support of it. In other words the accused cannot say to the judge at the end of stage 1 of a trial that the prosecution have failed to satisfy their evidential burden because they have not disproved every specific defence that could be available on that particular charge. The accused is required to adduce some evidence to raise that defence as a possibility in the instant case. Having done this his evidential burden is satisfied. The judge will direct the jury that they should convict only if satisfied that the prosecution have by their evidence disproved the defence raised. This principle can be illustrated by returning to the case of Bill, charged with assaulting George. If Bill wishes to rely on a defence of self-defence he must adduce some evidence to support his claims (*R* v *Lobell* [1957] 1 QB 547). He cannot at the end of the prosecution case simply claim that they have failed to satisfy the evidential burden because they have not adduced evidence to disprove self-defence. Once the defence evidence is adduced the evidential burden is satisfied. The jury must now ask themselves whether on all of the evidence before them there is a certain degree of doubt that the prosecution have made out their case. A verdict of guilty should only be returned if the jury are satisfied that Bill was not acting in self-defence. Apart from self-defence, other defences to which this principle applies include duress (*R* v *Gill* [1963] 1 WLR 841), provocation (*Mancini* v *DPP* [1942] AC 1), mechanical defect as a reason for an accident rather than careless driving (*R* v *Spurge* [1961] 2 QB 205), and privacy, consent or exempted age as an answer to a charge of buggery or indecency between men (*R* v *Spight* [1986] Crim LR 817).

Certain situations will raise a *presumption of law* or *inference of fact* against a defendant. This means that unless the defendant adduces some contrary evidence the jury in some cases must, and in others are entitled to, find in favour of the prosecution on a particular fact in issue. These presumptions and inferences and their effect are fully discussed in Chapter 2. Examples include the presumptions of regularity, marriage and death and inferences of continuance and recent possession.

Everything discussed so far under the heading of evidential burden applies equally to a magistrates' court. The only difference is that as the justices have to decide questions of law and fact they must deal with the submission of no case to answer. Faced with such a submission the justices should ask themselves, not whether they believe the evidence that they have heard but whether it is sufficient to justify a conviction, if at the end of the case they decide to believe it. In practice it must be accepted that such feats of mental gymnastics are difficult to perform.

(*d*) Practical considerations

When considering the burden of proof in a practical context, a number of points are worthy of mention. These are:

(1) Consideration of the charge and the evidence required to prove it.
(2) When to make a submission of no case to answer.
(3) Specific defences and the evidential burden.
(4) Rebutting evidence.

Whether acting for prosecution or defence, a useful practice in preparing a case is to make a list of the *essential elements of the offence charged and of any defence and the evidence available to prove each element*. From a prosecution point of view this will provide a checklist designed to avoid the embarrassment of losing a case through failure to adduce evidence to prove a vital element of the offence. For the defence, if this note is kept as a checklist during the trial and used as the prosecution case progresses, it is fairly easy to see when a submission of no case to answer is appropriate.

The circumstances in which a *submission of no case to answer* should be made in a magistrates' court are when there has been no evidence to prove an essential element in the alleged offence or when the evidence adduced by the prosecution has been so discredited as a result of cross-examination or is so unreliable that no reasonable tribunal could safely convict on it. In the Crown Court a judge should direct the jury to acquit if there is no evidence that the crime alleged has been committed by the defendant or the prosecution evidence taken at its highest is such that no jury properly directed could properly convict on it (*R* v *Galbraith* (1981) 73 Cr App R 124).

Although the defence will normally adduce their own evidence in support of a *specific defence*, and thereby set the prosecution the task of disproving it, it is possible for this evidence to be elicited from prosecution witnesses during cross-examination by the defence. If that be the case this should be sufficient to satisfy the evidential burden on the defence and the judge in summing up should instruct the jury that it is for the prosecution to disprove the defence. In practice, however, the defence will usually want to call evidence to further strengthen their case.

Where the defendant has raised a specific defence to a charge the prosecution may, in the discretion of the court, adduce *rebutting evidence* to disprove that defence (see *R* v *Milliken* (1969) 53 Cr App R 330). This will not always be necessary in practice as often the evidence called by the prosecution to satisfy their evidential burden will suffice. However, if they are taken by surprise by a defence then an application can be made to call rebutting evidence.

1.2 Civil cases

(a) The legal burden of proof

In civil cases the legal burden of proof can often be split between plaintiff and defendant. The general rule is that a party who asserts a fact must prove it. In simple cases this does not give rise to any problem. Who is asserting a fact and who is denying it will be obvious from the substantive law and the pleadings in the case (as to which see head (c) below).

Example
Joe sues Arnold for damages for negligence. Joe claims that Arnold left his car parked in a dangerous position on an unlit road and as a result Joe ran into the car. Arnold denies that he was negligent, claiming that he took all reasonable precautions.

In this example Joe is asserting the facts in issue. As part of his negligence claim he must prove that Arnold broke his duty of care owed to other road users. By his defence Arnold is denying a breach of that duty. Therefore the legal burden of proof is on Joe.

Example
Ernie buys a television set from Fixit Stores. He sues them for damages claiming that the goods are defective. The store deny this.

Ernie is asserting the facts in issue. As part of his breach of contract claim he must prove that he was supplied with defective goods. Therefore the legal burden of proof is on Ernie.

However, the legal burden of proof will not always be determined that easily. In the first example imagine that Arnold, apart from claiming that he took all reasonable precautions, actually alleges that Joe was contributorily negligent. The legal burden of proving this will fall on Arnold. He is not now simply denying something which Joe, as a requirement of proving his case would have had to deal with, he is raising a new issue. In the second example imagine that Fixit Stores, rather than denying that the goods were defective, allege that they specifically pointed out the defects to Ernie. The legal burden of proving this will fall on Fixit Stores as they are introducing a new issue into the matter.

As in criminal cases some statutes expressly reverse the general rule on the legal burden of proof. One such statute is the Civil Evidence Act 1968, s 11.

Example
Alan sues Bill for damages for personal injuries after a road accident. Bill has been convicted of careless driving.

Subject to certain procedural requirements (see **8.1**) once Alan has adduced evidence that Bill has been convicted (normally by producing a certificate of conviction), Bill will be taken to have committed the offence until the contrary is proved. Thus if Bill wishes to dispute the conviction the legal burden of proof is placed on him by statute. This is of course an exception to the general rule as to the incidence of the burden of proof by which Alan would have been required to prove the conviction if it was denied.

In certain situations a presumption of law will come into operation having the effect of providing that a fact will be presumed in favour of a party and that the opponent has the legal burden of proving the contrary. These presumptions are fully discussed in Chapter 2. Examples are the presumption of legitimacy and the presumption of marriage.

(b) The evidential burden

As in criminal cases the party with the legal burden of proof also initially has the evidential burden. The case of Ernie and Fixit Stores referred to earlier can be used to illustrate the principle. Ernie has the legal burden of proof and therefore initially the evidential burden. At the close of the plaintiff's case there must be sufficient evidence before the judge to justify a finding in Ernie's favour. If Ernie has not satisfied this evidential burden then the defendant Fixit Stores can submit that there is no case to answer. (This is unusual in civil cases—see head (c) below.) Assuming, however, that the plaintiff satisfies his evidential burden it then moves to the defence. There is no rule compelling the defence to give evidence but of course their chances of success are not great if they fail to do so. If they do adduce evidence that the goods were not defective then the judge must take all of the evidence into account and decide whether or not the plaintiff has satisfied the legal burden of proof. If he is undecided which version of events to accept then the plaintiff will fail as he bears the legal burden of proof.

It has been seen above that some presumptions of law effectively place the legal burden of proof on a party. There are other presumptions and inferences that do not affect the legal burden of proof but place an evidential burden on the defendant in as much as if he does not adduce some evidence in rebuttal the court is entitled to find or infer a fact or facts against him. Again, these are further discussed in Chapter 2. Examples include presumptions of regularity, death, the inference of continuance and probably the doctrine of res ipsa loquitur.

(c) Practical considerations

Most actions in the Queen's Bench Division and the county court will have *pleadings* (see RSC Ord 18 and CCR Ord 9). The object of the pleadings is to enable the parties to set out the material facts on which they intend to rely. By looking at the pleadings it is possible clearly to identify the issues between the parties and in many cases who has the legal burden of proof.

If a defendant feels that the plaintiff has failed to satisfy the evidential burden he is entitled to make a *submission of no case to answer.* If this submission succeeds then the plaintiff has of course also failed to satisfy the legal burden of proof and has lost the case. However such a submission is unusual in civil cases because if it fails the judge will usually not allow the defendant to call any evidence. Therefore unless it is very clear that there is no case to answer it is better to adduce defence evidence and let the judge weigh up all of the evidence before him and decide at the end of the case whether the legal burden of proof is satisfied.

STANDARDS OF PROOF

1.3 Criminal cases

When the jury in the Crown Court or the justices are deciding at the end of the case whether or not the legal burden of proof has been satisfied what standard of proof must they look for? This depends on who has the legal burden of proof.

(a) The prosecution

The proof required of the prosecution is proof beyond all reasonable doubt. In explaining this to a jury and 'reminding' the justices, many judges and advocates will say that they must be sure of the guilt of the accused. This is one explanation that has been approved (*Walters* v *R* [1969] 2 AC 26 at 30). For a full list of explanations that have met with judicial approval and otherwise see Archbold, *Criminal Pleading, Evidence and Practice*, 43rd ed (Sweet & Maxwell 1988), paras 4–426—4–429.

(b) The defence

If the legal burden of proving a fact is on the defence the proof required is proof on a balance of probabilities, which can be explained as 'more probable than not' (see *R* v *Carr-Briant* [1943] KB 607 and *Miller* v *Minister of Pensions* [1947] 2 All ER 372).

If the defence bear an evidential burden then it is wrong to talk of a standard of proof. The requirement is simply to adduce enough evidence to allow the jury or justices to take the defence into account when deciding whether the legal burden of proof has been satisfied by the prosecution. If the evidence is sufficient to raise a reasonable doubt in the minds of jury or justices then the accused should be acquitted.

1.4 Civil cases

The party bearing the legal burden of proving a fact in issue in a civil case is required to prove it on a balance of probabilities. As with criminal cases where the legal burden of proof is on the defence this means that 'if the evidence is such that the tribunal can say "we think it more probable than not," the burden is discharged, but, if the probabilities are equal, it is not' (per Denning J in *Miller* v *Minister of Pensions* [1947] 2 All ER 372 at 374).

Chapter 2

Proof by Evidence

Having examined the question of where the legal burden of proof of any of the facts in issue will lie, it is clear that the party bearing the burden of proof will generally be required to adduce evidence to support the allegation he is making. It is important to decide what facts are in issue in the proceedings and to determine what evidence is available to establish such facts. This may be the evidence of a witness who has perceived the fact in issue or perhaps the evidence of a witness who has perceived other facts from which the fact in issue can be inferred. The former type of evidence could be termed direct and the latter circumstantial evidence. As to methods of proof see generally Chapter 4.

2.1 The facts in issue

(a) Criminal cases

In a criminal case the facts in issue are determined by reference to the charge and the substantive law. It is generally for the prosecution to prove all the facts in issue but subject to the exceptions in Chapter 1. If a fact is formally admitted then it is no longer in issue. In such circumstances evidence is neither necessary nor receivable as to the fact admitted. It is important to distinguish between formal admissions discussed here and informal admissions (confessions) which will be considered in Chapter 12. The requirements as to the manner in which formal admissions can be made should make it easy to differentiate between such admissions and the informal admissions (confessions) which may be found in unguarded statements made by a party when, for example, being questioned by police.

Practical considerations: How is a formal admission made for the purposes of a criminal case? Such an admission may be made only in the manner prescribed by the Criminal Justice Act 1967, s 10. The admission may be made in court. If made otherwise than in court it must be in writing signed by the person making it. A safeguard is provided for an individual who is a party to criminal proceedings in that any formal admission must be either made on his behalf by or approved by his solicitor or counsel.

A formal admission made in accordance with the provisions of s 10 is binding for the purposes of the proceedings in respect of which it is made and may be withdrawn only with leave of the court. It is worth noting here that the plea of 'guilty' to a criminal charge admits the offence but not the truth of the statement of facts read by the prosecutor or the contents of any depositions. The offender may wish to challenge such matters when putting forward his plea in mitigation.

(b) Civil cases

In civil proceedings the facts in issue are determined by reference to the pleadings (or in cases without pleadings by reference to the substantive law). Generally a party asserting a fact is required to prove that fact (see Chapter 1). A party is required to plead all the material facts upon which he relies. In a High Court case he will be precluded from relying upon any matters which he has not pleaded (RSC Ord 18). This strict rule does not prevent a litigant in the county court from raising issues at the trial which are not dealt with in his pleadings.

Example
Steve is bringing an action against Bernard for the price of goods sold and delivered. He pleads the contract for the sale, the delivery of the goods and his claim to the price. Bernard serves a defence alleging that goods which were delivered did not conform with the contract.

In a High Court case Bernard could not seek to establish at the trial that there was no contract or that no goods were delivered as these are allegations which he has not pleaded.

In civil cases just as in criminal cases the parties may make formal admissions for the purposes of the proceedings in respect of which the admission is made. Again the effect of the admission is that the fact admitted is no longer in issue and evidence as to that matter is neither necessary nor receivable. Again the requirements as to the manner in which such admissions should be made will make it an easy matter to distinguish between such admissions and informal admissions such as that made by the driver of a motor vehicle immediately after an accident in which he has been involved when he may say, 'I'm sorry, it was my fault, I wasn't looking'.

Practical considerations: There are a number of ways in which a formal admission may be made for the purposes of civil proceedings.

The most usual means adopted is to make the admission *in the* *pleadings*. In the example given above the effect of Bernard's failure to plead a matter is that he is precluded from adducing evidence on the point and he is taken to have admitted such facts as are alleged in the statement of claim and have not been specifically denied in his defence. This shows an admission made by inadvertence which is binding as a formal admission in the same way as if Bernard had expressly stated in his defence that he admitted the existence of the contract and its terms and that (some) delivery had been made. As to the subject of implied admissions in pleadings see further RSC Ord 18, r 13. There is no corresponding provision in the County Court Rules (see J O'Hare and R N Hill, *Civil Litigation*, 4th ed (Longman 1986), 175). Apart from inadvertence a party may positively decide to make an admission in the course of his pleading. This will reduce the length of the trial and reduce the costs of the case as the opponent will be saved the trouble and expense of proving the fact at the trial. The effect then of such an admission is to narrow and perhaps clarify the issues to be settled at the trial. Returning once more to the example given above, Bernard may admit all the matters alleged by Steve and plead that Steve is in breach of a term of the contract in that the goods delivered were defective. By making those admissions he has reduced the facts in issue to the question of whether the goods were or were not defective, and evidence will only be required on this point. It is clearly not necessary nor even desirable to dispute every allegation made by the other party and it is appropriate to make such admissions in order to reduce the complexity and costs of the proceedings.

If it is decided that it would be expedient to make formal admissions then there are other ways in which the same object can be achieved and which save the necessity of amending pleadings at a later stage. An admission may be made pursuant to RSC Ord 27, r 1 (CCR Ord 20, r 1). The admission is made *by notice in writing* to the other party. A formal document may be prepared but a letter is sufficient if the intention is clear. Rules of the

Supreme Court, Ord 27, r 2 (CCR Ord 20, r 2) provides for a party to bring pressure upon an opponent to admit a fact which is in issue in the proceedings. *A notice to admit facts* is served upon the other party requiring him to admit for the purposes of the current proceedings a specified fact. Failure to make an admission may carry a costs penalty. A party who unreasonably fails to comply with a notice to admit facts may have to bear the costs of proving the fact whatever the outcome of the proceedings.

There are similar though not identical provisions relating to *notices to admit documents* the authenticity of which would have to be proved in the absence of any formal admission. As to admitting the authenticity of documents see further RSC Ord 27, r 5 (CCR Ord 20, r 3) and also the trap for the unwary in RSC Ord 27, r 4. This topic is fully discussed in Chapter 4.

There remain two further ways of making a formal admission for the purposes of civil proceedings. An admission may be made *at the trial by the advocate* thus precluding any further evidence on a point. Finally, in a case in which leave is given to serve *interrogatories* on the other party the replies given may contain admissions and such will be binding as formal admissions on the party making them. As to the serving of interrogatories see further RSC Ord 26 and CCR Ord 14 and also J O'Hare and R N Hill, *Civil Litigation*, 4th ed (Longman 1986), p 336.

2.2 Proving the facts in issue

Although it is generally true to say that a party bearing the legal burden of proving a fact in issue must discharge his burden by adducing evidence in support of his case there are circumstances in which he is assisted in discharging such burden.

The principal exceptions to the general rule requiring the facts in issue to be proved by evidence are: facts judicially noticed; and facts which are, or may be, presumed.

2.3 Facts judicially noticed

Facts which fall within this category may be classified in various ways. Classifications are not generally very helpful. It will be sufficient to bear in mind in considering the examples which follow that sometimes the court is *required* to take judicial notice of a particular fact whereas at other times it exercises a *discretion* to do so; that sometimes enquiries are made before judicial notice is taken and at other times no such enquiries are necessary; finally, that sometimes a fact judicially noticed is taken to be conclusively proved whereas in other cases evidence is permitted to displace judicial notice.

The effect of judicial notice is that the court accepts the truth of a fact, without proof, on the ground that the fact is within the court's own knowledge. Every day the courts take judicial notice of matters of common knowledge, often without any thought on the part of the court or the advocates as to the reasons for the acceptance of facts falling within this category. The facts are so well known that there can be no serious dispute about them. Facts which have been judicially noticed include that a fortnight is an insufficient gestation period for a human being (*R* v *Luffe* (1807) 8 East 193), that the domestic reception of television is a common feature of life (*Bridlington Relay Ltd* v *Yorkshire Electricity Board* [1965] Ch 436), that the life of a criminal is unhappy (*Burns* v *Edman* [1970] 2 QB 541), that a particular device for testing the alcohol content of a person's breath had been approved by the Home Secretary (*R* v *Jones* [1970] 1 WLR 16) and that a flick knife is an offensive weapon (*R* v *Simpson* [1983] 1 WLR 1494). Such facts as these may be noticed either expressly or tacitly and are so well established that evidence to contradict them is hardly likely. The matters of which the court will take notice will of course change with the times as may be seen from cases such as *Hoare* v *Silverlock* (1848) 12 QB 624. In *Hoare* v *Silverlock* it had been said of the plaintiff that 'her friends had realised the fable of the Frozen Snake'. The meaning of this was far too clear to require proof of its defamatory nature. (In the fable referred to, a farmer had gone out on a frosty day and had come across a snake frozen stiff as a pole. He picked it up and took it home where he allowed it to thaw out in front of the fire. The reward for his act of kindness was to be bitten by the snake.)

Other examples show the courts taking a positive decision to take judicial notice of a fact after making some preliminary enquiries. Such enquiries may take the form of consulting established works of reference or experts called to assist the court. In such a case the expert is not a witness and is not subject to cross-examination, he is merely assisting the court in forming its own view of a fact supposedly within its own knowledge. It is difficult to distinguish between cases where a person is assisting the court in this way and cases where a witness in the true sense should be called. In *McQuaker* v *Goddard* [1940] 1 QB 687 the judge consulted reference works and heard experts before taking judicial notice of the tameness of camels.

After appropriate enquiries the court will take judicial notice of such matters as customs, commercial and professional practices.

Certain matters which fall to be decided by the courts are such that they are taken to be the province of the executive rather than the judiciary and a certificate from the Secretary of State will be taken to be conclusive as to such matters as the recognition of foreign states, the existence of a state of war, the extent of British territory.

Finally, there are certain facts of which the court is obliged by statute to take judicial notice. These include Acts of Parliament except for private Acts passed prior to 1850 or which contain express provisions excluding them from the operation of judicial notice (Interpretation Act 1979). Certain matters of European Community law are required to be judicially noticed by virtue of the European Communities Act 1972.

2.4 Presumptions

A party may be assisted in discharging a burden of adducing evidence if there is a presumption operating in his favour. He may be entitled to have his case left to the tribunal of fact (he has satisfied the evidential burden) even without evidence being adduced as to an essential fact in issue.

(a) Presumptions in criminal cases

A presumption in a criminal case does not affect the legal burden of proof which remains upon the party, in most cases the prosecution, who bore it at the commencement of the trial. Such presumptions as are said to shift the legal burden of proof are not strictly presumptions at all but simply rules of law as to the incidence of the legal burden. It is said that the accused is 'presumed' to be innocent until proven guilty but this is nothing more than a rule of law that the legal burden of proof rests with the prosecution. A person is 'presumed' sane until the contrary be proved. This is a rule of law that the burden of proof of insanity rests with the person who alleges it. Furthermore there are a number of rules of substantive law which are often spoken of as presumptions. There are 'irrebuttable presumptions' that a child under ten years of age cannot commit a criminal offence and that a boy under 14 years cannot commit the offence of rape.

(b) *Presumptions in civil cases*

In civil cases presumptions may again assist a party in discharging an evidential burden. Certain presumptions may go beyond this and cast a legal burden upon the party seeking to rebut the presumption. In this way certain presumptions are elevated in civil cases to the status of rules of law concerning the incidence of the burden of proof.

(c) *When does a presumption arise and what is its effect?*

Instead of attempting a rigid classification of presumptions it is proposed to consider in turn the following questions:

(1) Is the presumption one which the court must draw or one which the court may draw?
(2) Is the presumption one which will come into play only after the proof of certain basic facts or will it arise independently of such facts?
(3) What evidence is required to rebut the presumption? Is it displaced merely by adducing evidence to the contrary or must the contrary be proved?

The answer to the first of these questions depends upon whether the presumption arises as a matter of law or merely because the facts support a particular inference. Presumptions of law result in an inference which must be drawn even though the facts may not support it.

2.5 Presumptions which the court must draw

Presumptions which the court must draw include the presumption of regularity often expressed in the maxim 'omnia praesumuntur rite esse acta'. A person who is acting in a public capacity is presumed to have been properly appointed.

Example
Where an inspector of the Health and Safety Executive was authorised to bring proceedings under the Health and Safety at Work Act 1974 he was not required to prove his appointment being permitted to rely upon the maxim 'omnia praesumuntur rite esse acta'. (*Campbell* v *Wallsend Slipway and Engineering Co Ltd* [1977] Crim LR 351)

Another presumption which the court must draw is that of legitimacy. Where a child is either born or conceived whilst the mother is lawfully married and not separated from her husband by court order the child is presumed to be legitimate.

Example

Following divorce proceedings Mary claims periodical payments from Harry for her child Chris. If the child has been born or conceived during the subsistence of the marriage then it will be presumed that Harry is the father of Chris. If Harry disputes that he is the father it will be for him to rebut the presumption.

The presumption of marriage arises on proof that the parties went through a ceremony of marriage. The court will presume that the marriage was valid. There is a second presumption of marriage which arises upon proof that the parties cohabited as man and wife and with the reputation of being married. The court will presume that they have at some time gone through a valid ceremony of marriage.

The presumption of a person's death arises upon proof that during a continuous period of seven years or more he has not been heard of by persons who would have been likely to have heard of him, that all due enquiries have been made and that there is no acceptable evidence that he was alive at some time during that period. The court will presume that at some time during that period he has died. As to this presumption see further *Chard* v *Chard* [1956] p 259.

Example

If a claim is made under a life assurance policy it may be possible to rely upon this presumption to show that the assured is dead and payment under the policy due.

2.6 Presumptions which the court may draw

A presumption drawn not as a matter of law but as a matter of logic is an inference drawn from the existence of certain facts that another fact is likely to be true. The inference is drawn because the tribunal of fact recognises the probability of the truth of the fact inferred. This amounts to nothing more than the acceptance of circumstantial evidence.

Although the layman may tend to be rather cynical about decisions which rely heavily upon circumstantial evidence this is largely due to a failure to appreciate the role which such evidence plays in a trial. It is not necessarily the case that circumstantial evidence is weak or unreliable. In criminal cases in particular a court is obliged to rely heavily upon circumstantial evidence as many crimes are by their nature committed in circumstances in which direct evidence is unlikely to be available. Burglars and murderers are unlikely to commit their crimes in the presence of witnesses.

Example
Bert is charged with burglary. There is no witness as to the entry into the premises or as to the theft of property. The prosecution call witnesses to show that he was seen in the vicinity at about the time of the crime, that he was in financial difficulties, that a plan of the raided premises was found in his flat, that he had been heard to say that the premises offered 'easy pickings' and that since the burglary he has been acting in a spend-thrift manner.

Each item of evidence in this example is circumstantial. The fact that so many items of circumstantial evidence supported the same conclusion shows a high degree of probability that the inference is correct and the fact in issue (that Bert was the burglar) is true.

Those presumptions that the court may make differ according to the nature of the case. As they are nothing more than inferences drawn from other facts they will be examined under that name.

(*a*) *Inferences of fact arising in both civil and criminal cases*

The presumption of continuance is an example of an inference which the tribunal of fact may draw in any proceedings. If it is shown that a state of affairs existed at a particular time it may be inferred that the same state of affairs prevailed at another reasonably proximate time. This is a conclusion which the tribunal of fact may be invited to reach where for example the fact to be proved is that two persons were carrying on a business together at a particular time or perhaps even that a person was alive at a particular time.

Example
The accused had been involved in a road accident in which his vehicle had collided with a vehicle travelling in the opposite direction. To prove the manner of his driving at the time of the accident evidence was received that a witness had seen him a third of a mile from the scene of the accident when he was two or three feet over the white line. The Divisional Court held that the evidence was rightly received although the justices had attached more weight to the evidence than they should have. (*Coles* v *Underwood* (1983) *The Times*, 2 November)

(*b*) *Inferences of fact arising only in criminal cases*

An inference which a jury will often be asked to draw is that a person who is found to be in possession of recently stolen goods is either the thief or a handler (see for example *R* v *Ball* [1983] 1 WLR 801). It appears that in most cases where the court is asked to draw this inference the more likely finding will be that he is the handler. In drawing the invited inference the court is said to be applying the doctrine of recent possession. The inference may be drawn only in a case in which the accused gives no explanation for his possession of the stolen goods or when the explanation which he does give is rejected by the jury (see *R* v *Smith* (1983) *The Times*, 22 November).

In a case in which the presence of mens rea is to be proved the prosecution will often give evidence as to the actus reus and will rely upon an inference to be drawn by the jury that the accused intended the consequences of his act. That the jury may draw such an inference is clear but there is no rule of law that such an inference must be drawn (Criminal Justice Act 1967, s 8). As to the inference of guilty knowledge on a handling charge see the Theft Act 1968, s 27(3), and **7.3** below.

(c) *Inferences of fact arising only in civil cases*

Perhaps the most important example of inferences of fact in civil cases is that found in negligence claims where the plaintiff relies upon the maxim 'res ipsa loquitur'. This is simply a plea that the facts as alleged by the plaintiff could not have arisen in ordinary circumstances without some negligence on the part of the defendant.

Example
Peter brings a claim for damages against David. He alleges that he was a pedestrian and David's vehicle mounted the kerb and hit him causing personal injury. Peter makes certain specific allegations of negligence but would also be able to rely upon the maxim res ipsa loquitur.

Example
A customs officer at the docks was passing in front of a warehouse when six bags of sugar fell on him. In a claim against the docks company he was able to rely upon the maxim res ipsa loquitur. (*Scott* v *London and St Katherine Docks Co* (1865) 3 H&C 596)

In *Scott* v *London and St Katherine Docks Co* Erle J explained the maxim by saying, at 667, that where a thing 'is shown to be under the management of the defendant . . . and the accident is such as in the ordinary course of things does not happen if those who have the management use proper care, it affords reasonable evidence, in the absence of explanation by the defendants, that the accident arose from want of care'.

2.7 What must be proved to give rise to the presumption?

Clearly inferences of fact based on circumstantial evidence will be drawn only on proof of those circumstantial facts. What then of presumptions which the court must draw as a matter of law? Apart from the presumptions of innocence and sanity which it has been noted (above) are not strictly presumptions but rules of law, presumptions of law arise only on the proof of certain basic facts. Examples can be found in the presumptions of marriage, legitimacy and death. The presumption of legitimacy arises only on proof that at the time of conception or birth the mother was married and not separated by court order from her husband. It can be seen therefore that presumptions never fully relieve a party of the burden of adducing some evidence in support of a case but simply assist him by providing that on proof of some facts others must be or may be presumed or inferred.

2.8 What evidence is required to rebut the presumption?

(a) Evidence to rebut presumptions in criminal cases

In a criminal case the burden of proof almost invariably rests with the prosecution and of course it is a burden which can be discharged only by adducing evidence to show beyond reasonable doubt that the accused is guilty. The effect of the prosecution relying on a presumption is to place upon the accused a burden of adducing some evidence to the contrary (an evidential burden). If some evidence is adduced to this end then the jury cannot convict unless satisfied beyond reasonable doubt that the prosecution has made out its case. The evidence put forward by the accused must have been rejected. Where the court is obliged to draw a particular conclusion the accused must adduce some evidence if he wishes to escape the consequences of the presumption or rely upon the jury finding that the basic facts giving rise to the presumption are not made out.

If the conclusion which the court is invited to draw is based on an inference of fact then the accused need not necessarily adduce any evidence to rebut the inference which may be drawn; he may hope that the jury will reject the basic facts giving rise to the inference or that the jury will decline to draw the inference. In most cases it will be desirable for the accused to adduce some evidence.

Example
Alan is charged with theft and in the alternative with handling. The prosecution adduce evidence of possession of recently stolen goods.

It is more likely that Alan will be convicted as a handler or even as the thief unless he puts forward some account of how he came to be in possession of the goods innocently. If his account raises a sufficient degree of doubt in the minds of the jury then again he will be entitled to an acquittal.

If the presumption is one which supports the accused's case then the prosecution will be required to adduce sufficient evidence to rebut the presumption beyond reasonable doubt.

(b) *Evidence to rebut presumptions in civil cases*

In civil cases many presumptions are such that if the judge is satisfied that the basic facts giving rise to the presumption are established then as a rule of law there will be a legal burden of proof on the other party. Such presumptions include those of legitimacy and marriage. If we return to the example given above of the presumption of legitimacy where Harry was disputing his paternity of a child born during his marriage to Mary (see **2.5** above), it can now be seen that Harry bears the burden of proof of illegitimacy, a burden which he must discharge to the usual civil standard.

In a case in which the presumption of death is relied upon it is necessary to show some acceptable evidence that the person was alive at some time during the requisite period. This is not so much a question of rebutting the presumption as of showing that the basic facts which give rise to the presumption are not established. The legal burden of establishing those facts rests with the party asserting them.

The presumptions of continuance, regularity and inferences of fact will all be displaced by evidence to the contrary and do not place a legal burden on the party seeking to avoid the effect of the presumption.

The position is less clear in relation to the maxim res ipsa loquitur. There is no direct authority as to the evidence required to displace the presumption of negligence in such cases. There appears to be no reason why a plaintiff who relies upon res ipsa loquitur should be in any better position than a plaintiff who has made out a prima facie case by giving evidence as to each separate element of the tort of negligence. It is suggested that the better view is that the presumption is rebutted by evidence as to how the accident may have occurred without negligence on the part of the defendant so that the legal burden remains on the plaintiff throughout.

Example
The defendant's barge hits a bridge causing damage. This is admitted. The plaintiff has the legal burden of proof of negligence and relies upon res ipsa loquitur. All that should be required of the defendant to rebut the presumption is a reasonable explanation consistent with the accident having occurred without negligence. (*The Kite* [1933] P 154)

As the nature of the onus on the defendant in such cases is not free from doubt some mention should be made of the alternative view. This view is that the onus on the defendant is that of proving the accident to have been caused by something not amounting to negligence on his part. The authority given for this view is *Barkway* v *South Wales Transport Co Ltd* [1948] 2 All ER 460. In that case Scott LJ says that the presumption of fault is rebuttable by 'the same defence as is open to any defendant accused of negligence against whom the plaintiff's evidence has made out a prima facie case. When the plaintiff has done that, the onus is said to shift to the defendant. In a case where res ipsa loquitur applies the onus is on the defendant at the outset to prove affirmatively that he has exercised all reasonable care'.

It is suggested that the onus to which the majority of the Court of Appeal referred was merely the burden of adducing some evidence by way of explanation. The decision in that case did not turn upon this point as the defendants were able to show that they had exercised reasonable care.

Chapter 3

Corroboration

There is no general requirement in English law that evidence should be corroborated. In the absence of any such requirement it is clear that the tribunal of fact may decide an issue in favour of the party bearing the burden of proof of that issue even on the uncorroborated evidence of a single witness.

Example
Following a road accident involving two vehicles driven by Peter and David, Peter brings a claim against David in negligence and David counterclaims. The witnesses for the plaintiff are Peter himself, his girl friend who was a passenger in the car, and an elderly independent witness. The judge may be unimpressed by Peter's evidence, decide that his girl friend is unreliable and unable to give a fair account of how the accident came about and find that the independent witness is so confused and forgetful that her evidence should be disregarded. On the other hand the defendant may impress him as an honest and reliable witness. In such a case the judge could find in favour of David without looking for further evidence to corroborate his account. The plaintiff's action would be dismissed because he had failed to discharge the legal burden of proof of negligence and David may even succeed on his counterclaim.

The question to be determined in such a case is simply whether or not the witness is to be believed. It is the requirement that a party should adduce cogent evidence in support of the facts he asserts which makes it desirable, wherever possible, that there should be some support for the evidence which a witness gives. When considering the credibility of a witness's testimony the tribunal will no doubt look at the evidence in the context of all other matters placed before it to see whether there is support for his account.

In exceptional cases, however, there are special requirements of corroboration. These requirements will be considered below but first some general points as to the nature of corroboration in a case in which there are such special requirements.

It is important to appreciate that corroboration is not a means of improving the evidence given by a witness who appears confused or forgetful or even dishonest. If a witness is found not to be creditworthy then his testimony should be rejected and the question of corroboration is then beside the point. Corroboration becomes relevant when a witness has given credible testimony and because of special rules discussed below the court is obliged to look for corroboration. Just as the testimony of the witness requiring corroboration must be creditworthy so must that of the witness giving the corroboration. In *DPP* v *Kilbourne* [1973] AC 729 at 746, Lord Hailsham LC said: 'corroboration is only required or afforded if the witness requiring corroboration or giving it is otherwise credible. If his evidence is not credible, a witness's testimony should be rejected and the accused acquitted, even if there could be found evidence capable of being corroboration in other testimony.' It has, however, been held that there is no need for a judge to specifically direct a jury that a witness must be independently credible before any question of corrobration can arise. (*A-G of Hong Kong* v *Wong Muk-Ping* [1987] 2 All ER 488)

Example
Tom is charged with procuring Alice, by false pretences, to have sexual intercourse with him. (As will be seen at **3.1**(*a*) below there is a special requirement that the evidence of Alice be corroborated.) If Alice appears to give reliable evidence then corroboration of her story must be sought. If Alice is not a convincing witness so that the court is disinclined to believe her the question of corroboration does not arise.

Special rules concerning corroboration are almost exclusively confined to criminal cases. The requirements in civil cases are considered at the end of this chapter.

Corroboration in Criminal Cases

In *R* v *Baskerville* [1916] 2 KB 658 at 667 Lord Reading CJ said: 'corroboration must be independent testimony which affects the accused by connecting or tending to connect him with the crime. In other words, it must be evidence which implicates him, that is, which confirms in some material particular not only the evidence that the crime has been committed but also that the prisoner committed it.' In *R* v *Olaleye* (1986) 82 Cr App R 337 the evidence against the principal offender was corroborated. The Court of Appeal had to consider whether the rules about corroboration had to be re-applied to the evidence of the same witness given against a secondary party. The jury must have found the witness to be reliable and trustworthy when convicting the principal offender. It would be 'absurd' to re-apply the rules on corroboration to her evidence against the secondary offender to prove what had already been shown ie that she was a reliable and trustworthy witness (per Watkins LJ at 340).

It should be noted that the corroborative evidence must be independent. 'If there is any real chance that there has been collusion between the makers of the two statements we should not accept them as corroborative' (per Lord Reid in *DPP* v *Kilbourne* [1973] AC 729 at 751).

Example
On a number of charges of indecently assaulting young boys, the prosecution try to show a system of committing the offence (see **7.2**). Here evidence of one of the boys on one count in the indictment may be taken as corroborating evidence of other boys in relation to different counts. This would not be so if the judge or jury found as a question of fact that the boys had prepared their stories in collusion.

3.1 Special rules

Special requirements of corroboration fall into two categories. There are cases where the law demands corroboration and there are cases where the judge is required to give a warning to the jury as to the dangers of convicting in the absence of corroboration.

Cases which involve disputed identification are considered separately (**3.9–3.11**).

(*a*) *Cases where corroboration is necessary*

If corroboration is required as a matter of law then the jury cannot convict on evidence which is uncorroborated. The jury could convict only if they were prepared to accept the evidence of the witness requiring corroboration and found cogent evidence to corroborate it. In the absence of any corroborative evidence the prosecution will have failed to make out a prima facie case and the defence would be entitled to succeed on a submission of no case to answer at the close of the prosecution case.

The cases in which corroboration is required as a matter of law include:

(1) On a charge of treason.

(2) On a charge of personation at elections.

(3) On a charge of perjury.

(4) For certain offences under the Sexual Offences Act 1956 including procurement by threats or by false pretences of a woman for sexual intercourse, administering drugs to facilitate intercourse and procuring girls under 21.

(5) Where a person is charged with an offence of speeding.

An accused cannot be convicted of speeding on the opinion evidence of one witness (Road Traffic Regulation Act 1984, s 89). There may, however, be a conviction on the evidence of a single witness if his evidence as to the speed of the vehicle is derived not from opinion but from an instrument reading.

In *Crossland* v *DPP* [1988] 3 All ER 712 a Divisional Court upheld a conviction for speeding based upon the evidence of a single police constable who had carried out a reconstruction of an unwitnessed accident based upon scientific calculations after inspecting the car and tyre marks. The court held that s 89 was not intended to apply to the present situation because the accused 'is not in jeopardy on the strength only of the unsupported visual impression of a single witness'.

It should be noted that by virtue of Criminal Justice Act 1988, s 34(1) it is no longer necessary for there to be corroboration of a child who gives unsworn evidence for the prosecution.

(b) Cases where a warning must be given to the jury

In addition to the cases where corroboration is a requirement of law there are two categories of witness in respect of whom there is a rule of practice, which has now matured into a rule of law, which requires the judge to give a warning as to the particular dangers of convicting on the uncorroborated evidence of the witness. The supposedly inherent unreliability of the witness may well not be apparent to the jury and the matters which may affect his evidence need to be spelt out to the jury. The nature of the direction which should be given to the jury was considered by the House of Lords in *R* v *Spencer* [1986] 3 WLR 348 per Lord Ackner at 358:

(1) The jury should be warned of the danger of relying upon the sole evidence of an accomplice or of the complainant in a sexual case.

(2) The warning must explain why it is dangerous so to act but the jury are told that they may do so if they feel sure that the uncorroborated witness is telling the truth.

(3) Where there is evidence before the jury which they can properly consider to be corroborative evidence, the trial judge must identify such material leaving it to the jury to decide whether to treat such evidence as corroboration.

(4) The judge must warn the jury against treating as corroborative evidence that which may appear to them to be such but which is not so in law.

(5) Where the prosecution are relying upon the lies of the accused as potentially corroborative evidence a 'particularly careful direction is needed' (*R* v *Lucas* [1981] QB 720 — see **3.6**).

The two categories of witness referred to are:
(1) Accomplices.
(2) Complainants in cases of sexual offences.

For various reasons it is considered that there is increased risk of inaccuracy in the testimony of such witnesses. The two categories will now be treated separately.

Where an *accomplice* is called as a witness for the prosecution the jury must be warned that although they may convict on the testimony of an accomplice it is dangerous to do so unless it is corroborated (*R* v *Thorne* (1977) 66 Cr App R 6). If no accomplice warning is given, the judge should state his reasons for not doing so in open court (*R* v *Wilson* (1988) *The Times*, 23 April).

Example
Gordon who is of previous good character was an accomplice in a burglary. He has made a frank admission as to his involvement and has pleaded guilty to charges arising out of the incident. Archie is charged with burglary and Gordon gives prosecution evidence. He describes the planning and execution of the offence and implicates Archie.

Example
Robert and Robin were both charged with robbery and causing grievous bodily harm. Both have a number of previous convictions. During the course of the raid a shopkeeper was violently assaulted and sustained severe injury. Robert has pleaded guilty to the charge and is giving evidence for the prosecution against Robin. He implicates Robin in the crime and lays the blame for the acts of violence at Robin's door.

In either of these cases the jury would be entitled, following an appropriate warning from the judge, to convict the accused on the uncorroborated evidence of his accomplice. However, it is far more likely that they would do so in the first case where the prosecution witness is of previous good character and has shown remorse for his criminal act than in the second case where the prosecution witness is a known villain trying to minimise his part in a serious crime.

These examples did not give rise to any doubt that the prosecution witness was an accomplice of the accused and that the warning was therefore necessary. However, it is not always clear that a witness is an accomplice. The question was considered in *Davies* v *DPP* [1954] AC 378 at 400, when Lord Simonds LC laid down three classes of person who would be considered to be accomplices *if called to give evidence for the prosecution*:

(1) Persons participating in the crime (including secondary offenders) whether charged or not.

(2) Handlers, on the trial of the thieves from whom they received the goods.

(3) In cases where evidence of other offences committed by the accused is admissible as similar fact evidence, participants in those offences.

It is for the trial judge to rule whether there is evidence that a particular witness is an accomplice. If such evidence exists, the jury must decide, as a matter of fact, whether he is one. It is important to note that the rule applies only to witnesses called by the prosecution. It does not apply between co-defendants (*R* v *Barnes and Richards* [1940] 2 All ER 229). See, however, **3.2** below.

Example
David and Donald are both accused of murder. The fatal blow was delivered in the course of a robbery. The prosecution have made out a prima facie case. The defendants each elect to give evidence (which is also evidence both for and against the co-defendant—see **4.2(d)**) and during the course of his evidence Donald says that David delivered the fatal blow and that he (Donald) did not realise that David was carrying the weapon, or that David contemplated the use of violence.

It is, as always, a matter for the jury as to what weight they attach to that part of the evidence. In giving this evidence Donald does not fall within the classes of person treated as an accomplice because he is not a prosecution witness and there is no requirement that the judge should warn the jury of the dangers of convicting on this evidence if it is uncorroborated. In a case such as this the judge has a discretion as to the nature of the direction given to the jury but 'he is at the least expected to give the customary clear warning to a jury where defendants have given damaging evidence against one another to examine the evidence of each with care because each has or may have an interest of his own to serve' (per Watkins LJ in *R* v *Knowlden* (1981) 77 Cr App R 94 at 100).

The jury must be given a warning that it is dangerous to convict on the uncorroborated evidence of the *complainant in sexual cases*. As in the case of accomplices, having been given an appropriate warning, the jury may convict even in the absence of corroboration if satisfied as to the truth of the complainant's testimony.

Example
Roger is charged with rape. The complainant, Vicky, gives evidence. The issue in the case is that of consent. Vicky's mother gives evidence of a complaint made by her daughter immediately upon arriving home after the incident and also of her distressed condition.

The mother's testimony as to the complaint is not independent of, and cannot therefore corroborate, the evidence of the complainant herself. (This part of the mother's testimony may however be admissible to show the consistency of the complainant's conduct—see **14.5**.) The mother's evidence as to the distressed condition of the victim is relevant and admissible but caution must be exercised where the distress is part and parcel of the complaint (see *R* v *Knight* [1966] 1 WLR 230). Whilst corroboration may be found in the fact of the victim's distress, no corroboration of her testimony can be found in the fact that she made a complaint.

It is to be emphasised that the case in the example turned on the issue of consent. In *James* v *R* (1970) 55 Cr App R 299 the prosecution were required to prove that intercourse took place, that it was without the consent of the complainant and that it was the accused who had intercourse with the complainant. The Privy Council, hearing the appeal from the Court of Appeal of Jamaica quashed the conviction of the accused. The trial judge had not made it clear to the jury that medical evidence showing that intercourse had taken place could not corrobrate the complainant's evidence that intercourse was without her consent, nor that it was the accused who had intercourse with her.

Whilst the rule in sexual cases is well established, it is clear from *R* v *Chance* (1988) 87 Cr App R 398 that a warning is not required in each and every case that comes before the court. The reason for the rule is 'because human experience has shown that in these courts girls and women for all sorts of reasons do sometimes tell an entirely false story which is very easy to fabricate but extremely difficult to refute' (per Salmon LJ in *R v Henry* (1968) 53 Cr App R 150 at 153). In *R v Chance* the Court of Appeal held that:

(1) There is no need for a warning in respect of identification where there is no real dispute that the accused was, at the material times, with the complainant.

(2) That there is no need to advise a jury to seek corroboration that the complainant was raped when there is no real dispute that she was raped by somebody.

(3) That where identification is in issue and there is no reason to think that the sexual nature of the offence distorted the complainant's evidence, there is no need for a formal warning. (As to the rules in any type of case involving disputed identification evidence see **3.9**.)

By virtue of Criminal Justice Act 1988 s 34(2) it is no longer necessary for a full corroboration warning to be given in respect of the sworn evidence of a child. The abolition of this rule is not as far reaching as might be thought. The 1988 Act states that the corroboration warning requirement is 'abrogated in relation to cases where such a warning is required by reason only that the evidence is the evidence of a child'. If a child gives evidence (sworn or unsworn) as the complainant in a sexual offence, a full corroboration warning will still be required. Similarly, a warning is necessary if it is decided that the child is an accomplice.

3.2 The witness who has a purpose of his own to serve

In a case where it is considered that a witness may have a purpose of his own to serve in giving evidence it is a matter for the trial judge to determine whether the jury should be warned of such purpose and whether any direction should be given concerning corroboration.

Example
Whitaker was charged with the murder of Robert Ogden, a boy of three years. The killing was in such circumstances that the child must have been killed either by Whitaker or by Mrs Ogden who gave evidence for the prosecution. (*R v Whitaker* (1976) 63 Cr App R 193)

The Court of Appeal refused leave to appeal against conviction. It must have been clear to the jury that they had to choose between the evidence of Whitaker and Mrs Ogden and that Mrs Ogden had a purpose of her own to serve in giving evidence against Whitaker. Further it was no ground for criticism that the trial judge did not deal with the question of corroboration.

It was once thought that a corroboration warning was required in all cases where the witness had a purpose of his own to serve in giving his evidence (see *R* v *Prater* [1960] 2 QB 464). The courts however refused to extend the requirement of a corroboration warning to include every such witness (*R* v *Stannard* [1965] 2 QB 1; *R* v *Beck* [1982] 1 WLR 461). In *R* v *Beck* the Court of Appeal did however say that the judge should 'advise a jury to proceed with caution where there is material to suggest that a witness's evidence may be tainted by an improper motive' (per Ackner LJ at 469). This is clearly a much less technical direction than the 'full' corroboration warning.

3.3 Other categories of witness

Although the courts have on a number of occasions refused to extend the categories of witness in respect of whom a 'full' corroboration warning is required there have been a number of cases where it has been said that the judge was under an obligation to warn the jury to treat the 'suspect' evidence with caution. In *Nembhard* v *R* [1981] 1 WLR 1515 the Privy Council said that the judge was under a 'duty' to leave the jury with a clear consciousness of their need for care in assessing the significance of a 'dying declaration' made by a homicide victim and identifying his killer.

In *R* v *Spencer* [1986] 3 WLR 348, the House of Lords held that patients under the Mental Health Acts did not form a new category of witness in respect of whom a 'full' corroboration warning was required. However, in cases where the prosecution evidence is solely that of a witness who, though not in one of the two accepted categories (see **3.1 (b)**), nevertheless by reason of his particular mental condition and criminal connection fulfilled analogous criteria, the judge must warn the jury that it is dangerous to convict on his uncorroborated evidence. The use of the words 'danger' or 'dangerous' is not essential. In such cases, the extent to which the judge should make reference to potentially corroborative material depends on the facts of each case and the overriding rule is that he must put the defence fairly and adequately.

By Police and Criminal Evidence Act 1984, s 77, where the case against an accused depends wholly or substantially on a confession made by him and (*a*) the court is satisfied that he is mentally handicapped; and (*b*) the confession was not made in the presence of an independent person; the judge must warn the jury (or the magistrates must warn themselves) that there is a special need for caution before convicting in reliance on the confession. (See further **12.5**).

In *R* v *Simmons* (1987) Crim LR 630 the Court of Appeal foresaw 'considerable danger' arising from 'an unwarranted extension of the categories in which the warning had to be given'.

Since the abolition of corroboration requirements for the evidence of children giving testimony for the prosecution, there has been no judicial suggestion that an alternative warning as to the need for caution should be given. If, however, there is a clear suggestion that a child has perhaps been manipulated by an adult, then it may be appropriate for some comment to be made to a jury.

3.4 Mutual corroboration

Can two witnesses in respect of each of whom the court is obliged to look for corroboration, satisfy the requirement of corroboration in relation to the testimony of each other? In general there is no objection to such corroboration.

Example
Rodney is charged with rape. The prosecution evidence consists of the testimony of the complainant, Carol, and of her twelve year old daughter, Donna. In such a case the jury are entitled to find corroboration of Carol's story in the testimony of Donna and vice versa.

Even in the case of two child witnesses there is no rule excluding the possibility of mutual corroboration.

Example
The accused was charged with indecently assaulting a twelve-year old girl. She gave sworn evidence and her nine year old sister gave unsworn evidence in support of the complainant's story.

These are the facts of *DPP* v *Hester* [1973] AC 296 in which the House of Lords held that the evidence of one child was capable of corroborating the other. The Criminal Justice Act 1988, s 34(3), confirms this point and extends the law further by providing that the unsworn evidence of a child may corroborate unsworn evidence given by another person.

Accomplices

Where two or more participants in a crime with which the accused has been charged each give prosecution evidence then there is a particular danger in accepting their evidence as mutually corroborative. The witnesses may have combined together to throw blame on the accused and the requirement that corroborative evidence must be independent will not be satisfied. The real danger, as Lord Hailsham LC said in *DPP* v *Kilbourne* [1973] AC 729 at 747, is of a conspiracy to commit perjury.

The Lord Chancellor also instanced other circumstances where there may be a danger of such a conspiracy and said at 748, that where this possibility exists 'it is right to direct the jury not to treat as corroborative of one witness the evidence of another witness who may be part of the same conspiracy'.

3.5 What can and cannot amount to corroboration?

Corroboration may be provided by a combination of pieces of circumstantial evidence, each innocuous on its own, which together tend to show that the defendant committed the crime. See *R* v *Hills* (1988) Cr App R 26 in which Lord Lane CJ gave the following example:

Example
In a rape case where the accused denies having had intercourse with the complainant, it may be possible to prove:
— by medical evidence, that she had sexual intercourse within an hour or so before the examination,
— by other independent evidence that the accused and no other man had been with her during that time,
— that her underclothing was torn and that she had injuries to her private parts.

Whilst none of those facts would itself amount to corroboration the combined effect of those items of evidence would be capable of corroborating the complainant's evidence. For a further example of cumulative corroboration see *R* v *McInnes* (1989) Crim LR 889.

The points to consider in deciding whether evidence is capable of amounting to corroboration are (per Lord Lane CJ in *R* v *Hills*):
  (1) What are the real issues in the case?
  (2) What the evidence tendered as corroboration does in fact prove.

(3) Whether that evidence comes from a source independent of the witness in respect of whom corroboration is sought and goes some significant part of the way towards showing that the offence was committed and that the accused committed it.

3.6 Corroboration from the conduct of the accused

Most categories of corroborative evidence (for example the testimony of another witness) give rise to no particular difficulty. However, a jury may be tempted to find corroboration of a prosecution witness in the conduct of the accused in telling lies or exercising his right to remain silent. These possibilities are now treated separately.

(a) Lies

Where an accused is proved to have told lies or admits to having done so this may provide corroboration for the testimony of a prosecution witness. If it is to amount to corroboration the lie must be deliberate and must relate to a material issue; it must be told because of the realisation of guilt and fear of the truth; finally, it must be proved to be a lie by evidence other than that of the witness whose testimony is to be corroborated (see *R* v *Lucas* [1981] QB 720; also *R* v *West* (1984) 79 Cr App R 45).

Example
Bob is charged with burglary. Graham has pleaded guilty to the offence and now gives prosecution evidence. He is therefore within the definition of 'accomplices' for the purpose of the corroboration requirement. Graham says that he and Bob drove to the home of Graham's former girl friend, broke in and stole property. Bob denies any involvement and says that he lent Graham his car supposedly to enable Graham to go and see his girl friend and that he knew nothing of Graham's real purpose. There is no other evidence connecting Bob with the crime.

If the jury believe Graham and disbelieve Bob then the fact that Bob has been found to have told lies cannot corroborate Graham's testimony. There is no evidence of the lie other than that given by the witness requiring corroboration. Suppose however that Bob changes his story and admits that he was lying and admits driving the vehicle but remains adamant in his denial of involvement in the burglary or alternatively that another prosecution witness is able to identify him as the driver of the vehicle. In either case there is proof from someone other than Graham that

Bob was lying. His lies may be taken to be corroboration of Graham's testimony provided the jury is satisfied that his lies were deliberate, material and made in the realisation of guilt and fear of the truth. Even having been warned as to these requirements the jury must be reminded that people sometimes lie to bolster a good cause or to conceal behaviour from family and friends and that the lie should be accepted as corroboration only if the jury is satisfied as to the motive for it (see *R* v *Lucas*).

(b) Fabricated alibi

One common way in which an accused may lie is by setting up a false alibi. Again caution must be exercised in finding corroboration in the fact that an alibi is rejected. A fabricated alibi may amount to corroboration but not if the falsity was due to mistake, panic or stupidity (see *R* v *Thorne* (1977) 66 Cr App R 6).

Example
Leonard is accused of the murder of his mistress, Mary. He was seen leaving her flat on the night of the murder, by a boy of twelve who gives sworn evidence for the prosecution. He puts forward an alibi that he was out drinking with friends at the material time. It later transpires that the alibi is false and Leonard admits to having seen Mary on the night in question but claims that she was well when he last saw her and denies killing her. When asked the reason for his earlier lies he says he did not want his wife to know of the affair.

If the jury disbelieve his evidence as to his motive for lying and decide that the lies were told to deceive the jury, then (and only then) can the jury find in the fabricated alibi corroboration of the boy's evidence.

(c) Silence of the accused

It seems that neither the silence of the accused when charged nor his failure to give evidence can amount to corroboration of a witness's testimony (R v *Keeling* (1942) 28 Cr App R 121). Whilst the recent report of the Working Group On The Right To Silence has recommended modification of the right, it does not go so far as to suggest that silence should be capable of amounting to corroboration.

If silence is such as to amount to a confession, as in the face of an accusation by someone on even terms with the accused, then it may provide corroboration of other testimony. As to silence and confessions, see **12.1**.

(d) Refusal of an intimate body sample

An intimate body sample may only be taken from a suspect if a superintendent authorises it and the suspect gives his consent (Police and Criminal Evidence Act 1984, s 62). If the suspect refuses to give a sample and does not have good cause for the refusal, s 62(10) provides that the refusal may be treated as capable of amounting to corroboration of any other evidence in the case to which the refusal is material.

3.7 Corroboration from the appearance of the accused

In *R v Willoughby* (1989) 88 Cr App R 91, it was held that 'the physical appearance of the defendant, however singular and however closely it corresponded with a description given by the victim, could not without more, amount to corroboration of her evidence'.

Example

W was charged with kidnapping and indecent assault. The victim gave evidence that her assailant had spots on his face. The fact that W had spots could not corroborate the evidence of the victim as there was nothing independent of her to confirm that the assailant had spots.

3.8 Practical considerations

Where questions of corroboration arise in a case tried in a magistrates' court there can of course be no question of a corroboration warning as the justices are the tribunal of both law and fact. Nevertheless in cases where a warning would normally be required the justices should have regard to the dangers of convicting in the absence of corroborative evidence. Such cases are usually better tried in the Crown Court when possible.

In cases tried in the Crown Court the failure of the trial judge to give a suitable warning is likely to result in the conviction being quashed on appeal; the proviso to the Criminal Appeal Act 1968, s 2 (enabling a conviction to stand if, notwithstanding that there are grounds for appeal, there has been no miscarriage of justice) will only be applied in exceptional cases. (See *R v Trigg* [1963] 1 WLR 305)

In almost all cases where a corroboration direction is called for, it is desirable that the trial judge should listen to submissions from counsel (in the absence of the jury) on the elements of the offence which required corroboration and what evidence there was available that was capable of amounting to corroboration (*R* v *Ensor* [1989] 1 WLR 497).

 EVIDENCE OF IDENTIFICATION IN CRIMINAL CASES

One of the main causes of wrong convictions is mistaken evidence of identification. In cases turning upon disputed identification evidence the judge must take special care in directing the jury. There is no requirement that the evidence of a witness as to identification must be corroborated nor is there a rule of law requiring the judge to warn the jury of the dangers of convicting in the absence of corroboration. But, recognising the risk and perhaps especially the risk that a witness who is honest and well-meaning may impress the jury even though he is in fact mistaken, the Court of Appeal has laid down guidelines to be observed by the trial judge when summing up in such cases (*R* v *Turnbull* [1977] QB 224).

3.9 The Turnbull guidelines

Wherever a case depends wholly or substantially on the correctness of identification evidence which is disputed, the judge should himself assess the quality of the evidence of identification and decide whether the evidence is good enough to be left to the jury.

Example
Susan is charged with the theft of goods from a supermarket. She says there must be some mistake and that she was not at the store. The principal prosecution witness is a store detective who says that he watched Susan for some fifteen minutes during which she took goods from her trolley and placed them in another bag and then left the store without attempting to pay for those goods. The witness tried to apprehend her but Susan pushed him aside and ran out of the store.

In such a case the judge may think that the evidence as to the accused's identity is good enough to be left to the jury. The jury will eventually have to assess the evidence for themselves and may convict on that evidence. If the judge considered the evidence to be poor then it should not be left to the jury unless there is some other evidence capable of lending support to the evidence of identification.

Example
Peter is charged with the theft of a wallet and its contents. The principal prosecution witness is the victim who turned around as the wallet was taken from his pocket and caught a brief glimpse of the thief as he disappeared into the crowd.

In this case it is likely that the judge would not allow the evidence of identification to be left to the jury in the absence of some supporting evidence.

In any case where disputed identification evidence is to be left to the jury, the judge should direct the jury very carefully as to the special need for caution before convicting in reliance upon it and should refer to the possibility of a witness or even a number of witnesses making an honest mistake. Provided that such a warning is given, the trial judge is entitled to direct the jury that an identification by one witness could provide support for the identification by another (*R* v *Breslin* (1985) 80 Cr App R 226).

The judge should then direct the jury to examine closely the circumstances in which the original observation was made:

(1) Over what period?
(2) In what conditions?
(3) In what light?
(4) At what distance?
(5) Was the witness recognising someone he already knew?
(6) Was he identifying a stranger?
(7) Does the description given to the police match the appearance of the accused?

Example
When questioned about his movements at the time of the theft, Peter (the pickpocket in the previous example) puts forward an alibi which is later admitted to have been false.

The judge may feel that in view of the support for the otherwise poor evidence as to identification the case can safely be left to the jury. In a case where such supporting evidence is sought the judge should identify to the jury the evidence which is capable of supporting the disputed identification evidence. Furthermore he should identify other evidence which the jury may think could support the evidence of identification but which cannot do so.

Example
Thomas is accused of taking and driving away a motor car without the consent of the owner. A prosecution witness gives evidence of identification having had a brief glimpse of the offender as he got into the car. The judge may form the view that this evidence alone was insufficient to

leave to the jury. Another prosecution witness gives evidence that a coat was found in the vehicle when it was recovered and that Thomas has admitted that the coat belonged to him. Thomas does not give evidence in his own defence.

In such a case the judge should direct the jury that they may find support for the identification evidence in the fact that a coat belonging to the accused has been found in the car. The judge should also make it clear to the jury that the accused is not obliged to give evidence and that his decision not to do so cannot amount to support for the disputed evidence of identification.

The court should be particularly careful about finding support for disputed identification evidence in the fact that they reject an alibi. False alibis may be put forward for a variety of reasons and witnesses as to alibi may make genuine mistakes. It is only if the jury are satisfied that the alibi was fabricated to deceive them that support for the evidence of identification can be found (see also **3.6(b)** above).

It should be noted that in all these examples the evidence to support the poor identification evidence is evidence to support the disputed testimony. It does not necessarily fulfil the criteria required of corroboration and discussed at **3.1** above.

Example
A witness catches only a fleeting glance of the thief's face as the thief runs off. The witness sees the thief entering a nearby house. Later, the witness picks out the accused on an identity parade. This identification evidence is supported by evidence that the house belongs to the father of the accused.

This is an example given by Lord Widgery CJ in *R* v *Turnbull*. The supporting evidence cannot here amount to corroboration of the witness's testimony but nevertheless makes it more likely that the identification was not mistaken. The judgment of the Court of Appeal repays careful reading and contains a number of further examples.

As to the courts' discretion to exclude identification evidence, see **5.5(d)**.

3.10 Failure to observe the guidelines

Although the guidelines are intended to lay down a rule of practice rather than of law it is clear that the failure of the trial judge to observe them is likely to result in the conviction being overturned by the Court of Appeal if it is considered that the conviction is unsafe or unsatisfactory.

3.11 When does the warning cease to be required?

The guidelines laid down in *R v Turnbull* are intended to reduce the risk of an innocent person being convicted by being wrongly identified as the person seen by a witness on the material occasion. If the accused has not been positively identified by the witness or admits being at the scene but denies any involvement the guidelines do not strictly apply. In such a case a prudent jury would no doubt take into account the circumstances in which a witness observed the matters to which he is deposing. In his summing up the judge would no doubt direct the minds of the jury to matters making the testimony of the witness more or less reliable.

Example
An elderly lady reports the theft of her handbag and gives a description of the culprit. The police interview the accused who makes statements amounting to an admission of his involvement in the offence. He is arrested and agrees to take part in an identification parade. The victim is unable to pick him out.

If the accused later denies the offence there would be no need for the trial judge to give a *Turnbull* warning. No doubt the court would attach little weight to the evidence of the victim in so far as it linked the accused to the crime. The prosecution would be heavily dependent upon the self-incriminating nature of the statements made by the accused.

Example
Oakwell was charged with assaulting a police officer in the execution of his duty. He admitted being present at the time of the assault but claimed that the police officer had confused the person who actually knocked him to the floor with Oakwell who was standing there as he got up again. (*R v Oakwell* [1978] 1 WLR 32)

The court was perhaps surprised to find that identification was thought to be in issue and that the *Turnbull* guidelines were claimed to apply. The police officer had not mistaken the accused for someone else. The real issue was what the police officer had seen the accused do. Accordingly, the trial judge had given an adequate direction even though he had not followed the guidelines in *Turnbull*. A similar decision was reached in *R v Curry* [1983] Crim LR 737. The court did however make it clear that even where *Turnbull* does not apply but there is a risk of error the judge should make reference to weaknesses in the evidence.

CORROBORATION IN CIVIL CASES

The presence or absence of corroboration of the testimony of a witness in civil proceedings goes to the weight of his evidence but the court may act upon the uncorroborated testimony of a single witness. The only important exception to this general principle was to be found in the Affiliation Proceedings Act 1957, s 4, but this was repealed when Part II of the Family Law Reform Act 1987 came into force on 1 April 1989.

3.12 Matrimonial offences

So far as matrimonial offences are concerned, there is no requirement that the evidence of the petitioner or complainant must be corroborated before the court may act upon it. Nevertheless the court should look for corroboration and should consider the dangers of acting on the uncorroborated testimony of the 'aggrieved' spouse. The vast majority of divorce petitions are undefended and in cases relying upon the proof of adultery the respondent will often provide corroboration by a written confession. In proceedings for maintenance under the Domestic Proceedings and Magistrates' Courts Act 1978, the complainant is rarely required to prove a matrimonial offence and will rely instead upon failure by the respondent to provide reasonable maintenance.

Chapter 4

Methods of Proving a Fact in Issue

The first two chapters established what must be proved by evidence, to what standard and which party actually has the burden of proof. The purpose of this chapter is to consider how the facts in issue in a case can be proved in a court of law. There are four methods of proof available:

(1) Evidence given orally by witnesses.
(2) Evidence given in written statements by witnesses.
(3) Other documentary evidence.
(4) Real evidence.

When investigating a case it is necessary to know which methods of proving a fact are acceptable to the court and to appreciate the technical rules that apply to each particular method.

Oral Testimony

By far the most common method of proving a fact in issue is to call a witness to give oral evidence. A number of questions have to be considered. How does the witness give his evidence? Can the witness be compelled to attend? Are there any restrictions on the type of witness that can be called?

4.1 How oral evidence is given

When a witness appears in court, the first step is for him to take the oath or affirm. The general rule in both civil and criminal cases is that the evidence must be given under the sanction of an oath or solemn affirmation. Witnesses who object to being sworn will be allowed to affirm instead (Oaths Act 1978, s 5).

(a) Examination in chief

The witness will then begin his evidence. The rule against hearsay (see Chapter 11) prohibits a witness from giving evidence of any fact of which he has no personal knowledge. Bearing this in mind it is the task of the advocate calling the witness to coax him into relating to the court facts that will support the case. The evidence must of course be restricted to those facts which are both relevant and admissible (see Chapter 5). Witnesses are unpredictable creatures and the most obvious way of ensuring satisfactory answers is to ask questions of the witness that require nothing more than a simple 'yes' or 'no'. To do this is to ask a leading question and such questions are generally not allowed.

Example
Tommy is charged with the theft of a watch from Fixit Stores. William allegedly saw Tommy do it. It is not permissible to ask William, 'Did you see Tommy take a watch from Fixit Stores?' The advocate would have to ask William where he was at the relevant time, whether he saw anyone there, and what he saw that person do.

Another way of ensuring that a witness gives the evidence that is expected of him is to give him a prepared statement to read out. Obviously this will not be allowed. The witness is required to speak from his own recollection. Quite apart from any strict rule of evidence prohibiting it (see Chapter 14) common sense alone dictates that reading a prepared statement would be extremely artificial.

Although a witness may not read from a prepared statement, he is allowed to refresh his memory in the witness box before giving evidence on a particular point by referring to a document. There are two conditions which must be satisfied:
(1) The document must have been made or verified by the witness.
(2) The document must have been made contemporaneously with the events to which the witness is testifying. (See *Attorney-General's Reference No 3 of 1979* (1979) 69 Cr App R 411)

As to the first of these two tests, a document is made by a witness if he has written it himself. It is verified by him if it has been prepared by a third party but the witness has checked that what has been written is correct.

Example
Gerald witnesses a bank robbery. As the culprits drive away Gerald calls out the registration number of a getaway car. Harry, a passer-by, scribbles the number on a piece of paper.

If Gerald checks at the time that what Harry has written down is correct by reading it or asking Harry to read it out then Gerald has verified the document and will be allowed to refresh his memory in the witness box before giving evidence of the registration number of the car. Had Gerald not checked Harry's note, then the document being neither made nor verified by Gerald could not be used by him to refresh his memory whilst giving evidence (see further *R* v *Kesley* (1982) Cr App R 213). For the sake of completeness it should be mentioned at this stage that Harry would not be allowed to relate to the court what Gerald had called out to him as it would be hearsay evidence (see Chapter 11).

In *R* v *Townsend* [1987] Crim LR 411, the victim of an attempted robbery tried to write down the registration number of the getaway vehicle but unfortunately the ink ran out. Examination of the paper with specialist equipment revealed the imprint of the writing. The original paper was not retained. Nevertheless, the witness was permitted to refresh her memory from the result when she gave evidence.

The second of the above tests poses the question of when a document will be taken to be contemporaneous. The answer is that this will be a question of fact in every case depending upon whether the facts are sufficiently fresh in the mind of the witness at the time he made the document (see *Attorney-General's Reference No 3 of 1979* above).

Example
A police officer witnesses an accident. He writes up his notes of the events fifteen days later during which period he has attended eight other incidents.

Example
Winifred witnesses an accident. She goes home and thinks of nothing else for fifteen days and then decides to make a detailed note of everything she saw.

Which document is contemporaneous with the event to which the witness is testifying? It will be for the court to decide whether either document is sufficiently contemporaneous with the events but despite the fact that the time lapse is identical in each case there is considerably more likelihood of objection being taken to the police officer refreshing his memory than Winifred.

Finally it should be noted that there is no rule to prevent a witness from reading his statement before he goes into court to give evidence. If this is done it is customary to notify the other party that this is the case (see *R* v *Richardson* [1971] 2 QB 484).

There is no requirement that such a statement should be strictly contemporaneous, though this is clearly of relevance in assessing the credibility of the subsequent oral evidence. Such a non-contemporaneous statement must be removed from the witness before he gives his evidence and he should not be permitted to refer to it again (see *R* v *Da Silva* (1989) *The Times*, 17 August). The judgment of the Court of Appeal in this case extended the principle so as to permit a witness to read his non-contemporaneous statement even though he had started to give his evidence if the judge in his discretion considered such a course of action to be in the interests of justice. The judge must be satisfied that:
— the witness could not now recall the details of the events because of the lapse of time;
— much nearer to the time of the events he had made a statement which represented his recollection at that time;
— he had not read the statement before going into the witness box; and
— he wished to have an opportunity to read the statement before continuing his evidence.

Practical considerations: There are three practical points to note concerning the examination in chief. These relate to:
(1) The rule against leading questions.
(2) The memory refreshing rule.
(3) The witness who fails to give the evidence expected of him.

In spite of the rule stated above, *leading questions* are asked in examination in chief. It is accepted practice to lead the witness on preliminary matters such as the witness's name and qualifications. Leading questions can also be asked on matters which are not in dispute. However, some advocates take the view that they will ask leading questions until they are stopped! It is necessary to be prepared to make objection to such questioning as the need arises.

How does the court decide whether or not a witness should be allowed to *refresh his memory* from a document? Questions will be put to the witness to ascertain when the document was made. If there is a substantial period between the event and the making of the document, it may be advantageous to find out what the witness had been doing during this intervening period (for example a police officer may have attended a number of incidents, thus reducing the likelihood of the facts being fresh in his memory). A point that is often overlooked is that the opposing advocate has the right to inspect the document *before it is used* (*Attorney-General's Reference No 3 of 1979* above). This can be particularly useful in relation to a police officer's notebook. If, for example, his day by day account of events is not written up in chronological order, it may show that the witness did not write them when he claims to have done so. It may also be possible to spot discrepancies between the witness's evidence and the document from which he is refreshing his memory. If it is intended to cross-examine the witness on the contents of the document it is important to bear in mind the rule that although cross-examination on that part of the document referred to by the witness does not make the document evidence against the cross-examiner, if the cross-examination is extended to take in other parts of the document then the whole document becomes evidence (see *Gregory* v *Tavernor* (1883) 6 C & P 280 and the Civil Evidence Act 1968, s 3(2)). The effect of this in a criminal case would be that the document would become an exhibit for the jury or magistrate but would be admissible merely to show consistency in the witness producing the note (see *R* v *Britton* [1987] 2 All ER 412). This case serves as a useful reminder that the defence can take advantage of the memory refreshing rule as well as the prosecution. In a civil case the document would be admissible to prove the truth of the matters stated.

If a witness refreshes his memory from a notebook whilst outside the court but does not use the document in the witness box the defence are entitled to examine the contents of the document and cross examine on relevant matters in it (*Owen* v *Edwards* (1983) 77 Cr App R 191).

However well prepared a case may be, there is always a danger of the *witness giving his evidence in chief failing to give the evidence expected of him*. This may be through nervousness or forgetfulness (the unfavourable witness) or because the witness actually refuses to tell the truth in accordance with a statement given previously (hostile witness). How to cope with this situation is dealt with in detail in Chapter 9. Suffice it for the moment to say that a witness who is ruled to be hostile can be cross-examined on certain matters by the party calling him whereas a witness who is merely unfavourable cannot.

(b) Cross-examination

When the witness has completed his evidence the opposing advocate has the chance to cross-examine. In cross-examination the advocate will be setting out to achieve one or more of three objectives:

(i) To discredit the evidence in chief. (It is necessary to consider carefully how this is to be approached. Broadly the choice is between showing the witness to be mistaken and showing that he is deliberately setting out to mislead the court. It may be that the witness is honest but mistaken as where he appears confused, forgetful or his evidence conflicts with accounts given by other witnesses or an earlier statement given by himself. If the witness is lying, then the likelihood of his being dishonest and his motive for so being, can be shown, for example, by highlighting his interest in the proceedings, any connection he may have with the parties, and his previous record of dishonesty.)

(ii) To clarify certain facts to put them in a more favourable light and to elicit facts favourable to the client and which the witness may not have volunteered.

(iii) To put his own client's case to the witness. (Failure to do so can lead to an allegation that the opponent's version of events has been accepted—see *R* v *Hart* (1932) 23 Cr App R 202 and *O'Connell* v *Adams* [1973] RTR 150.)

These are the aims of cross-examination. It does not follow that cross-examination will always be successful but the chances of achieving the objectives are greater if the advocate knows when he gets on his feet why he is cross-examining the witness. Unlike the examination in chief it is permissible to ask leading questions in cross-examination. The art of cross-examination is one requiring detailed study and the subject is more fully discussed in D Napley, *The Technique of Persuasion*, 3rd ed (Sweet & Maxwell 1983).

Practical considerations: In criminal cases it should always be borne in mind that as a consequence of cross-examining a prosecution witness and casting imputations on his character the defendant's own previous convictions can, in some circumstances, be put to him. This is dealt with in detail in **9.4** below. If there is a danger of this happening it should be carefully explained to the client beforehand and ideally his instructions should be obtained in writing.

(*c*) *Re-examination*

The advocate who called the witness is given the chance to try to repair any damage that may have been done in cross-examination. The re-examination should be confined to points arising out of cross-examination and leading questions are not allowed.

4.2 Special rules for witnesses in criminal cases

(*a*) *The general rule*

The general rule in criminal cases is that witnesses are both competent and compellable to give evidence. 'Competent' means that the witness is permitted to give evidence. 'Compellable' means that the court can enforce his attendance.

Practical considerations: In the magistrates' court a request should be made to the witness to attend. If this does not prompt a satisfactory reaction then request the clerk to the justices to arrange for a *witness summons* to be issued. In the Crown Court the procedure is to enforce the attendance of a witness by asking the examining justices to make a *witness order* at the committal proceedings or to make a request to the Crown Court office.

The general practice in criminal cases is that *witnesses do not sit in court before giving evidence*. There is no rule of law governing this and it is suggested that if a witness has been listening to other evidence before being called to give his own evidence then that is a matter which would go to the weight rather than the admissibility of his evidence.

The general rule on competence and compellability stated above is displaced in respect of particular types of witness.

(*b*) *Child witnesses*

If a child of tender years is to give evidence (there are no fixed age limits but 14 years is a useful guideline), the court should consider two questions:

(1) Should the child be allowed to give evidence at all?

(2) If yes, should the evidence be sworn or unsworn?

The test to be applied for the first question is simply whether the child is of sufficient intelligence to give evidence and understands the duty to tell the truth. If this hurdle is overcome, the child will be allowed to give evidence. Whether the evidence should be sworn or unsworn depends upon the test laid down in *R v Hayes* [1977] 1 WLR 234, namely whether the child appreciates the solemnity of the occasion and the special duty to tell the truth on oath as opposed to the general duty to do so in everyday life. If the child does not pass this test then the Children and Young Persons Act 1933, s 38, allows a child (a person under the age of 14) to give unsworn evidence.

Practical considerations: How does the court decide whether or not a child should give sworn evidence or indeed any evidence at all? It is a question for the justices or the judge to decide before the child actually gives evidence. Questions should be put to the child to ascertain whether the tests described above can be satisfied. The questions need not be of a religious nature. In the Crown Court such questioning should be in the presence of the jury and the questions and answers should be recorded in the trial transcript (*R v Khan* (1981) 73 Cr App R 190).

A witness under the age of 14 may give evidence, through a live television link on a trial on indictment in certain types of case including offences of assault, cruelty to children and sexual offences to which Criminal Justice Act 1988, s 32(1)(*b*), applies. The success of pilot schemes is such that this method of giving evidence is likely to become commonplace in the Crown Courts as the facilities are introduced more widely. It is possible that the system will be adopted in other cases where witnesses may be traumatised by having to give their evidence in the witness box, particularly victims of sexual assault. The voice-activated system allows the witness to see the person who is speaking. All the participants in the trial are able to see the witness via monitor screens. The procedure appears to be very much more satisfactory than erecting screens in the courtroom between the dock and the witness box as happened in *R v X, Y and Z* (see (1989) *The Times*, 3 November).

If it is desired to keep the identity of the child witness anonymous then an application for a direction to that effect can be made to the court under the Children and Young Persons Act 1933, s 39. This application is of course unnecessary in a juvenile court where s 49 of the Act imposes restrictions on reporting anyway.

(c) *Persons of unsound mind*

There is no provision for such persons to give unsworn evidence. The test to be applied therefore is whether the witness is able to comprehend what he is doing and, as with a child, whether he understands the nature of the oath. The procedure to be followed will be the same as for a child (see *R* v *Dunning* [1965] Crim LR 372).

(d) *The accused and co-accused*

At the trial of an accused who is charged alone with committing an offence the rules are very simple. The accused is competent to give evidence in his own defence but cannot be compelled to do so (Criminal Evidence Act 1898, s 1). This is an important point. The prosecution is not permitted to comment upon the fact that the accused has chosen not to give evidence in his own defence (Criminal Evidence Act 1898, s 1(*b*)). The trial judge can comment on this fact provided that he informs the jury of the accused's *right* not to give evidence and makes it clear that the jury are not to infer guilt from this (*R* v *Bathurst* [1969] 2 QB 99). An unusual point arose in *R* v *Harris* (1987) 84 Cr App R 75 in that the accused appealed on the ground that the judge had not made any comment to the jury on his failure to give evidence. The defendant's reasoning was that an experienced juror (such specimens are to be found at the Crown Court at Southwark!) would infer guilt from this. It was held that provided the judge makes it clear that no one is bound to give evidence any further comment is a matter of discretion.

It has always been the usual practice to call the accused to give evidence before calling other defence witnesses. The Police and Criminal Evidence Act 1984, s 79, now provides that the defence must call the accused before any other witness of fact.

Complications arise when two or more people are charged as co-accused. In this case it is necessary to consider not only their competence and compellability as witnesses in their own defence but also their competence and compellability as prosecution witnesses.

The first situation to consider is where the co-accused gives evidence for the prosecution. This may seem a strange notion and requires explanation. If two people are charged with the same crime it is quite possible that one will be prepared to give evidence for the prosecution against the other. The general rule is that if

they are being tried together one co-accused is not competent
to give evidence for the prosecution against the other (see *R* v
Richardson (1967) 51 Cr App R 381).

Example
Alan and Joe are jointly charged with burglary and are to be tried
together. Alan denies participating in the crime but is prepared to lay
the blame on Joe. Alan is not a competent prosecution witness.

However this is only the general rule and there are exceptions.
Alan would be a competent and compellable prosecution witness
in the following circumstances:
   (1) If he has pleaded guilty.
   (2) If, instead of being tried together, Alan is to be tried separ-
       ately.
   (3) If the charges against him are dropped (see, for example,
       R v *Governor of Pentonville Prison, ex parte Schneider*
       (1981) 73 Cr App R 200).
If any of these three situations applies and Alan does give evidence for the prosecution, there are specific rules on corroboration
of his evidence (see **3.1(b)**).

When co-accused are tried together they are of course competent to give evidence on their own behalf although as in the
case of a single accused they are not compellable (Criminal Evidence Act 1898, s 1). In giving evidence on their own behalf it is
quite possible that one co-accused will implicate the other.

Example
Alan and Joe are to be tried together on a charge of burglary. In his own
defence Alan may go into the witness box and say: 'I was approached
by Joe in a pub to help in a burglary. I refused. I then saw Joe leave the
pub, throw a brick through a shop window and climb in. I had nothing
to do with it—I was not present.'

In this example, in giving his own defence Alan has implicated
Joe. This will be evidence against Joe and can be used by the
prosecution (*R* v *Rudd* (1948) 32 Cr App R 138).
   The idea that the co-accused cannot say something against his
fellow accused for the prosecution but can say it in his own defence
and it then becomes evidence that can be used by the prosecution
is one that tends to confuse. It is perfectly simple to understand
if the procedural progress of a trial is borne in mind.
   Imagine that the horizontal line below represents the progress
of the trial of Alan and Joe. The evidence is presented to the
court in the stages shown, prosecution first, defence second. The

rules discussed above make Alan incompetent to give evidence at stage 1. At stage 2 Alan can give evidence for himself and anything he says becomes evidence against Joe if it incriminates him. Of course the prosecution are not going to proceed against Joe simply on the basis that Alan is going to implicate him when giving his own evidence. If this were the only prosecution evidence, Joe could make a successful submission of no case to answer at the end of stage 1 of the case (see **1.1(*d*)**) and the question of Alan's evidence being used against Joe would not then arise. The converse of this situation, which is sometimes overlooked however, is that anything said by one co-accused that helps his fellow accused is evidence for his fellow accused.

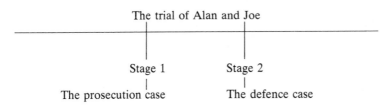

It was at one time thought that a co-accused who wishes to give prosecution evidence should be sentenced before giving such evidence. In *R* v *Weekes* (1980) 74 Cr App R 161, 167, it was stated that the better sentencing policy is not to sentence before the co-accused gives prosecution evidence but to wait until all persons charged can be sentenced together.

Practical considerations: Where two people are being tried together and in giving defence evidence one of them or indeed both will be implicating the other, application can be made to the justices or judge for *separate trials*. The matter is in the discretion of the court and it should be noted that the mere fact that one accused will implicate the other does not create any right to a separate trial. Indeed the attitude of the court is that unless it would be contrary to the interests of justice it is preferable, from the point of view of time, cost and consistency of verdict, to hold just one trial (see *R* v *Moghal* (1977) 65 Cr App R 56).

Under the Criminal Evidence Act 1898, s 1(*f*)(iii), if one co-accused in giving defence evidence implicates the other he can be cross-examined as to any previous convictions. This is more fully considered in **9.4**.

(e) *The spouse of the accused*

The Police and Criminal Evidence Act 1984, s 80(1)(*b*) and 80(2), makes the wife or husband of the accused competent and compellable to give evidence for the defence. The only exception to this rule is provided by s 80(4) which covers the situation where husband and wife are tried together. In such circumstances the rules are as for any other two persons who are co-accused, namely that the spouse is competent to give evidence but is not compellable. It should be noted that the failure of a spouse of an accused to give evidence cannot be commented on by the prosecution (s 80(8)). The judge, in his discretion, may comment and if the prosecution, in breach of s 80(8) make adverse comment on the failure of a spouse to give evidence, the judge is under a duty to remedy the situation (see *R* v *Naudeer* [1984] 3 All ER 1036).

The husband or wife of an accused is also a competent and compellable witness for any co-accused if the offence charged is one of those listed in s 80(3) (see below). This is again subject to s 80(4) where husband and wife are tried together.

As a prosecution witness the general rule used to be that a spouse of the accused was not competent to give evidence. This was subject to a number of exceptions but in none of those cases was the spouse compellable to give evidence. Section 80(1)(*a*) makes a significant change to the general rule by providing that the wife or husband of the accused is competent to give evidence for the prosecution subject to the exception in s 80(4). This exception applies where husband and wife are co-accused and are tried together, in which event neither is a competent witness for the prosecution unless he or she has pleaded guilty, is to be tried separately or the charges have been dropped. Section 80(3) further provides that a wife or husband of the accused is a compellable witness for the prosecution if the offence charged is covered by s 80(3)(*a*), (*b*) or (*c*). Subsection 3(*a*) deals with an assault on, or injury or a threat of injury to, the spouse of the accused or a person who at the time of the offence was under 16 years of age. Subsection 3(*b*) deals with a sexual offence alleged to have been committed in respect of a person who at the time of the offence was under 16 years of age. A sexual offence is defined by s 80(7) and includes offences under the Sexual Offences Acts 1956 and 1967 and the Protection of Children Act 1978. Subsection 3(*c*) deals with attempts or conspiracies to commit, aid, abet, counsel, procure or incite the commission of, an offence falling within subsection 3(*a*) or 3(*b*). These are the only offences in which the spouse is a compellable witness for the prosecution.

Example
Alan is charged with assaulting his wife Doreen. She is a competent and compellable witness for the prosecution.

Example
Fred is charged with stealing money from his wife Mavis. She is competent to give evidence against Fred but not compellable as theft is not one of the offences listed in s 80(3).

Example
R v *Deacon* [1973] 1 WLR 696 would now be decided differently. The accused was charged with attempted murder of his wife and the murder of *X*. The court held that the wife was competent in relation to the offence against her but not in the offence against *X*. As a result of s 80(1) the wife would now be competent but not compellable in respect of the offence against *X*.

Finally mention should be made of s 80(5) of the Act which provides that if a former husband and wife are no longer married then each spouse is competent and compellable to give evidence against the other as if they had never been married.

Practical considerations: Before the Police and Criminal Evidence Act 1984, it was desirable (see *R* v *Pitt* [1982] 3 WLR 359) if one spouse was to give prosecution evidence against the other, that the judge should advise the witness that there was no obligation to give evidence but that if he or she chose to do so then the normal rules relating to witnesses would apply. In the Crown Court this warning should be given to the witness in the absence of the jury. *Pitt* will not apply to those offences covered by s 80(3) of the Act but will continue to be applicable in other cases.

The Theft Act 1968, s 30(4), which provides that proceedings cannot be instituted against a husband or wife for stealing or damaging property belonging to the other spouse without the consent of the DPP is not affected by the Police and Criminal Evidence Act 1984.

(f) Witnesses outside the United Kingdom

When the Criminal Justice Act 1988, s 32(1)(*a*) is brought into force, it will be possible for a person outside the United Kingdom to give evidence through a live television link in criminal proceedings in the Crown Court.

4.3 Special rules for witnesses in civil cases

(a) The general rule

The general rule is that all witnesses are both competent and compellable to give evidence. The attendance of a witness can be enforced by subpoena in the High Court and witness summons in the county court (RSC Ord 38, r 14 and CCR Ord 20, r 12).

(b) Child witnesses

There is no provision for unsworn evidence in civil cases. Therefore the child must satisfy the test described in **4.2(b)** above and the same procedure will apply.

(c) Persons of unsound mind

The position is the same as for witnesses in criminal cases.

(d) Exclusion of witnesses from court

A feature of civil cases as opposed to those in a criminal court is that witnesses normally sit in court and listen to the proceedings before giving evidence. However, a witness may, in the discretion of the court, be excluded before giving evidence on the application of either party.

WRITTEN STATEMENTS OF WITNESSES

It is of course always preferable for a witness to attend court to give oral evidence. He can then be cross-examined and the court decides how much weight to attach to his evidence after looking at factors such as his manner, appearance and how he stands up to cross-examination. However, there will be occasions in both civil and criminal cases when a witness will not be able to attend, through ill health or death, for example. The parties to a case may also agree that attendance is not necessary. There are specific rules to cope with these situations. Before looking at them it should be noted that written statements are a particular type of documentary evidence and are therefore subject to the general rules discussed below (**4.7**). However, the rules relating to authenticity and originality should rarely, if ever, present a problem.

4.4 Written statements in criminal proceedings

(a) Statements admissible by agreement

A written statement of a prosecution or defence witness can be admissible in a criminal case without calling the maker provided the party tendering the statement in evidence has served notice in the proper form on all parties to the proceedings and no objection is raised within seven days (Criminal Justice Act 1967, s 9).

Practical considerations: The form of notice required for a s 9 statement is illustrated in case studies A and B, which will be found at the back of this book. The requirements are set out in s 9(2) and (3) of the Criminal Justice Act 1967. The most important are summarised below:

(1) The statement must be signed by the witness.
(2) The statement must contain a declaration that it is true and that the witness is aware of his liability to prosecution if the statement is tendered in evidence and he has wilfully stated anything in it which is untrue.
(3) If any document is referred to as an exhibit a copy should be attached or information given as to facilities for inspection.

Section 9 statements need not contain all of the witness's original statement. Indeed they should not contain any inadmissible or prejudicial matter. However if the prosecution edit out material evidence they are under a duty to notify the defence (see *Practice Direction (Evidence: Written Statements)* (1986) 83 Cr App R 212).

Section 9 statements are used by both prosecution and defence in the magistrates' court and the Crown Court. Their most common use is in agreeing non-controversial evidence when the opposing party does not wish to cross-examine the witness.

Example
Bill is charged with theft of goods from a shop. The prosecution have a statement from the manager of the shop identifying the goods and stating that Bill had no authority to remove them from the store without paying for them. Bill's defence is that he was not acting dishonestly but forgot to pay.

The prosecution in this case will almost certainly serve on the defence the manager's evidence in s 9 form. The defence are likely to agree the statement.

(b) Depositions from committal proceedings

A deposition of a witness taken at committal proceedings before justices or a statement tendered in evidence at such proceedings in accordance with the Magistrates' Courts Act 1980, s 102, is admissible in evidence on the trial of an accused in certain situations laid down in the Criminal Justice Act 1925, s 13(3).

The first situation is if a conditional witness order has been made in respect of a witness and he has not been asked to attend the trial.

The second is if the witness is dead, insane, too ill to travel or, on a more sinister note, has been kept out of the way by the accused. On this last point, it should be noted that the onus lies on the prosecution to establish by admissible evidence that the witness has been kept out of the way by the accused. It is not sufficient that the statements to be introduced contain allegations that threats have been made to the witness, as such evidence is hearsay (*R* v *O'Loughlin and McLaughlin* (1987) 85 Cr App R 157).

Practical considerations: The function and purpose of and the procedure at committal proceedings are outside the scope of this book but these matters are fully considered in P Rowe and S Knapp, *Evidence and Procedure in Magistrates' Courts*, 3rd ed (Longman 1984). Here it is sufficient to note that when a witness gives oral evidence at committal proceedings, has the evidence reduced into writing and signs it, it becomes his deposition. As an alternative to the giving of oral evidence at committal proceedings a witness's statement may be tendered in evidence provided it complies with the requirements of the Magistrates' Courts Act 1980, s 102. These conditions are broadly similar to those for statements admitted under the Criminal Justice Act 1967, s 9 (see **4.4(a)** above). However the fact that a defendant accepts a s 102 statement at committal proceedings does not necessarily mean that he would not wish to cross-examine the witness at the subsequent trial. It could therefore happen that if a witness dies for example between committal and trial the defendant could find extremely damaging evidence being read out from a s 102 statement without the chance to challenge it by cross-examination. In *R* v *Blithing* (1983) 77 Cr App R 86 the Court of Appeal stated that in this type of situation a court could use its discretion to exclude the statement notwithstanding the provisions of the Criminal Justice Act 1925, s 13(3).

The procedure for taking depositions is laid down in the Magistrates' Courts Rules 1981, rr 6–11.

(c) Depositions of witnesses who are dangerously ill

The Criminal Law Amendment Act 1867, s 6, allows a justice to take a deposition from a witness who is dangerously ill and unlikely to recover and this deposition can be admitted in evidence at a trial in the magistrates' court or the Crown Court.

Practical considerations: The deposition will only be admitted in evidence if the Magistrates' Courts Rules (r 33) are followed. The essential feature of these is the giving of notice to the other parties to the proceedings to enable them to attend to cross-examine the witness. Rules 6 to 11 also apply.

(d) Depositions of children and young persons

The Children and Young Persons Act 1933, s 42, provides that a justice may take a deposition from a child or young person relating to any offence referred to in the first schedule to the Act (examples of which include murder and manslaughter of a child or young person, any offence involving bodily injury to a child or young person and certain sexual offences) provided a doctor testifies that the giving of evidence in court would involve serious danger to the witness's life or health. The deposition can then be admitted in evidence at a trial in the magistrates' court or in the Crown Court.

Practical considerations: The deposition will only be admitted in evidence if the procedure laid down in s 43 of the Act is followed. The essential feature of this is again the giving of notice to the other parties to enable them to cross-examine the witness. The Magistrates' Courts Rules, rr 6–11 apply.

(e) Criminal Justice Act 1988, ss 23, 24

Subject to detailed conditions, written statements are admissible under the Criminal Justice Act 1988. These provisions require an appreciation of the rule against hearsay and are discussed in detail at **12.9**.

4.5 Written statements in civil proceedings

(a) Evidence by affidavit

Although affidavit evidence is admissible at various stages of civil proceedings (for example interlocutory applications, special procedure divorce cases, at the hearing of a High Court action begun by originating summons, originating motion or petition) a specific order of the court will be required if affidavit evidence is to be accepted at the trial of a High Court action commenced by writ or a county court action (see RSC Ord 38, r 2 and CCR Ord 20, r 6). An order will not normally be made if evidence is strongly contested by another party to the case.

Practical considerations: The application should be made by interlocutory summons in the High Court or on notice in the county court, attaching a copy of the affidavit.

(b) Depositions

Courts have a discretion in civil proceedings to allow evidence to be given at a trial by deposition (see RSC Ord 39, r 1 and CCR Ord 20, r 13). This will involve a judge or other court officer hearing the evidence out of court and reducing it into writing. The witness signs the document and it becomes his deposition.

Practical considerations: The court will usually exercise its discretion in favour of an applicant if the witness concerned is unable to attend the trial through ill health, old age, pregnancy or if the witness is going abroad before the trial date. There are also special rules (for example Ord 39, r 2) enabling a deposition to be taken in certain foreign countries.

An application to take evidence by deposition is by interlocutory summons in the High Court and on notice in the county court together with an affidavit setting out the grounds of application. As in criminal cases opposing parties must be given the opportunity of being present when the deposition is taken for the purpose of cross-examination.

(c) Unsworn written statements

Subject to complying with the correct procedure, the Civil Evidence Act 1968, ss 2 and 4, enables a party to civil proceedings to adduce in evidence certain written statements of witnesses. Sections 2 and 4 require an understanding of the difference between first-hand and multiple hearsay evidence. See **13.1** and **13.2**.

(d) Unsworn written statements in the magistrates' court

Magistrates' courts are still awaiting a statutory instrument bringing into effect the Civil Evidence Act 1968. At the moment the Evidence Act 1938 applies. Section 1 of the 1938 Act enables

certain written statements to be adduced in evidence provided
that the statement was not made by a person interested at a time
when proceedings were pending or anticipated involving a dispute
as to any fact which the statement might tend to establish. Section
1 again requires an understanding of first-hand and multiple hearsay and is therefore further discussed in **13.7**.

DOCUMENTARY EVIDENCE

If a party to a case wishes to adduce in evidence a document,
three points should be borne in mind:
  (1) The party producing the document may be required to
      prove its authenticity.
  (2) The document should if possible be original.
  (3) The contents of the document should not contravene any
      of the rules of admissibility discussed in Chapter 5. This is
      something that is easily overlooked but a document can for
      example contravene the rule against hearsay in the same
      way as oral testimony.
Documentary hearsay is discussed further in Chapters 12 and
13.

4.6 Public documents

A mixture of common law and statutory provisions relating to
public documents effectively deal with the above mentioned points
if the document to be adduced in evidence falls into this particular
class.

A public document is one that is made by a public officer for
the purpose of the public making use of it and being able to refer
to it. See *Sturla* v *Freccia* (1880) 5 App Cas 623. Examples of
public documents are numerous. Certificates of birth, marriages
and death are some of the most common. A full list can be found
in Archbold, para 10–1. Public documents are presumed to be
authentic by virtue of numerous statutes governing particular
classes of public document (see Archbold, para 10–1). As an
exception to the rule requiring originality in documents, certified
or office copy public documents are normally admissible by virtue
of a wide variety of statutes (for example the Public Records Act
1958, s 9(2)). In spite of the rule against hearsay, public docu-

ments are admissible in evidence of the truth of the facts contained therein. In criminal cases this is so by virtue of common law (*Sturla* v *Freccia*) and numerous statutes (Archbold, para 10–1). In civil cases the position is covered by the Civil Evidence Act 1968, s 9.

Practical considerations: The practical effect of the law relating to public documents is that they are usually simply handed to the court by counsel or solicitor as evidence.

4.7 Private documents

Private documents cannot according to the strict rules of evidence be adduced in evidence as easily as public documents.

(a) Authenticity

The person who made the document must be called to prove (eg) his signature or handwriting. If that person is not available another witness should be called for this purpose. As an exception to this rule so-called ancient documents are presumed authentic. An ancient document is one that is at least twenty years old and is produced from the place where it might be expected to be, having regard to its nature (Evidence Act 1938, s 4).

(b) Originality

The so-called 'best evidence' rule required that a document produced in evidence should be the original and not a copy. The effect of the numerous exceptions discussed in (*d*) below is that the rule itself is now of minor importance.

(c) Admissibility of contents

Confusion sometimes arises as to the admissibility of a document in evidence. This can be avoided by bearing in mind that documents are subject to the general rules of admissibility of evidence in the same way as oral evidence from a witness. Thus some documents, such as contracts or leases, may be admitted as direct evidence of the existence of the contract or lease. Other documents (such as records where it is sought to prove the truth of a matter referred to therein) will only be admissible if they fall within a recognised exception to the rule against hearsay (see **13.1** and **13.7**). Objection may also be taken to a document if it contravenes any other general principle of admissibility (eg it contains inadmissible opinion evidence).

(d) Practical considerations

The evidential rules relating to private documents can be avoided in certain circumstances.

In civil cases the *parties will frequently agree* that certain documents be admitted in evidence without further formality. If this is the case an agreed bundle of documents can be prepared with copies for the advocates, the court and witnesses. Because of the sheer volume of documents in many civil cases and the inconvenience caused to both parties in proving them this particular practice is popular and it is facilitated by discovery and inspection of documents (see **6.13**). In criminal cases there are normally fewer documents, there is generally no discovery and inspection and the very nature of criminal proceedings means that agreement is less likely. Indeed, such agreement may sometimes not even be accepted by the court (see *R* v *Nicholls* (1976) 63 Cr App R 187).

By RSC Ord 27, r 4, a party to High Court proceedings on whom a list of documents has been served (see **6.13**) is deemed to *admit the authenticity of documents* listed unless he states otherwise. Thus the onus is on the opponent to say whether he wishes to invoke the rule on authenticity.

In the county court by CCR Ord 20, r 11 the presumption of authenticity of ancient documents described above is deemed to apply to all documents of whatever age provided they are produced from proper custody, appear genuine and no objection is taken by the other side in the case.

A further practice is provided by RSC Ord 27, r 5 and CCR Ord 20, r 3 whereby a *notice to admit documents* can be served on an opponent. This requires a party to state in writing that he disputes the authenticity of a document and a failure to do so means that it is deemed to be admitted as authentic.

The legal and practical effect of the Civil Evidence Act 1968, ss 2, 4 and 5, which deal with documentary hearsay are fully discussed in Chapter 13. It is appropriate to mention at this stage however that a copy document is sufficient for the purposes of the Act. By s 6 of the Act a document may be authenticated in any manner the court may think fit.

In both civil and criminal cases the *loss of an original document* means that a copy can be adduced in evidence. It is for the party wishing to adduce the evidence to prove that the original is lost.

In both civil and criminal proceedings a third party in possession of a document can be compelled to attend court to produce it by using one of the methods described at **4.2(a)** and **4.3(a)** above. If a witness is able to claim privilege from producing the original (see Chapter 6) then the party wishing to call him may nevertheless be able to adduce a copy in evidence if he has been able to obtain one.

In criminal proceedings, where a statement contained in a document is admissible, it may be proved by production of the document or by the production of a copy authenticated in such manner as the court may approve (Criminal Justice Act 1988, s 27). This is so irrespective of the number of stages by which the copy is removed from the original.

The Bankers Books Evidence Act 1879, ss 3–9 (as amended by the Banking Act 1979), makes special provision for the admissibility of copies of bank ledgers and accounts in both civil and criminal proceedings.

REAL EVIDENCE

4.8 Matters directly perceived by the court

Apart from considering oral testimony, written statements and other documents it is often necessary for the court to look at people and objects which are relevant to the case. This is commonly referred to as real evidence. There are numerous examples of real evidence (see for example R Cross and C Tapper, *Cross on Evidence*, 6th ed (Butterworths 1985), 40–44). Some are noted below in their practical context.

Example
Fred is injured in a factory accident. The court may decide to look at the scene of the accident as real evidence.

Example
A case hinges on which of two conflicting stories the court prefers. One of the considerations must be the demeanour of the witness when giving evidence. The court will be considering real evidence.

Example
Bill is charged with committing an act of gross indecency in a public convenience. He contends that the witness who claims to have seen the incident could not possibly have seen anything from the position described. The court may decide to view the scene of the alleged crime as real evidence.

Example
Alice is badly scarred in an accident. At the trial of her action for damages the court may look at the extent of her injuries as real evidence.

Whilst there are no special rules relating to the admissibility of real evidence, if the object viewed requires some technical explanation then expert evidence will be needed. See *Buckingham* v *Daily News* [1956] 2 QB 534.

If the judge considers that a viewing of the scene of the crime is relevant, then it should take place under the control of the judge and in the presence of counsel, the jury and other participating members of the court (*R* v *Albarus and James* [1989] Crim LR 905).

PHOTOGRAPHS, PHOTOFITS, TAPE RECORDINGS AND VIDEO RECORDINGS

Having established the different methods of proof available to a party to litigation, this section examines the attitude of the courts to photographs, photofits, tape recordings and video recordings. A separate section has been devoted to this topic as it is one that can present difficulties for both student and practitioner. Furthermore, in *R* v *Cook* [1987] 2 WLR 775, it was suggested that these types of evidence are in a class of their own.

4.9 Photographs

A photograph of, for example, the scene of a crime, the scene of an accident or of a person allegedly committing a crime are admissible in evidence on proof that they are relevant to the issues involved in the case and that the prints are taken from untouched negatives (*R* v *Maqsud Ali* [1966] 1 QB 688). This will involve the photographer giving evidence as to the circumstances in which the photographs were taken, producing the untouched negatives and confirming that the prints were taken from them.

In *R* v *Dodson* [1984] 1 WLR 971 it was held that photographs taken by an automatic security camera of an attempted robbery of a building society were admissible. It would again be necessary to adduce evidence as to the way in which the camera operated. It is then for the jury or magistrates to decide whether they are sure that the photographs are of the defendants on trial.

Evidence that the accused has been identified from a photograph is admissible (*R* v *Byrne and Trump* [1987] Crim LR 689), but such evidence would be inadmissible where the photograph is identified as coming from police records and thereby discloses to the jury that he has a criminal record (*R* v *Wainwright* (1927) Cr App R 52).

4.10 Photofit pictures

A photofit picture is usually composed by a police officer from a description given by a witness of a person who has allegedly been seen committing a crime. In *R* v *Cook* [1987] 2 WLR 775 it was held that such pictures are admissible evidence before a jury. It was suggested that a photofit is effectively another kind of camera at work rather than a statement by the witness. As such they are admissible in evidence and considerations such as hearsay evidence do not arise. It is a curious result which follows from this manner of treating photofit pictures that, in the absence of other evidence amounting to a positive identification, there is no requirement for a warning to be given in accordance with the Turnbull guidelines (as to which see **3.8** above) (*R* v *Constantinou* [1989] Crim LR 572). Consequently, there must be some risk that a jury may attach undue weight to the photofit evidence.

4.11 Tape recordings

In *R* v *Maqsud Ali* [1966] 1 QB 688 it was held that tape recordings of a conversation are admissible in evidence provided that the accuracy of the recording can be proved (presumably by evidence from the person who made it), the voices can be properly identified and the evidence is relevant and otherwise admissible. The Police and Criminal Evidence Act 1984, s 60, provides for the tape-recording of interviews with suspects. A Code of Practice has been issued by the Home Secretary under the provisions of s 60(1). It is usual for a record of the interview to be used in a Crown Court trial and the Lord Chief Justice has issued a Practice Note ([1989] 2 All ER 415) which sets out the procedure to be followed both before and at trial. In particular, the defence must be given an adequate opportunity to consider any amendment to the record or the preparation of any transcript or the editing of any tape for the purpose of playing it back in court.

4.12 Video recordings

A video recording of the scene of a crime is admissible in evidence in the same way as a photograph. In *R* v *Thomas* [1986] Crim LR 682, the court admitted a recording of the route of a car chase between the police and a man subsequently charged with reckless driving.

It is also settled law that a video recording of a person allegedly committing a crime is admissible and that there is no need to produce the original recording provided that a copy is authenticated (*Kajala* v *Noble* (1982) 75 Cr App R 149). For the position when the defendant disputes the fact that he is the person identified from the recording see **3.7—3.9**.

It should be stressed that a video recording will only be admissible if it contains relevant and otherwise admissible evidence. Thus it has been held for example that it is not permissible to introduce a recording of what happened at a street identification held in a shopping precinct to try to improve the quality of the identifying witnesses' evidence (see *R* v *Smith and Doe* [1987] Crim LR 267; (1987) 85 Cr App R 197).

In *Taylor* v *Chief Constable of Cheshire* [1987] 1 All ER 226 it was held that the evidence of police officers which they had derived from viewing a video recording (the recording not being available to the court) was admissible and did not contravene the rule against hearsay. Evidence of the contents of the video recording was direct evidence of what was seen to be happening. It was, however, necessary that there should be sufficient evidence to connect what was seen on the video recording to the alleged actions of the accused.

It was held in *Ash* v *Buxted Poultry Limited* (1989) *The Times*, 29 November, that the High Court has an inherent jurisdiction to order one party in a personal injury action to allow the other to make a video of an industrial process so that the trial judge could see and understand the process.

4.13 Criminal Justice Act 1988, s 31

In Crown Court cases involving complicated issues of fact or technical terms there is now provision, with leave of the court or on the court's request, for evidence to be given in any form notwithstanding the existence of admissible material from which such evidence would be derived (Criminal Justice Act 1988, s 31).

The section specifically covers the preparation of glossaries and is wide enough to extend to drawings, photographs, video recordings and other documents.

Part II

Admissibility of Evidence

Chapter 5

General Principles of Admissibility

5.1 Introduction

The question of admissibility is one that arises not only during the course of a trial but also at the preparatory stage of a case. For example, in a criminal case it will be necessary to consider the admissibility of one's own evidence when preparing either the prosecution or the defence case for trial. In Crown Court cases (and in the magistrates' court if advance disclosure of the prosecution case is given by written statements) the defence will have an opportunity to examine the prosecution statements well before the trial. It will be necessary to look out for evidence to which objection will be taken on the grounds of inadmissibility. In civil cases the question of admissibility must be considered when preparing the case for trial on behalf of plaintiff or defendant, although usually it will not be possible to look at the evidence to be adduced by the other side.

Practical considerations: How are the problems of admissibility to be dealt with? The actual procedure will depend upon the type of trial. In criminal proceedings in the Crown Court any argument about admissibility will be determined by the judge in the absence of the jury. In this way the jury is prevented from hearing inadmissible evidence which it would then be told to disregard. The position is less satisfactory in the magistrates' court where the justices are the tribunal of both fact and law. The advocate may be aware before the trial that a point of evidence is going to arise. This may be so either as a result of advance disclosure of the prosecution case or because the matter has been specifically drawn to an advocate's attention before the trial by his opponent. In such circumstances it may be possible, in the case of more straightforward points, to reach agreement before the case is heard. In other cases the justices will have to rule on admissibility with the resulting difficulty of having to disregard evidence which they have heard but ruled inadmissible.

In a civil case where the trial is usually by judge alone, the judge will have to rule on points of admissibility.

The final possible problem is that a witness will, without warning, say something whilst giving his evidence that is plainly inadmissible. Objection will be raised by the opposing party. In the Crown Court the judge will tell the jury to put the matter out of their minds. In the magistrates' court and in civil cases the justices or judge, as the case may be, will have to attempt to put the evidence out of their own minds.

These points of procedure are re-examined in the chapters that follow whenever it is necessary to see precisely how a point of admissibility is dealt with.

5.2 The general principles of admissibility

The following points are the foundation of all specific rules of admissibility to be examined in this part of the book:
(1) If evidence is not relevant then it is not admissible.
(2) If evidence is relevant then it may or may not be admissible. Some categories of relevant evidence are rendered inadmissible by a rule of law.
(3) There is a discretion in criminal cases to exclude relevant evidence in the circumstances laid down in the Police and Criminal Evidence Act 1984, s 78. The courts appear to have claimed no such exclusionary discretion in civil cases at common law and there is no such statutory provision. Each of these points will now be examined in turn.

5.3 Relevance

Evidence is said to be relevant if it renders a fact in issue in a case more likely or less likely as the case may be or if it affects an issue that goes to the credibility of the witness. The evidence may consist of direct evidence from someone who actually perceived a fact or it may be circumstantial evidence from which a fact can be inferred.

Example
Jimmy is charged with murdering Jane who was found strangled. His defence is that at the relevant time he was drinking at a pub 15 miles away and that he did not know the victim. Part of the prosecution evidence consists of the testimony of a witness that he saw Jimmy running away from the scene of the crime shortly after the murder. This is evidence of a relevant fact, namely whether Jimmy was anywhere near the scene of the crime at the relevant time. It makes it more likely that this was the case if the evidence is believed and is therefore relevant. Further evidence is adduced that a strand of hair matching Jimmy's was found on the clothing of the victim. This is circumstantial evidence but again is relevant as it makes it more likely that Jimmy had been in contact with the victim.

Example
Mabel is charged with shoplifting. The prosecution allege that she took a pair of trousers from a major chain store and ran home without paying. Mabel's defence is that on the day in question she did not go to the store. This is plainly relevant since, if believed, it makes it less likely that Mabel is guilty of the offence charged. A store detective gives evidence that he had seen Mabel in the store five days before the crime looking at trousers. This evidence should not have been admitted as it is irrelevant. The fact that Mabel had been in the store five days previously does not make it more probable that she was in there on the day of the crime.

Example
Graham sues Mick for damages for personal injuries sustained as a result of a road traffic accident. One of the allegations of negligence is that Mick was exceeding the speed limit, a fact which is denied. Graham wishes to call a witness to say that when he saw Mick driving four days before the accident he was speeding. This is irrelevant. The evidence given does not make it more probable that Mick drove negligently on the day in question.

Res gestae

It has been seen that evidence is generally confined to the facts in issue in a case and to such other facts as are relevant in that they render more or less probable the existence (or non-existence) of the facts in issue. It is not always possible to determine the moment at which the relevant fact begins or ends.

Example
The employees at a timber camp started drinking on a Saturday morning and continued drinking heavily until late in the evening. During this drunken orgy the defendant had without provocation violently assaulted a number of people, striking them sharply about the head. At about midnight *B* retired to his sleeping quarters. The following morning he was found dying, having been struck several times about the head with

a bottle. His clothes had been soaked in paraffin and set alight. The defendant had in his possession a bottle, and a sweater belonging to the defendant had been found near *B*'s sleeping quarters. The defendant was charged with murder and at his trial evidence was admitted as to the earlier assaults. The part which the defendant had taken in the drunken orgy was relevant to the question whether the defendant had attacked *B* and whether at the time he had the intention which would make him guilty of murder. There was a series of connected occurrences commencing on the Saturday and culminating in *B*'s death early the following day. (*O'Leary* v *R* (1946) 73 CLR 566 — High Court of Australia)

Furthermore it could be highly artificial to restrict evidence simply to the fact in issue and to exclude the surrounding circumstances. For example in a murder case it may assist the jury if the evidence is not confined to the acts of firing a gun or inserting a knife but extends to the surrounding circumstances so that the jury may know in a broader sense what actually happened. See *Ratten* v *R* [1972] AC 378, 388 where this illustration was given by Lord Wilberforce.

The doctrine of res gestae renders admissible evidence of a series of facts of which the fact in issue is a part and also evidence of surrounding facts which accompany and explain a fact in issue.

Commonly, the surrounding fact will be a statement and it is in such cases that the most difficult questions of admissibility arise.

If the statement is relevant (irrespective of truth) then it is generally admissible.

Example
The deceased died in her kitchen from a gunshot wound. The accused held the shotgun but maintained that it had been fired accidentally. The prosecution case depended on proof that the killing had been deliberate. At 1.09 pm the accused had spoken to his father. The conversation lasted about three minutes. The voice of the deceased woman had been heard by the accused's father. At 1.15 pm a telephone call was made from the house. According to the evidence of the telephonist at the local exchange the woman on the line was hysterical and sobbing and asked for the police. At 1.20 pm a police officer arrived, by which time the woman had been shot. The evidence of the telephonist was relevant to show that a telephone call had been made (which was denied by the accused) by a woman, who could have only been the deceased and as showing that she was in a state of emotion or fear moments before she was shot. (*Ratten* v *R*)

Under the doctrine of res gestae a statement may also be receivable which would otherwise be excluded under the rule against hearsay (see Chapter 13) or under the rule against self-made evidence (see **14.2**).

5.4 Relevant evidence which is excluded

The fact that evidence is logically relevant does not mean that it will necessarily be admissible. Various categories of evidence are excluded on some other ground. These are all examined in some detail in the chapters that follow but it is useful to provide examples of the types of evidence involved and the reasons for exclusion. It should be stressed that these categories of evidence are rendered inadmissible as a matter of law, rather than at the discretion of the court.

Similar fact evidence (as will be seen in Chapter 7) is evidence that the accused in a criminal trial (or a party to a civil action) has done something similar in the past. Such evidence is not considered to be legally relevant and is therefore excluded. The character and convictions of the defendant in a criminal case are generally inadmissible for similar reasons. They are only admissible in exceptional circumstances (see Chapters 7 and 9).

Some relevant evidence is excluded as a matter of policy. Examples include hearsay evidence, self-made evidence, evidence subject to private privilege and evidence excluded as a matter of public policy.

5.5 The discretion to exclude evidence in criminal cases

At common law the judge has a discretion to exclude two types of relevant evidence: evidence obtained illegally and unfairly; and evidence the prejudicial effect of which outweighs its probative value (*R* v *Sang* [1980] AC 402).

In the Police and Criminal Evidence Act 1984, s 78, Parliament has, for the first time, conferred a statutory discretion to exclude otherwise relevant evidence. It was unclear whether this provision would be interpreted by the courts as merely a re-statement of the common law position (*R* v *Mason* (1988) 86 Cr App R 349), or whether the section conferred a new discretion and was therefore to be given its natural meaning without reference to earlier decisions (*R* v *Fulling* [1987] QB 426).

Section 78 provides as follows:

(1) In any proceedings the court may refuse to allow evidence on which the prosecution proposes to rely to be given if it appears to the court that, having regard to all the circumstances, including the circumstances in which the evidence was obtained, the admission of the evidence would have such an adverse effect on the fairness of the proceedings that the court ought not to admit it.

(2) Nothing in this section shall prejudice any rule of law requiring a court to exclude evidence.

Subsection (2) clearly preserves existing exclusionary rules of law, but it does not appear to extend to rules conferring a discretion on the judge being expressly limited in its operation to those rules *requiring* a court to exclude evidence'. Section 82(3) deals with existing discretionary powers by providing that nothing in Part VIII of the Act 'shall prejudice any power of a court to exclude evidence (whether by preventing questions from being put or otherwise) at its discretion'.

If s 78 were to be interpreted as a restatement of the pre-existing common law position then, s 82(3) in particular would have been redundant. It follows that s 78 should not be treated as prejudicing the rule under the common law that if, in the court's opinion, the prejudicial effect of evidence was likely to be greater than its probative value, the court in its discretion might exclude it (*R v O'Leary* (1988) *The Times* 18 May). The section therefore confers a new discretion to be exercised concurrently with the common law discretion identified in *R v Sang*, albeit that there is a considerable overlap between the statutory provision and the common law principles.

In the exercise of the statutory discretion the court should take into account all the circumstances of the case and then answer the question: 'Will the admission of the relevant evidence have such an adverse effect on the fairness of the proceedings that I, the court, ought not to admit it?' (per May LJ in *R v O'Leary*).

(a) Illegally and unfairly obtained evidence

It is not an uncommon occurrence for allegations to be made that evidence in a criminal case has been obtained in a manner which is unfair or even illegal.

Example
The police conduct a search of premises without a warrant or other authorisation. They discover a number of stolen items and as a result bring criminal proceedings against the occupier of the property.

In *R v Sang* the House of Lords considered illegally and unfairly obtained evidence generally. Lord Diplock said (at 437) that 'save with regard to admissions and confessions and generally with regard to evidence obtained from the accused after the commission of the offence, he [the trial judge] has no discretion to refuse to admit relevant admissible evidence on the ground that it was obtained by improper or unfair means'. At first sight, the phrase 'evidence obtained from the accused after commission of the offence' appears to include all evidence obtained by an illegal or improper search. But this was not Lord Diplock's intention (see 436). His Lordship explained that the underlying rationale of this branch of the criminal law is to be found in the maxim *nemo debet providere se ipsum*: no one can be required to be his own betrayer. There is in colloquial terms, a right to silence. Consequently there is a discretion to exclude evidence that is tantamount to a self-incriminatory admission but there is no discretion to exclude evidence discovered as a result of an illegal search.

The mere fact that evidence has been obtained as the result of an illegal search is unlikely to lead to its exclusion under the statutory jurisdiction. To exclude evidence on this basis would simply be to discipline the police within criminal proceedings. Clearly, there are more appropriate procedures open to persons aggrieved by police conduct. To this extent it is improbable that s 78 will affect the principles in *Sang*.

It is clear from *R* v *Sang* that the common law discretion is more likely to be exercised where evidence is obtained by some trickery, deception or other unfair means.

Example
Payne was charged with drunken driving. At the police station he allowed a police doctor to examine him on the understanding that this was merely to ascertain whether he was suffering from any illness and not to find out whether or not he was fit to drive. The Court of Appeal held that the evidence of unfitness to drive subsequently given by the doctor had been unfairly obtained by trickery and should not have been admissible. (*R* v *Payne* [1963] 1 WLR 637)

This is the case referred to by the Lord Chancellor during Parliamentary debate as one example of the type of situation that the new Act is intended to cover.

The case of *R* v *Mason* (1988) 86 Cr App R 349 illustrates the use of the statutory discretion to exclude evidence. The police told the defendant and his solicitor that the defendant's fingerprints had been found on a bottle used to start a fire. This was untrue. In the face of this new 'evidence' the solicitor advised the defendant to answer police questions following which he made a confession. The Court of Appeal held that the judge should have taken into consideration the deceit practised on the solicitor and that had he done so 'he would have been driven to the opposite conclusion, namely, that the confession be ruled out'.

In that case the deceit practised on the solicitor was considered to be the vital factor. Another case in which the defendant was tricked into providing evidence to incriminate himself was *R* v *H* [1987] Crim LR 47. The defendant was interviewed about a complaint of rape. He alleged that the complainant had consented to sexual intercourse and was released pending further enquiries. The complainant then made telephone calls to the defendant which were recorded on equipment installed by the police. The trial judge exercised his discretion under s 78 to exclude the evidence of the tape recordings. The defendant had been tricked into incriminating himself.

The case of *R* v *Mason* was distinguished in *DPP* v *Marshall* [1988] 3 All ER 683 where Woolf LJ said that in *R* v *Mason* 'there was an express misrepresentation and a clear deception practised and . . . it could have an adverse effect on the fairness of the trial, but here it is difficult to see how the fact that the police officers did not reveal their identity could have any effect on the trial'. In that case two plain-clothed police officers had entered a shop where they had made test purchases of alcoholic liquor without revealing their identity. As a result, the defendant was charged under the Licensing Act 1964.

In *R* v *Sang*, the House of Lords had held that entrapment was no defence and this rule of substantive law could not be circumvented by the device of excluding the evidence of the commission of the offence. Similarly, the Court of Appeal in *R* v *Harwood* [1989] Crim LR 285 held that s 78 being contained in a statute dealing with evidential matters could not be interpreted in a way which concluded that the substantive rule of law could be abrogated by evidential means.

The statutory discretion contained in Police and Criminal Evidence Act 1984, s 78, has been applied so as to exclude evidence of confessions (see **12.4**), evidence of identification (see below), evidence of the convictions of another or of the guilty plea of a co-accused (see **7.6**). The circumstances to be taken into account in the exercise of the discretion vary infinitely, and the Court of Appeal has said that it is 'undesirable to attempt any general guidance as to the way in which a judge's discretion under s 78 . . . should be exercised'. (*R* v *Samuel* [1988] 2 WLR 920)

(b) *Where the prejudicial effect of the evidence outweighs its probative value*

The courts always have a discretion to exclude evidence if its prejudicial effect outweighs its probative value. This is the second principle laid down in *R* v *Sang*. It relates to all evidence, not just that which has been obtained illegally or unfairly. This rule is included in the new statutory provision (see for example *R* v *O'Connor* [1987] Crim LR 260). If the court considers that the prejudicial effect of the evidence outweighs its probative value then it follows that the reception of the evidence will have an adverse effect on the fairness of the proceedings.

How does this principle fit in with the other rules looked at in this chapter? It has been established that certain categories of evidence are excluded as a matter of law rather than at the discretion of the court.

The character and convictions of the defendant were cited as an example. However, as will be seen from Chapters 7 and 9 there are circumstances in which a defendant's convictions, as an exception to the general rule, can be admitted. Nevertheless if one of these circumstances arises there is still a discretion to prohibit the introduction of the convictions if the judge feels that the reception of the evidence would have an adverse effect on the fairness of the proceedings.

What of evidence obtained as a result of an illegal search? Although a court is not likely to exclude such evidence on the grounds of the manner in which it was obtained it can be excluded on the ground that the reception of the evidence would have an adverse effect on the fairness of the proceedings.

Example
A witness to a robbery describes one of the participants in a robbery as wearing a blue anorak and grey trousers. The police receive an anonymous tip off that the person involved was Albert. They raid his house without a warrant, arrest him and to help prove evidence of identity take away a pair of grey trousers and a blue anorak.

The court is unlikely to exclude the evidence of the clothing on the ground that it was obtained as a result of an illegal search. However it may be prepared to exclude the evidence on the basis that its reception would have an adverse effect on the fairness of the proceedings. The items of clothing involved are so common that their probative value is very slight. There is a danger however that the jury will attach more weight to it than they should, thus causing unfair prejudice to Albert.

(c) Irregularities in identification procedures

Irregularities in identification procedures may result in the exclusion of evidence. That this was the position at common law is illustrated by R v Leckie [1983] Crim LR 543.

Example
Two defendants, both West Indians, were charged with robbery. On their arrest they refused to take part in an identification parade. They were then taken to a police station with a view to holding a parade. They were not given the information on their rights relating to such parades and were refused access to a solicitor. They were then placed in a cell and surrounded by three white police officers. Two witnesses then looked through the cell door and identified the defendants. (R v Leckie [1983] Crim LR 543)

The identification evidence was ruled inadmissible because of the way in which it had been obtained but it could equally have been excluded on the ground that its reception would have an adverse effect on the fairness of the proceedings. The way in which the evidence of identity was obtained rendered it virtually worthless. There was a chance that the jury would be prejudiced by the identification and attach more weight to it than was proper.

Following the introduction of the Police and Criminal Evidence Act 1984 and the Code of Practice for the Identification of Persons by Police Officers issued by the Home Secretary under s 66 (Code D), the courts have taken a very strict approach in dealing with evidence of identification.

The Code makes the holding of a parade mandatory unless it is impracticable. Thus, in R v Gaynor [1988] Crim LR 242, there had been difficulty in assembling a sufficient number of people of suitable appearance to hold a parade in compliance with the Code of Practice. On being informed that he would otherwise be confronted with the witness, the defendant agreed to a group identification. It was held that more could have been done to arrange an identity parade and that accordingly there was a breach of the Code. The evidence was excluded under s 78.

The case of R v Britton and Richards [1989] Crim LR 144 goes further. Two defendants of Afro-Caribbean extraction had been bailed to appear at police stations on consecutive days for the purpose of taking part in an identity parade. On the day fixed for the parade, each was told that it was impracticable to hold a parade, or even a group identification, as no perons had been found who were willing to take part. Accordingly, it was proposed that a confrontation was to take place. R's solicitor made no representations, but on the following day B's solicitor asked for a week in which he would try to find people to take part in the parade. The offer was declined. In both cases confrontations took place at which the defendants were identified. It was held not only that the identification officer should have allowed B's solicitor the opportunity to try to find suitable persons to participate in the parade, but that he should also have considered himself whether R's solicitor could have helped assemble the parade. There had been a breach of the Code, and as the identification evidence would have had such an adverse effect on the fairness of the trial, that evidence would not be admitted.

According to the Code of Practice, arrangements for an identification parade must be the responsibility of a uniformed officer not below the rank of Inspector who is not involved in the investigation. Furthermore, no officer involved in the investigation of the case against the suspect may take any part in the arrangements for, or the conduct of, the parade. In *R* v *Gall* (1989) *The Times*, 2 May, an investigating officer came into the room, looked at the parade and then had an opportunity to speak to a witness who was then introduced to the parade. The Court of Appeal held that the judge should have taken the view that this was a breach of the Code of Practice, and having reached that conclusion he should have exercised his discretion to exclude the evidence.

Evidence that a witness has been able to identify the defendant in the dock had been excluded under the common law discretion, as in the case of *R* v *Horsham JJ, ex p Bukhari* (1982) 74 Cr App R 291, where it was considered that the prejudicial effect of the evidence would outweight its probative value. Similarly, following the introduction of the Code of Practice, such evidence was excluded in the case of *R* v *Eatough* [1989] Crim LR 289 on the same ground (though the statutory discretion could equally have been relied on). The concern over dock identifications had been further recognised by the Code of Practice which required first that an identification parade be held if possible.

Practical considerations: In the Crown Court an application to exclude evidence under s 78 is made to the judge in the absence of the jury. It is clearly desirable that consideration be given to the exercise of the discretion before the evidence is given. Furthermore, the wording of s 78 demands this, and once evidence has been given, only the common law discretion remains. It may be necessary to hold a voir dire, but the judge is not obliged to do so (*R* v *Beveridge* (1987) 85 Cr App R 255) and nor does the defendant have the right to insist on a trial within a trial in magistrates' court proceedings (*Vel* v *Chief Constable of North Wales* [1987] Crim LR 496). The issue can usually be resolved by considering depositions, exhibits and the submissions of counsel.

It should be noted that whilst the exclusionary discretion applies to all criminal trials, magistrates have no discretion to exclude evidence at committal proceedings (*R* v *Horsham Justices ex p Bukhari* (1982) 74 Cr App R 291).

Subject to unreasonableness, the Court of Appeal will be loath to interfere with the exercise of the judge's discretion (*R* v *O'Leary* (1988) *The Times*, 18 May). An appeal may be successful in cases where a judge has reached a conclusion as a result of which he fails to exercise his discretion at all. This occurred in *R* v *Samuel* [1988] 2 WLR 920 where the trial judge ruled that the police had been justified in refusing the solicitor access to the defendant. Had he ruled otherwise he would have been unlikely to exercise his discretion in such a way as to admit the evidence.

5.6 The exclusionary discretion and civil cases

The lack of authorities suggests that in civil cases the courts do not claim a general exclusionary discretion. Thus, in civil cases generally there is no discretion to exclude relevant evidence even though it has been unlawfully or improperly obtained. See for example *Calcraft* v *Guest* [1898] 1 QB 759.

The problem of illegally or unfairly obtained evidence may arise in respect of documents which are subject to legal professional privilege. It will be seen in **6.11** that if privileged documents or copies thereof fall into the hands of an opponent then there is nothing to prevent copies of the documents being adduced in evidence. This rule applies even if the documents have been obtained by improper means.

However in *ITC Film Distributors* v *Video Exchange Ltd and others* [1982] Ch 431 the court considered a situation in which the defendant to an action had actually taken documents belonging to the plaintiff whilst they were in court, and then sought to adduce copies of them in evidence. In this case the court stated first of all that the reason for admitting evidence obtained by improper means was the public interest in the ascertainment of the truth in litigation. In the instant case, however, this was outweighed by the public interest that litigants should be able to bring their documents into court without fear that they may be filched by their opponents by stealth or trick and then used in evidence. Warner J ruled that the evidence was inadmissible. The decision must be taken to be one turning on its particular facts and does not affect the general principle stated above.

Practical considerations: Although generally there is no power to exclude evidence of privileged documents if they have been obtained by an opponent even by improper means, it may be possible to seek an injunction under the equitable jurisdiction in confidence restraining the use of the documents (see further **6.12**).

Chapter 6

Public Policy and Privilege

A claim to privilege is a claim that a witness should not be obliged to give some oral evidence or should not be obliged to produce some document or thing. If the claim is upheld, then the result is, of course, that relevant evidence may be witheld from the court. In the development of rules relating to privilege the courts and the legislature have to balance the competing interests of, on the one hand, allowing the tribunal of fact to have before it all relevant evidence so as to do justice between the parties and, on the other hand, the interest to be protected by the privilege. The public interest in the administration of justice is an interest which generally requires that a court should have access to all evidence relevant to the issues to be decided. There are however circumstances where the public interest is better served by excluding evidence. Sometimes the purpose in excluding evidence is to assist the court in reaching a fair verdict in the case before it: hearsay evidence is generally excluded because of its unreliability, evidence of the bad character of the accused in a criminal trial is excluded because it is of only marginal relevance and the tribunal would be in danger of attaching undue significance to it. In other cases there are wider considerations of policy calling for the exclusion of relevant evidence. It is these cases which will be considered in this chapter.

PUBLIC POLICY

6.1 Immunity from disclosure on grounds of public interest

(a) Civil cases

A claim to withold evidence of a communication on grounds of public interest will be made where the public interest in the

88

administration of justice is alleged to be outweighed in the circumstances of the case, by some greater public interest.

Example
The plaintiff's claim arose from the sinking of the submarine '*Thetis*' during trials in Liverpool Bay. Ninety-nine lives were lost. In the course of a negligence claim brought against the shipbuilders, the plaintiffs sought discovery of certain documents concerned with the construction of the submarine. The Admiralty instructed the defendant company to resist disclosure of these documents on grounds of public interest. The claim was upheld by the House of Lords. Disclosure of the documents would have been against the interests of national security which in the circumstances of the case outweighed the public interest in the administration of justice and the interests of the individual litigants. (*Duncan* v *Cammell Laird & Co Ltd* [1942] AC 624)

The objection to disclosure may be made on the ground that the disclosure of the contents of a specific document would be contrary to the public interest (as was the case in *Duncan* v *Cammell Laird & Co Ltd*). These may be termed the 'contents' cases. More commonly, disclosure will be resisted on the ground that the document is one of a class of documents, the disclosure of which would be contrary to the public interest irrespective of the contents of an individual document. These may be termed the 'class' cases. Such documents as cabinet papers, foreign office papers, documents concerned with the administration of the armed forces or the functioning of the Civil Service may all be the subject of class claims. In either case the objection to disclosure will be taken by, or on the instructions of, the head of the department of government which is affected. The distinction between these two categories may no longer be of real significance (see *Conway* v *Rimmer* [1968] AC 910 and *Burmah Oil* v *Bank of England* [1980] AC 1090) but it did enable the House of Lords in *Duncan* v *Cammell Laird & Co Ltd* to lay down a wide general principle that whether the claim be a 'class' or a 'contents' claim the courts are bound by the decision of a Minister of State to withhold evidence provided that it appears that the objection was in proper form and taken on proper grounds.

This aspect of the decision was not accepted by the House of Lords in *Conway* v *Rimmer*. Although the courts will give great weight to the objections put forward by the Minister, especially where it appears that he has inspected a certain document and has formed the opinion that the disclosure of its contents would be against the public interest, a ministerial certificate or affidavit in support of a claim to withhold evidence will not be regarded as conclusive. In each case it will be for the court to weigh the competing public interests. It will need to know what harm would be done by disclosure and may therefore ask the Minister to be more specific about his objection to disclosure, requiring him to swear a further affidavit or even to appear before the court to press his objections. The court will also need to know the effect of non-disclosure in the particular case it is dealing with. Would the effect of non-disclosure be a complete denial of justice (as it may well have been in *Duncan* v *Cammell Laird & Co Ltd*) or would the evidence be of little value anyway?

In a case in which the court is not satisfied that the documents should be withheld the court may first inspect the documents privately before ordering disclosure (see *Air Canada* v *Secretary of State for Trade* [1983] 2 AC 394). The burden rests on the party resisting disclosure to show that the interest to be protected outweighs the interests of justice and in a case where the competing public interests appear to the court to be balanced it seems that disclosure should be ordered (per Lord Edmund Davies in *D* v *NSPCC* [1978] AC 171 at 246).

It was once thought that a claim to withhold documents on grounds of public interest would be effective only to protect from disclosure matters concerned with the organs of central government. It is now clear that the protection extends to other matters of public concern and that 'the presence (or absence) of involvement of the central government in the matter of disclosure is not conclusive either way' (per Lord Edmund Davies in *D* v *NSPCC* at 245).

In recent years many of the cases involving claims that entire classes of documents should be immune from disclosure on grounds of public interest have been concerned with the preservation of confidences. However, 'confidentiality is not a separate head of privilege' (per Lord Cross in *Alfred Crompton Amusement Machines Ltd* v *Commissioners of Customs and Excise (No 2)* [1974] AC 405 at 433) although his Lordship did go on to say that it 'may be a very material consideration to bear in mind when privilege is claimed on the ground of public interest'. In that case the Commissioners' objection to the disclosure of documents was upheld by the House of Lords. The Commissioners relied upon information supplied to them in confidence in carrying out their statutory duties. If it was known that the sources could be disclosed in subsequent proceedings, then the supplies of information might dry up. In the circumstances an order for disclosure would have the effect of inhibiting the Commissioners in carrying out their statutory purpose. This consideration of public interest prevailed.

Similarly, the courts found it necessary to afford protection to statements made solely for the purpose of an investigation under the Police Act 1964, s 49, again because liability of the statements to disclosure would discourage those who could supply information from coming forward. This would make it difficult for the Chief Constable to carry out his statutory duty in relation to the investigation of complaints against the police (*Neilson* v *Laugharne* [1981] 2 WLR 553; cf *Peach* v *MPC* [1986] 2 WLR 1080).

In *Gaskin* v *Liverpool City Council* [1980] 1 WLR 1549 the prospective plaintiff was a young man who had been brought up in the care of the local authority following the death of his mother when he was six months of age. He had a bad criminal record and suffered from a psychiatric disorder. He alleged that his misfortunes were caused by the negligence of the social services department in the manner in which he had been cared for. He brought an action for discovery of reports and case notes kept by the social services department. The Court of Appeal held that the documents were protected by public interest immunity and that disclosure could not be ordered. In *Re M (a minor)* (1990) *The Times*, 4 January, the Court of Appeal held that the reports of social workers and analogous documents were in a special category of immunity justified by the particular circumstances of the welfare of the children. There is, however, no absolute rule against disclosure. It might for example be necessary for local authorities in child care cases, for the benefit of the child concerned, to volunteer disclosure of certain records, such as contemporaneous notes in a neglect case, or the actual notes of interviews in a sexual abuse case.

Disclosure was also ordered in *Campbell* v *Tameside Metropolitan Borough Council* [1982] QB 1065. A teacher was assaulted by an eleven year old boy. She suffered serious injuries which necessitated early retirement. She was proposing to bring a claim against the local education authority. She brought an action for discovery of various reports about the boy. The education authority sought to withhold these reports claiming public interest immunity. The Court of Appeal ordered the documents to be produced. Lord Denning MR thought that on balance the public interest required disclosure. Ackner LJ was of the view that dis-

closure would not impede the public statutory purpose for which
the documents came into existence and that, therefore, there was
no consideration of public interest requiring the documents to be
withheld.

In *Science Research Council* v *Nasse; Leyland Cars (BL Cars
Ltd)* v *Vyas* [1980] AC 1028 the complainants had each made
unsuccessful applications for certain posts. In order to prove their
allegations of discrimination each sought discovery of records and
interview notes concerning other employees. Disclosure of these
documents was resisted. The employers in each case wished to
preserve the confidentiality of the reports. It was held that documents were not protected by any public interest immunity. The
House of Lords emphasised again that confidentiality is not of
itself a ground for withholding evidence. In neither case was any
public function affected by the disclosure of the reports.

The difference between the immunity from disclosure now
under consideration and the rules concerning private privilege
considered below lies in the fact that in the former claim it is a
public interest which is to be protected rather than the interest of
an individual. If evidence is withheld on grounds of public interest,
then it is not open to the individual to waive the immunity or to
introduce secondary evidence of the matter (see *Gain* v *Gain*
[1961] 1 WLR 1469).

In every case where there is a claim to withhold evidence on
grounds of public interest, the court must balance the conflicting
public interests involved. From the fact that a particular document
or class of documents was ordered not to be disclosed in one
case it does not automatically follow that those documents would
receive the same protection in later proceedings. In cases where
some reliance has been placed on the need to preserve confidences
it may be that the person who supplied the information is prepared
to give evidence. In those circumstances there is perhaps no public
interest which will be threatened by disclosure. (See also *Alfred
Crompton Amusement Machines Ltd* v *Commissioners of Customs
and Excise (No 2)* [1974] AC 405, 434, where Lord Cross
described this as 'waiver'.)

(b) Criminal cases

Protection has for many years been given to evidence which, if
disclosed, could have the effect of deterring informers from assisting the police in the detection of crime (see, for example, *Marks*
v *Beyfus* (1890) 25 QBD 484). Thus the police will not normally

be compelled to reveal the identity of an informer. In certain cases, however, the public interest will be outweighed by the need for disclosure to enable the defence to properly present their case.

Example
W was charged with conspiracy to rob. He was arrested whilst hiding on office premises in a cupboard. W had a shotgun with him in the cupboard. W claimed that he had been recruited to steal from the offices by X, but that he did not know that force was to be used. W further claimed that X had planted the gun in the cupboard whilst working in his capacity as office cleaner, and had then informed the police of W's intentions to rob the offices. The police were obliged to state in court whether or not X was the informer, as if he was, he clearly had a chance to plant the rifle in the cupboard and had a motive to do so, as it enhanced his value as an informer. (*R* v *Williams and Bellfantile* [1988] Crim LR 114)

The principle of non-disclosure in the public interest has also been held to apply to the location of police observation posts and to the identity of the owners/occupiers of such premises. The public interest here is in protecting those who are prepared to assist the police, and in *R* v *Johnson (Kenneth)* [1988] 1 WLR 1377 the Court of Appeal stated that, in order to enable a judge to determine whether non-disclosure was desirable, the following minimum evidential requirements had to be satisfied:

(1) The police officer in charge of the observations to be conducted must testify (in the absence of the jury) that he has ascertained the attitude of occupiers of the relevant premises, not only to the use to be made of them, but also as to the possible disclosure to a court of their location.

(2) A police officer must testify (in the absence of the jury) that immediately before the trial he visited the premises used for observation to ascertain whether the occupants were still the same and what their attitude to disclosure in court would now be.

The court are clearly taking precautions to establish that there is genuinely an interest to protect, and in *R* v *Daley* (1988) 87 Cr App R 52, it was held that the police could not refuse to disclose the colour and make of an unmarked police car which had been used for surveillance purposes as the question of protection of the owner did not arise.

6.2 Without prejudice communications

It is an aspect of public interest in the administration of justice that the parties to a dispute should be encouraged to settle wherever possible. Clearly, the prospects of settlement would be greatly reduced if a party were not able to discuss the basis of a proposed settlement (perhaps involving some admission) and its terms for fear that should negotiations break down, his case may be prejudiced by the proof of communications made in the pursuit of a settlement.

Clearly, there is no problem where, as is often the case, an offer of settlement is made 'without admission of liability'. Suppose however that following a road accident one of the parties brings a claim for personal injuries and the defendant alleges contributory negligence. Any settlement will inevitably be on the basis of an agreed apportionment of liability.

It is in such cases that the 'without prejudice' privilege is important. Where the privilege exists the effect is that the privileged communication must not be disclosed to the court without the consent of both parties.

The existence of the privilege depends upon the purpose of the communications and the intentions of the parties (see, for example, *South Shropshire District Council* v *Amos* [1986] 1 WLR 1271 and *Hawick International Ltd* v *Caplan* (1988) *The Times* 11 March, in which it was held that 'without prejudice' privilege does not apply to a communicaton made in furtherance of crime or fraud). It is customary to make communications expressly 'without prejudice' by including those words (or other words to similar effect). It is not however absolutely necessary that these words should be inserted at every stage of the correspondence.

Problems have arisen in cases involving more than one defendant. If a settlement is negotiated between the plaintiff and one defendant, can the defendant who is still involved in the litigation seek production of the correspondence that led to the settlement? In *Rush and Tompkins Ltd* v *G L C* [1988] 3 All ER 737, the House of Lords decided that if one defendant has come to an agreement with the plaintiff, then the 'without prejudice' correspondence that led to the settlement remains privileged in relation to the second defendant in the litigation, and indeed, in any subsequent litigation with the same subject matter.

If a settlement is reached (a contract of compromise is concluded) then the 'without prejudice' communications are admissible as evidence of such agreement.

Example
Paul has brought an action in negligence to recover damages for personal injuries alleged to be caused by the negligent driving of Norman. Norman makes an offer of settlement without prejudice on the basis of a 70/30 per cent apportionment of liability. Neither party can give evidence of this communication without the consent of the other. However if the offer is accepted there is a concluded contract of compromise. If Norman fails to pay then Paul could bring proceedings to enforce the contract. In those proceedings he would be entitled to prove the contract by introducing evidence both of Norman's offer and of his own acceptance.

In making a 'without prejudice' offer a party may in some cases reserve the right to draw the offer to the attention of the court when, after verdict, the question of costs is considered. This will be appropriate in cases in which a payment into court is not possible or appropriate but the party making the offer wishes to minimise any liability for costs (*Cutts* v *Head* [1984] 2 WLR 349). See now RSC Ord 62, r 9.

Example
Peter is a pedestrian who has been injured in an accident. He brings proceedings against Derek the driver of the vehicle which struck him and he in turn joins Thomas as a third party to claim contribution from him towards any damages he may be ordered to pay. Thomas is prepared to accept that he is partly responsible and gives notice to Derek that he is prepared to contribute forty per cent of the total damages. Although this offer may not be proved by either party in the course of the third party proceedings, Thomas will be able to draw the offer to the attention of the judge when he considers what order should be made as to the costs of the third party proceedings. (See RSC Ord 16, r 10)

Similarly a party wishing to make an offer of settlement in proceedings for financial provision following divorce may reserve the right to refer to the offer when the question of costs is to be considered. See *Calderbank* v *Calderbank* [1976] Fam 93. Communications between the parties to a marriage with a view to promoting the prospects of reconciliation enjoy a similar privilege. Furthermore, where the communications are made through, or in the presence of, a third person who is acting as a conciliator then neither party to the marriage nor the conciliator may give evidence of the communications unless both parties agree. See *McTaggart* v *McTaggart* [1949] P 94.

The conciliator will commonly be a probation officer, clergyman or marriage guidance counsellor but may be any private individual. Furthermore, it seems that where the privilege exists evidence of the communications may not be given by another person who heard the conversation (*Theodoropoulas* v *Theodoropoulas* [1964] P 311).

In determining whether or not a communication is protected by any head of private privilege, there are a number of questions to consider. What is the relationship between the parties to the communication? What was the purpose of the communication? What was the nature of the communication?

If it appears that the communication is privileged, then it is necessary to consider two further questions. To whom does the privilege belong? Who may waive it?

If a claim to privilege is made and upheld, then is it possible to introduce evidence of the communication in some other way?

6.3 Legal professional privilege

Under this head of privilege there is protection for communications between a legal adviser and his client and also for certain communications with third parties. The privilege in these cases belongs to the client and it is for the client to decide whether or not a claim to privilege should be made.

(a) Communications between legal adviser and client

Where communications pass between a client (or his agent) and his solicitor (or the solicitor's clerk) and counsel to enable the client to obtain legal advice such communications will be protected in two ways:

(1) The client will not be obliged to give evidence of the communications himself.
(2) The legal adviser may give such evidence only with the consent of the client.

Were it not for the existence of this privilege, the client would be unable to instruct his legal adviser without the risk that the latter might be obliged to give evidence of what had passed between them. This would make it difficult to prepare litigation or to advise adequately in non-contentious matters.

Although the giving or seeking of advice is an important ingredient if a claim to privilege is to be upheld, it does not follow that every document or communication for which a claim is made must have specifically sought or given advice. The test is whether in the course of a solicitor and client relationship a communication is made confidentially for the overall purpose of legal advice. This includes communications made with a view to keeping both parties informed so that advice could be given or sought as required (see *Belabel* v *Air India* [1988] 1 WLR 1036).

The privilege applies only where the legal adviser is consulted formally in that capacity. The privilege would not (for example) extend to a conversation at the local golf club when a member may casually seek advice from a solicitor/friend (see *Minter* v *Priest* [1930] AC 558).

The privilege applies in the same way to communications between 'in-house' lawyers and other members of a company's staff. The communication must be for the purposes of giving and receiving legal, as opposed to general, advice (*Alfred Crompton Amusement Machines Ltd* v *Commissioners of Customs and Excise (No 2)* [1974] AC 405).

Although the privilege covers both oral and written communications, there will be no protection for a document handed over to a solicitor which would not have been privileged in the client's hands (*R* v *Peterborough Justices, ex parte Hicks* [1977] 1 WLR 1371).

The privilege is overridden by the interests of justice in securing the acquittal of an innocent person. Where a solicitor had in his possession certain documents which were relevant to the defence of the accused in a criminal trial he was obliged to produce the documents even though his clients would in other circumstances have been able to claim legal professional privilege (*R* v *Barton* [1973] 1 WLR 115). In *R* v *Ataou* [1988] 2 All ER 321 the principle was extended so as to allow a witness to be cross-examined on a document which was, on the face of it, protected by legal professional privilege.

Example

H and Ataou were charged with conspiracy to supply a controlled drug. They consulted the same solicitor and H told the solicitor that Ataou was not involved. H later changed solicitors, pleaded guilty and gave prosecution evidence against Ataou. The trial judge refused to allow counsel for the defendant to cross-examine H about the interview with Ataou's solicitors, as it was protected by privilege. The Court of Appeal held that the legitimate interests of the defendant in seeking to breach the privilege outweighed that of H in seeking to maintain it.

(b) Communications between legal adviser (or his client) and third parties

'Evidence obtained by the solicitor, or by his direction, or at his instance, even if obtained by the client, is protected if obtained after litigation had been commenced or threatened, or with a view to the defence or prosecution of such litigation' (per Jessel MR in *Wheeler* v *Le Marchant* (1881) 17 Ch D 675 at 682).

The protection afforded to communications with third parties is narrower than that afforded to communications between legal adviser and client. Litigation must have been commenced or must at least be in the contemplation of the client at the time of the communication if it is to be protected.

This head of privilege will cover interviews and correspondence with prospective witnesses. This is the case whether the witness is a witness of fact, a witness as to character or an expert witness. A report prepared by an expert witness is therefore privileged. (The privilege does not attach to documents prepared before litigation is contemplated or pending and which are sent to the expert for comment—see *R* v *King* [1983] 1 WLR 411). In the case of a document prepared by a third party it will be privileged if brought into existence for the purposes of litigation. This need not be the sole purpose for which the document was commissioned or prepared provided that it is the dominant purpose.

Example
An employee of the British Railways Board had been killed in an accident. A report on the circumstances of the accident had been prepared. In an action against the Board the widow of the deceased wished to see the report. The defendants claimed to withhold the document on grounds of legal professional privilege. It appeared that the report had been prepared for two purposes. Firstly, the Board wished to discover the cause of the accident. Secondly, it wished to submit the report to its solicitor for use in any subsequent litigation. (*Waugh* v *British Railways Board* [1980] AC 521).

The House of Lords held that for the important public interest in disclosure to be overriden by a claim of privilege, the purpose of submission to the party's legal advisers in anticipation of litigation must be at least the dominant purpose for which it had been prepared. It was not, however, necessary that this should be the sole purpose. This 'dominant purpose' test was also preferred in the case of *Re Highgrade Traders Ltd* (1983) *The Times*, 20 December.

(c) Privileged communications for unlawful purposes

Legal professional privilege will not extend to a communication which is in itself unlawful as where advice is sought as to the best way to commit a crime (see *R* v *Cox* (1884) 14 QBD 153). This principle is also now contained in statutory form. Legal professional privilege can defeat a police claim to seizure of material under the Drug Trafficking Offences Act 1986 or the Police and Criminal Evidence Act 1984. By s 10(2) of the 1984 Act 'items held with the intention of furthering a criminal purpose are not items subject to legal privilege'. In *R* v *Central Criminal Court ex p Francis and Francis* [1989] 3 WLR 989 a Divisional Court held that the relevant criminal intention did not have to come from the person holding the document in question (in this case the solicitor) but could include the intention of the client and that of a third party if the client was the innocent instrument or beneficiary of the third party's criminal purpose.

Example
The police suspected A of drug trafficking and further suspected that A had used some of the proceeds to purchase property for X who was innocent of knowledge as to the source of the money used. The police sought production of the files held by A's solicitors relating to the purchase of the property. Although the files were privileged this privilege was defeated as A had a criminal purpose.

(d) Expert reports and privilege

It has already been established that an expert's report is a privileged document if prepared for use in litigation (see **6.3(*b*)**). Confusion sometimes arises as to the relationship between this privilege and procedural rules of court that may require disclosure of such reports to an opponent. Both the High Court and the county court rules normally require, as a condition of calling an expert, that a party disclose the substance of his report to all other parties involved in the case (see RSC Ord 38, r 36 and CCR Ord 20, r 27.) In criminal cases before the Crown Court advance disclosure is again usually required. It is important to appreciate that these rules require only that reports which are to be relied upon be disclosed. A report which is perhaps unfavourable to the party commissioning it remains privileged and does not have to be disclosed to anyone. See further **10.2**.

(e) Witness statements and privilege

A witness statement (including a statement taken from a party) will be protected from disclosure to third parties by legal professional privilege. In civil cases, however, this privilege must again be examined in conjunction with procedural rules of court.

By RSC Ord 38, r 2A, in any case proceeding in the High Court, the court may direct a party to serve on the other parties to the case, written statements of the oral evidence which the party intends to lead at the trial on any issue of fact to be decided. In *Comfort Hotel Ltd* v *Wembley Stadium Ltd* [1988] 1 WLR 872 it was confirmed that this rule is procedural in effect only, and does not alter the fact that statements are privileged. The rule is similar to the one relating to expert evidence. Any statement that is not to be relied upon need not be disclosed. If a party wishes to lead evidence from a witness, however, (in which case the content of his evidence would then become public knowledge) then the rules require advance dislosure of the substance of his evidence.

In *Richard Saunders and Partners* v *Eastglen Ltd* (1989) *The Times*, 28 July, it was held that an order for exchange was the normal procedure, but may not be appropriate in cases alleging fraud or where exchange would be oppressive.

6.4 Other confidential relationships

The courts have refused to extend the protection of the law of privilege to relationships such as those between medical practitioner and patient, priest and penitent, accountant and client. Similarly there was no protection for communications made to journalists, who could always be compelled to disclose their sources of information (see for example *British Steel Corporation* v *Granada Television Ltd* [1981] AC 1096). Such communications do now enjoy a limited privilege under the provisions of the Contempt of Court Act 1981, s 10. The courts may however order a journalist to disclose his sources where this is necessary 'in the interests of justice or national security or for the prevention of disorder or crime'.

In *Secretary of State* v *Guardian Newspapers Ltd* [1984] 3 WLR 986 Lord Diplock said: 'I have not found it possible to envisage any case that might occur in real life, in which . . . it would be necessary in the interests of justice to order delivery up of a document'. Such a case arose, however, in *X* v *Morgan Grampian*

(Publishers) Ltd (1989) *The Times*, 13 December, in which the Court of Appeal required confidential information improperly given to a journalist to be disclosed to plaintiffs to enable them to commence proceedings to prevent further disclosure.

Statute has also intervened to provide some protection for communications between a client and his patent agent. The privilege is analogous to legal professional privilege and the relevant provisions are now contained in the Patents Act 1977, s 104.

In the absence of such statutory provisions the witness will be obliged to disclose confidential communications made to him if the evidence is relevant and necessary to the proceedings. The fact that a communication was made in confidence is not of itself sufficient to found a claim to privilege. It is however a relevant consideration where privilege is claimed on some other ground such as public interest immunity.

Practical considerations: The powers of the police to enter premises and to search for and seize material which is likely to be relevant evidence are now contained in the Police and Criminal Evidence Act 1984, Pt II. Items which are held in confidence by journalists are examples of 'excluded material'. If the police seek access to excluded material they must apply to a circuit judge for an order that the person in possession of the material should give them access to it (see Sched 1 to the Act).

6.5 Communications between spouses

A witness was formerly not obliged to disclose any communication which had been made to him during the subsistence of a marriage, by his spouse. This head of privilege was abolished in relation to civil cases by the Civil Evidence Act 1968, s 16(3). In criminal cases the privilege survived until the Police and Criminal Evidence Act 1984 (s 80(9)).

Whether or not evidence will be received will of course depend upon the rules as to the competence and compellability of the spouse witness. These matters were considered in **4.2(*e*)**.

6.6 Marital intercourse

The former privilege which relieved a witness of the obligation to give evidence that marital intercourse did or did not take place between himself and his spouse during a given period was abolished for the purposes of civil proceedings by the Civil Evidence Act 1968, s 16(4). In criminal proceedings the privilege has been abolished by the Police and Criminal Evidence Act 1984, s 80(9).

6.7 Privilege against self-incrimination

The general rule in respect of self-incrimination was set out by Lord Goddard LJ in *Blunt* v *Park Lane Hotel Ltd* [1942] 2 KB 253 at 257: 'no-one is bound to answer any question if the answer thereto would, in the opinion of the judge, have a tendency to expose the deponent to any criminal charge, penalty or forfeiture which the judge regards as reasonably likely to be preferred or sued for'.

For the purposes of civil proceedings, the privilege applies only 'as regards criminal offences under the law of any part of the United Kingdom and penalties provided for by such law' (Civil Evidence Act 1968, s 14(1)). It is unclear whether at common law the same restriction applies in criminal proceedings or whether privilege may be claimed where an answer is potentially incriminating under foreign law. The reference to forfeiture is now applicable only in criminal proceedings (Civil Evidence Act 1968, s 16(1)).

There are a number of limitations to the privilege against self-incrimination, the most important of which is found in the Criminal Evidence Act 1898, s 1(*e*). In criminal proceedings in which the accused elects to go into the witness box and give evidence he will be obliged to answer questions put to him in cross-examination even though the tendency may be to incriminate him as to the offence with which he is then charged. In so far as an answer may tend to incriminate him as to any other offence he may still claim the privilege.

6.8 Privilege against incrimination of spouse

In a civil case the privilege against self-incrimination is expressly extended to relieve the witness of the obligation of answering a question which would tend to incriminate his spouse (Civil Evidence Act 1968, s 14(1)(*b*)).

It is unclear whether a similar privilege exists at common law which still governs criminal cases. The absence of authority is due to the combined effect of the privilege attaching to communications between spouses and of the rules governing the competence and compellability of the spouse to give evidence. With the abolition of this privilege (Police and Criminal Evidence Act 1984, s 80(9)) and the introduction of new provisions concerning the competence and compellability of the spouse witness (see **4.2(e)** and s 80(3) of the 1984 Act) it cannot be long before the point falls to be decided.

In proceedings in which the spouse is a defendant it seems improbable that the witness (whether testifying voluntarily or not) would be permitted to rely upon the privilege in respect of the offence being tried. It is perhaps more doubtful how the courts would deal with a situation such as the following:

Example
Wendy is giving evidence in proceedings against Alf. Her husband, Harry, is not directly involved in the proceedings but Wendy is afraid that the answer to a question put to her would tend to incriminate her husband by showing that he had assisted in the removal of stolen goods.

6.9 Limits of the privilege against self-incrimination and incrimination of spouse

A number of statutory provisions place limitations upon the right of the witness to claim privilege against incrimination of himself or his spouse. One of these provisions has been considered above (Criminal Evidence Act 1898, s 1(*e*)). Other relevant provisions include those contained in the Bankruptcy Act 1914 and the Theft Act 1968, s 33, which are concerned with the examination of the debtor in bankruptcy proceedings; those of the Theft Act 1968, s 31, and the Criminal Damage Act 1971, s 9, which are concerned with proceedings for the recovery or administration of any property, for the execution of a trust or for an account of any property or dealings with it; and those of the Supreme Court Act 1981, s 72, which is concerned with proceedings in respect of intellectual property.

6.10 Documents prepared for use in previous proceedings

Talbot J said in *Distillers Co v Times Newspapers* [1975] 1 QB 613 at 621:

Those who disclose documents on discovery are entitled to the protection of the court against any use of the documents otherwise than in the action in which they are disclosed. I also consider that this protection can be extended to prevent the use of the documents by any person into whose hands they come unless it be directly connected with the action in which they are produced.

The court may however grant leave to use documents obtained on discovery for some other purpose (*Sybron Corpn* v *Barclays Bank plc* [1984] 3 WLR 1055).

For a case in which documents disclosed in earlier proceedings were no longer privileged in a subsequent action see *Earle* v *Medhurst* [1985] CLY 2650. Conversely, the Court of Appeal has held that a document which was privileged in earlier proceedings as having been prepared in contemplation of litigation remained privileged in subsequent proceedings involving the party on whose behalf it had been prepared or his successor (*The Aegis Blaze* (1985) *The Times*, 2 November). It did not matter that the second action did not involve the same parties or the same subject matter.

Documents created for the purpose of civil proceedings and covered by legal professional privilege remain privileged in civil proceedings despite their dislosure to the police for the purposes of a criminal investigation and their likely use in criminal proceedings (see *British Coal Corporation* v *Dennis Rye Ltd* (*No 2*) (1988) *The Times*, 7 March).

6.11 Admissibility of other evidence of privileged matters

The fact that a witness is able to claim privilege from disclosing a communication does not always lead to the result that all evidence of the privileged communication is excluded. The evidence may be given by another witness who is either not entitled to claim privilege or who is prepared to waive it. A letter passing between a solicitor and his client need not be proved by the client and may not be proved by the solicitor without the consent of his client (see **6.1(a)** above) and communications between spouses were protected until the Police and Criminal Evidence Act 1984, s 80 came into force. However, if a privileged document falls into the hands of another then that person may give evidence of the communication.

Example
During a trial the accused passed a note to his counsel which contained incriminating statements. The note had been dropped and was later found by the prosecutor. When the accused later gave evidence in his own defence he was cross-examined on the contents of the note. (*R* v *Tompkins* (1977) 67 Cr App R 181)

Where letters are written to the client and to the opposing party on the same day it is important to check that they are placed in the correct envelopes!

Example
The accused had written a letter to his wife. Neither he nor his wife would have been compellable to give evidence of the statements contained in the letter. The letter was intercepted and read by the police and found to contain incriminating material. The prosecution used the letter in evidence. (*Rumping* v *DPP* [1964] AC 814)

In dismissing the appeal the House of Lords held that the evidence had been rightly received.

In a case in which the original document remains in the possession of a witness who is able to claim privilege from producing it the document may be proved by secondary evidence such as by the proof of a copy (see *Calcraft* v *Guest* [1898] 1 QB 759). This principle has been re-affirmed in the case of *Goddard* v *Nationwide Building Society* [1986] 3 All ER 264 in which May LJ said: 'If a litigant has in his possession copies of documents to which legal professional privilege attaches, he may nevertheless use such copies as secondary evidence in his litigation.'

Whether it is sought to prove the communication by primary or by secondary evidence the court will not, in general, be concerned with the means by which such evidence was obtained. The material may be used whether the person relying upon it has come by it innocently or by unlawful means. However, in *ITC Film Distributors* v *Video Exchange Ltd and others* [1982] Ch 431 the court ruled evidence inadmissible which had been taken from an opponent who had brought the documents into court (see **5.6**). For the considerations where the accused in a criminal trial has been tricked into providing evidence against himself (see **5.5**).

6.12 Restraining the use of privileged material

If privileged material (or a copy) has fallen into the hands of the opposing party objection can rarely be taken to its reception in evidence. As indicated above the court is not generally concerned with the means by which the evidence was obtained. It may however be possible to bring separate proceedings for the return of the documents and any copies and an injunction may be granted to restrain the other party from making use of any copies of, or of the information contained in, the document (see *Lord Ashburton* v *Pape* [1913] 2 Ch D 469). This is the case no matter how the evidence is obtained. 'The right of the party who desires the protection to invoke the equitable jurisdiction does not in any way depend on the conduct of the third party into whose possession the record of the confidential communication has come.' (per Nourse LJ in *Goddard* v *Nationwide Building Society* [1986] 3 All ER 264, 271.)

It should be noted that the relief is granted in separate proceedings brought to claim the protection and is not available in the proceedings in which the evidence is sought to be introduced. Nowadays the courts would at most require an undertaking to issue a pro forma writ but the protection must be sought before the other party has adduced the confidential communication in evidence or otherwise relied on it at the trial (per Nourse LJ in *Goddard* v *Nationwide Building Society* at p 271).

In the case of a public prosecution the remedy will be unavailable as no injunction will lie against the Crown and the court will not grant a declaration to prevent the evidence from being introduced (*Butler* v *Board of Trade* [1971] Ch 680). As to the exclusion of evidence the reception of which would have an adverse effect on the fairness of the proceedings see **5.5**.

6.13 Practice in civil proceedings

As to the practice in civil proceedings with regard to the disclosure of documents see RSC Ord 24 and CCR Ord 14. Where a party is required to give discovery of documents he must generally prepare a list of all the relevant documents which are, or have been, in his possession or control. The list consists of two schedules, the second describing the documents which are no longer in his possession or control. The first schedule is divided into two parts. The first part sets out the documents which the other party will be allowed to inspect whilst the second part lists the documents which are privileged and which the party preparing the list does not wish his opponent to see. See further O'Hare and Hill *Civil Litigation* 4th ed (Longman, 1986).

If privileged documents are mistakenly included in Sched 1 Pt I of the list and are therefore inspected by the other side, secondary evidence of their contents will be admissible. The list may be corrected at any time before inspection by notifying the other party that there are documents which the litigant objects to produce, per Hoffman J in *Re Briarmore Manufacturing Ltd* [1986] 1 WLR 1429. Once inspection has taken place it is too late for the party who sought to claim privilege to attempt to correct the mistake by applying for injunctive relief (*Guiness Peat Properties Ltd* v *Fitzroy Robinson Partnership* [1987] 2 All ER 716 CA). It would be otherwise if the solicitor had procured inspection of the relevant document by fraud or if, on inspection, he realised that he had been permitted to see the documents only by reason of an obvious mistake.

Chapter 7

Evidence of Bad Character and Previous Convictions in Criminal Cases

This chapter is primarily concerned with the extent to which the prosecution may adduce evidence of the bad character and previous convictions of a defendant to a criminal charge to help prove his guilt. This is not to be confused with cross-examining a witness (including the defendant) on previous convictions to undermine the credibility of his testimony (as to which see Chapter 9). There is also a short section at the end of the chapter dealing with the admissibility of the convictions of someone other than the defendant to help prove the defendant's guilt.

EVIDENCE OF A DEFENDANT'S BAD CHARACTER AND PREVIOUS CONVICTIONS

If a defendant in a criminal trial is of bad character or has previous criminal convictions, evidence of these matters cannot, as a general rule, be adduced as part of the prosecution case. The reason for this is that normally the prejudice caused to the defendant when the jury or justices hear of such matters far outweighs any probative value of the evidence.

Example
Alan is on trial for theft. He has several previous convictions for dishonesty. The fact that he is of a dishonest nature does not go to prove that Alan committed the offence which is the subject of the charge. However, a jury or justices may come to the conclusion that Alan is guilty because of what he has done in the past.

If evidence is given by the prosecution in contravention of this rule (perhaps inadvertently) then in the court's discretion, a retrial can be ordered (*R* v *Weaver* [1968] 1 QB 353).

There are four main exceptions to the general exclusionary rule. These are:

(1) Previous convictions are admissible at common law to rebut an assertion of good character.

(2) Previous convictions and/or discreditable conduct may be admissible at common law under the similar fact rule.

(3) Previous convictions may be admissible under the Theft Act 1968, s 27(3).

(4) Previous convictions may be admissible under the Police and Criminal Evidence Act 1984, s 74(3).

7.1 Rebutting an assertion of good character

A defendant in a criminal trial may give evidence of his own good character. The term good character refers not only to reputation but also to disposition. Such evidence may be given by the defendant himself, by his witnesses or, more unusually, by cross-examination of prosecution witnesses. Any witness called to give evidence of the character of the defendant must restrict himself to evidence of general reputation and should not refer to specific acts (see *R* v *Rowton* (1865) Le & Ca 520). According to *R* v *Redgrave* (1982) 74 Cr App R 10 this rule applies equally to the defendant himself when giving evidence, although it seems that some degree of latitude is allowed (see for example *R* v *Samuel* (1956) 40 Cr App R 8). The distinction between giving evidence of general reputation as opposed to specific acts can be illustrated by reference to the facts of *R* v *Redgrave*.

Example
The defendant was charged with persistently importuning for immoral purposes. The prosecution case was that he had attempted to make homosexual contacts in a public lavatory. The defendant was not allowed to attempt to rebut this suggestion by referring to his specific sexual relationships with certain women. All that he was allowed to do was say that he was not the type of person who would do the alleged act.

If the defendant adduces evidence of his good character in one of the ways described and it is contended that the evidence is untrue, then the prosecution may adduce rebutting evidence. Similarly, if the evidence adduced by one defendant to establish his own good character becomes relevant to the guilt of the co-defendant, then the co-defendant should be permitted to introduce evidence in rebuttal including evidence of the defendant's previous record (see *R* v *Douglass* (1989) 89 Cr App R 264). It should be noted that if the defendant gives evidence of good character then rebutting evidence may include evidence of all previous convictions, not simply those that relate to the type of offence that is the subject of the charge (*R* v *Winfield* (1939) 27 Cr App R 139).

Example
Albert is charged with indecent assault. He adduces evidence to the effect that his morals are of the highest standard. Rebutting evidence may include, for example, convictions for assault and dishonesty.

It is worth noting here that there will be occasions when a defendant with previous convictions may be able to safely assert that he is a man of good character. The Rehabilitation of Offenders Act 1974 provides that after a certain period of time some criminal convictions become spent. Whether or not a conviction is spent is ascertained by looking at the sentence of the court and the period that has since elapsed (see ss 5 and 6). Although these provisions do not apply to criminal proceedings the court may, in its discretion allow a defendant with spent convictions to put himself forward as a man of good character. In *R* v *Nye* (1982) 75 Cr App R 247 the Court of Appeal gave some examples on the exercise of the court's discretion in this matter.

Example
Fred is thirty-five. He is charged with theft. His only previous conviction is for petty theft when eighteen. The conviction has been spent for many years. It is suggested that in a case such as this Fred can assert that he is a man of good character.

Example
Bill is twenty-six. He is charged with assault and has a previous conviction for assault that has just become spent. He should not say that he is a man of good character.

The Court of Appeal will not interfere with the proper exercise of the judge's discretion, even though the case may be such that most judges were likely to have exercised their discretion in the defendant's favour (*R* v *Bailey* [1989] Crim LR 723).

The common law rule concerning the rebuttal of assertions of good character is reinforced by the statutory provisions dealing with the cross-examination of the accused. Whilst the Criminal Evidence Act 1898, s 1(*f*) gives a defendant a general protection from cross-examination on his previous convictions (see **9.3**) an exception is provided where the defendant has 'personally or by his advocate asked questions of witnesses for the prosecution with a view to establish his own good character, or has given evidence of his good character'.

There is obviously an overlap between the common law provisions and s 1(*f*)(ii). Two examples will serve to illustrate the point.

Example
Alan is on trial for theft. He does not give evidence himself. However he calls a character witness.

Here, the prosecution will have to call their own rebutting evidence. They cannot rely on s 1(*f*)(ii) as the defendant has not gone into the witness box to give evidence. Therefore he cannot be cross-examined.

Example
John is charged with assault occasioning actual bodily harm. He gives evidence of his own good character.

Here the prosecution could call rebutting evidence but it will not normally be necessary. John is in the witness box. He has given evidence in chief and can therefore be cross-examined. By giving evidence of his own good character he has lost the basic s 1(*f*) protection and can therefore be cross-examined on his previous convictions.

A further point for consideration in relation to both the common law and statutory provisions is what should a court be told to make of the convictions which are put in evidence or revealed in cross examination? According to *R* v *Samuel* (1956) 40 Cr App R 8 the inference which may be drawn from the convictions is not simply that the defendant is not, as asserted, a person of good character but also that he is guilty of the offence charged.

The discretion to exclude prosecution evidence under the Police and Criminal Evidence Act 1984, s 78 (see **5.5**) is a general one and could no doubt be used to prevent the prosecution from adducing rebutting character evidence or cross examining a defendant under s 1(*f*)(ii). However the absence of reported cases either under s 78 or the common law discretion which preceded it tends to suggest that once a defendant has adduced evidence of good character that is not true there is little that can be done to prevent the prosecution from redressing the balance.

Practical considerations: If the prosecution wish to adduce rebutting character evidence then this may be done at the close of the defence case (*R* v *Butterwasser* [1948] KB 4).

Rebutting character evidence will obviously require the prosecution to prove the defendant's previous convictions. Similarly if a defendant is cross examined under s 1(*f*)(ii) and denies a conviction then the prosecution are put to proof of it. By the Police and Criminal Evidence Act 1984, s 73(1) a conviction may be proved by producing a certificate signed by the clerk to the relevant court and proving that the person named in the certificate is the defendant. It should be noted that any convictions which are proved will go before the court in the form of a description of the offence with particulars of the date and convicting court. The facts upon which the convictions were based are not relevant and details should not be provided.

7.2 Similar fact evidence

An application by the prosecution to adduce similar fact evidence means that they are seeking to put before the court details of the previous conduct of the defendant to prove his guilt of the offence charged. It should be stressed that it is not the fact of conviction that is relevant (unlike cases referred to at **7.1**) but the facts upon which the conviction was based. Indeed, as will be seen shortly, there is no requirement that the previous conduct should amount to a criminal offence.

Obviously, such evidence, if admitted, will be highly prejudicial to the defendant's case. A conviction may be almost inevitable. Consequently, the courts exercise great care in determining questions of admissibility of similar fact evidence. The leading case is *DPP* v *Boardman* [1975] AC 421, in which the House of Lords gave detailed consideration to the circumstances in which such evidence should be admitted. Lord Wilberforce said that it was necessary in each case to estimate how strongly the evidence as to the other facts tended to support the evidence of the fact in issue, and to consider the degree of prejudice to the defendant. The judge must be satisfied that the interests of justice require that the evidence be admitted: 'The admission of similar fact evidence . . . is exceptional and requires a strong degree of probative force. This probative force is derived, if at all, from the circumstance that the facts testified to by the several witnesses bear to each other such a striking similarity that they must, when judged by experience and common sense, either all be true, or have arisen from a cause common to the witnesses or from pure coincidence' (per Lord Wilberforce at p 444).

Clearly, the evidence must go beyond merely showing a tendency in the defendant to commit certain types of criminal act.

Example
In a trial on counts of buggery the similarities relied on by the Crown were: the ages of the complainants; that the boys were truanting from school at the time; that the offences occurred in Leicester; that in each case a reward was promised; and that in each case the offender was a middle-aged man with a flat cap, glasses and a leather jacket. (*R* v *Maher* (1989) *The Times*, 19 October)

The facts were all commonplace, and the similarities could not be said to be striking. The evidence could not be used to show that the same man was involved on each occasion, nor could evidence of his behaviour on one occasion lend support to evidence of his behaviour on another occasion. In *R* v *Jeffrey Wells* [1989] Crim LR 67, in which two separate raids on the defendant's premises had led to charges on drugs-related offences, the Court of Appeal held that the following evidence was far from satisfying the criteria laid down in *DPP* v *Boardman*: that in each case paper folds, scales and cocaine in 1g and 0.5g units had been found; that the cutting agent was the same; that there were felt tip markings on the paper folds (albeit in different colours); and that the percentage purity of the cocaine was 21% on the first raid and varied between 15% and 23% on the second. The defendant's case on the second count was that the evidence had been planted. The evidence of the earlier raid could not be relevant as it was not probative of the prosecution case and merely amounted to evidence of disposition.

Example
The defendant was charged with raping Anna. His defence was that he was not the person responsible. The prosecution case was that Anna had been picked up by a man with a beard who drove a Mini. The defendant had a beard and owned a Mini but Anna could not identify him as the person responsible. Forensic evidence increased the suspicion that the defendant was the person who committed the crime but was not conclusive. The prosecution called Gill and Fiona to say that a bearded man in a Mini had tried to pick them up but they had refused. The defendant admitted that he was the man involved in these two incidents. (*R* v *Tricolgus* (1976) 65 Cr App R 16)

The Court of Appeal held that this was not admissible similar fact evidence. All that it proved was that the defendant had a tendency to 'kerb crawl' looking for sex. It did not supply any cogent evidence of the defendant being the man who raped Anna in the peculiar way alleged by the prosecution.

There are, however, many cases where similar fact evidence was cogent enough to justify its admission.

Example
Smith was charged with murdering his wife. She was found drowned in her bath and Smith stood to gain from life assurance. His defence was that his wife had died from natural causes. Evidence was admitted that Smith had gone through a ceremony of marriage with two other women and that they too had been found dead in their bath, with Smith due to gain from life assurance. (*R* v *Smith* [1915] 11 Cr App R 229)

How does this differ from the cases above? It is possible that Smith was an extremely unlucky man with his wives. However, the overall circumstances of the case, in particular the striking similarity and uniqueness of the previous conduct, suggest that there was more than mere coincidence involved and that Smith was guilty of murder. Thus the evidence was sufficiently cogent, bearing in mind the facts in issue in the case, to justify the prejudice caused to the defendant.

Example
Makin was charged with murder of a child. The case against him was that he had adopted the child, murdered him and buried the body in his back garden. He claimed that the child had died of natural causes. Evidence was admitted that the bodies of other children adopted by the defendant had been found in the back gardens of other houses occupied by him. (*Makin* v *A-G for New South Wales* [1894] AC 57)

Again the facts of the case point to something more than coincidence. The court is not being asked to conclude that the defendant has a propensity to commit a fairly common act and therefore must be guilty this time. The overall circumstances, in particular the striking similarity and uniqueness of the previous conduct point to Makin having murdered the child, rather than there being an innocent explanation.

Example
Straffen was charged with the murder of a girl by manual strangulation. He admitted being in the vicinity of the crime at the relevant time and had escaped from Broadmoor. Evidence was admitted that the year before he had killed two other girls. In all three cases the method of death and precision of strangulation were identical, there was no sexual motive, no evidence of a struggle, and no attempt to conceal the bodies when this could easily have been done. (*R* v *Straffen* [1952] 2 QB 911)

This evidence was admitted not to show that Straffen was a professional strangler but to provide cogent evidence that because of the similar circumstances and hallmark of the crime, he was guilty of murder. It should be noted again, here, that the evidence was admissible because of its cogency in proving the facts in issue in the case.

Example
The defendant denied indecently assaulting three young girls. Their evidence was that in each of the three cases involved they were invited to baby-sit, on arrival were shown pornographic magazines, offered £200 to pose for indecent photographs and then indecently assaulted. The defendant alleged that the girls had got together and concocted the whole story. The prosecution called three more girls who alleged that they too had been asked to the defendant's flat on the pretence of baby-sitting, had been shown pornographic magazines and had been offered £200 to pose for indecent photographs. They did not allege any indecent assault. (*R v Barrington* [1981] 1 WLR 419)

This was again held to be admissible similar fact evidence, even though the Court said that the conduct alleged did not constitute a criminal offence (they overlooked the Protection of Children Act 1978, s 1(*a*)). The evidence had a strong probative value in that the latter three girls' similar story as to the circumstances surrounding the crimes being tried tended to refute the defendent's case that the whole story was a pack of lies. If on the other hand, Barrington had admitted all of the surrounding circumstances but denied indecent assault the evidence of the three other girls should not have been admissible in the prosecution case, notwithstanding suggestions to the contrary in the judgment of the court. That the previous conduct does not have to amount to a criminal offence was confirmed in *R v Butler* (1987) 84 Cr App R 13 (where evidence of previous consensual sexual conduct was admitted).

In all of the examples given above of admissible similar fact evidence the conduct involved is of a kind that could at the very least be described as unusual. However, it would be wrong to create the impression that only cases involving unique behaviour can fall into the category of admissible similar fact evidence.

Example
Bob is charged with theft of scrap metal from a derelict piece of land. His defence is that he thought that the property had been abandoned. He has two previous convictions for stealing scrap metal from precisely the same piece of land in the same way.

These facts are of course rather more mundane than some of

those to which references have been made. Nevertheless the principles are much the same. Are the prosecution seeking to adduce the evidence merely to prove that Bob has a tendency to steal scrap metal or has it a more positive probative value? It would appear that, in the example, this is admissible similar fact evidence. Looking at the facts in issue, the circumstances of the previous convictions go a long way to proving that the defence put forward by Bob is not true. The position would be different if Bob denied any involvement at all. The true facts in issue would not be whether Bob, having taken the goods, was acting dishonestly but whether or not he took the goods at all. In that situation the previous convictions would seem to show nothing more than a propensity to commit this type of crime and would not be admissible.

Example
Rance was the managing director of a building firm and was charged with bribing Ken, a local councillor. The cheque was signed by Rance and put through the accounts as a payment to a sub-contractor. Rance's firm only paid sub-contractors on production of a certificate signed by a company official that the work was satisfactorily completed. The certificate for Ken was signed by Rance, which was highly unusual. Rance's defence was that someone had tricked him into signing the documents. Evidence was admitted that Rance had made payments to two other councillors that had been covered by bogus notes of building work that had not been done and that these too had been signed by Rance. (*R* v *Rance and Heron* (1975) 62 Cr App R 118)

Again these are facts that cannot be said to be particularly unusual but which, given the facts in issue, do have a strong probative value. The evidence is not admitted to prove that Rance is not above bribing councillors but because the facts, considered as a whole, show a system which suggests that the defence put forward is not true, and that hence the defendant is guilty as charged.

Example
The defendant was charged with shoplifting. The prosecution case was that he went into a supermarket, carrying his own bag. He put some bacon into a wire basket provided by the store and then transferred the bacon into his own bag and left the store without paying. His defence was one of honest mistake. Evidence was admitted that a store detective had noticed the defendant in the store twice before. On the first occasion he put some bacon into a wire basket and went out of view. When he returned the bacon had disappeared. On the second occasion he put the bacon into his own bag but on realising that he was being watched, put it back on the display counter. (*R* v *Seaman* (1978) 67 Cr App R 234)

This is a difficult case. The Court of Appeal said that it was a borderline decision to admit the evidence. On balance, however, it was felt that the evidence of the store detective was cogent enough to show a particular method of operating over and above a propensity to shoplift and therefore helped prove that the defence of honest mistake was not true.

The fact that the 'similar fact evidence' comes from an accomplice does not make it inadmissible, but is merely one of the factors to take into account (*R* v *Lunt* (1987) 85 Cr App R 241). In that case, the Court of Appeal considered the line of cases commencing with *DPP* v *Boardman* and then laid down some further guidelines to be followed in cases where the prosecution sought to adduce 'similar fact evidence':

(1) The general rule is that the prosecution may not adduce evidence of other criminal acts of the accused or evidence showing a propensity to commit crimes of the kind with which he is charged.

(2) 'Similar fact evidence' will be admissible only if it goes beyond showing a tendency to commit crimes of the kind charged and is positively probative in relation to the present charge.

(3) To determine that question it is first necessary to identify the issue to which the evidence is directed.

(4) Having done so, the question is: will the 'similar fact evidence' be positively probative in the sense of assisting the jury to reach a conclusion on that issue rather than on the bad character of the accused or his disposition to commit the sort of crime with which he is charged?

(5) If the evidence is positively probative the judge will nevertheless have a discretion to exclude it under the common law principle, in *R* v *Sang* (see **5.5**), that the prejudicial effect of the evidence outweighs its probative value.

This case has been applied by the Court of Appeal in more recent decisions (see, for example, *R* v *Shore* (1989) 89 Cr App R 32, and *R* v *Beggs* [1989] Crim LR 898). In *R* v *Wells* [1989] Crim LR 67, it was again emphasised that the cases in which 'similar fact evidence' should be admitted are extremely rare and that judges should be cautious in succumbing to applications by the prosecution to be allowed to rely on such evidence.

Practical considerations: If the prosecution intend adducing similar fact evidence there are a number of possible methods available. If the evidence is of past crimes or misconduct not amounting to a crime then the prosecution will apply to the judge in the absence of the jury for leave to adduce the evidence. This application will usually be made by the prosecution in opening their case. The judge will decide whether the evidence comes within the similar fact principle and exercise his discretion as to admissibility.

Alternatively, if the defendant has allegedly committed a number of crimes of a similar nature then the prosecution will incorporate all of the offences into one indictment to enable them to be tried together. If the defence object then they should apply to the judge, again in the absence of the jury and before the start of the trial, to sever the indictment and have each offence tried separately. The judge has a discretion in this respect and will take into account the principles referred to above and also consider the possibility of the witnesses having got together to concoct a story. If he rules that the offences do come within the similar fact principle then the evidence on each offence may be capable of corroborating the others. For the sake of clarity it should be added that even if the judge decides that the offences in the indictment do not come within the similar fact principle he does not necessarily have to sever the counts but must warn the jury that the evidence on one count cannot amount to corroboration on another (see *R* v *McGlinchey* (1983) *The Times*, 12 October). The Court of Appeal will not usually interfere with the exercise of the judge's very wide discretion under Indictment Rules 1971, Rule 9 (*R* v *Wells* [1989] Crim LR 67).

The two methods described so far for admitting similar fact evidence both relate to the prosecution adducing the evidence as a part of their case. These common law provisions are reinforced by the Criminal Evidence Act 1898, s 1(*f*). It was seen at **7.1** above that s 1(*f*) gives a defendant a basic protection from cross-examination on his previous convictions. However, by s 1(*f*)(i) such cross-examination is permissible if 'the proof that he has committed or been convicted of such other offence is admissible evidence to show that he is guilty of the offence wherewith he is then charged'. The provision is of limited importance. If the prosecution wish to rely on the similar fact rule then the previous conduct must normally be proved as part of the prosecution case. Once this has been done, a defendant who gives evidence may be cross-examined under s 1(*f*)(i). If however the prosecution do not prove the previous conduct then cross-examination under s 1(*f*)(i) should not be permitted (*R* v *Coombes* (1960) 45 Cr App R 36).

Similar fact evidence in the magistrates' court could arise in any of the ways described above, although it should be borne in mind that the justices are arbiters of law and fact and would therefore have to hear the nature of the evidence to enable them to determine its admissibility. This makes such cases more suitable for trial on indictment wherever possible. ⚱

7.3 Theft Act 1968, s 27(3)

By the Theft Act 1968, s 27(3)(b) if a person is charged with handling stolen goods and evidence is given that he had them in his possession or undertook or assisted in their disposal, retention, realisation or removal then evidence may be given of any theft or handling convictions in the previous five years. The evidence is admissible to prove that the defendant knew or believed the goods to be stolen.

A further provision is contained in s 27(3)(a). This allows evidence to be given on a trial for handling stolen goods that other property, stolen within a period of twelve months before the offence charged, had been found in the possession of the defendant or that he had otherwise dealt with it in a way which would constitute the actus reus of handling. Again the evidence is admissible to prove that the defendant knew or believed the goods to be stolen.

Although the convictions are made admissible by statute, the trial judge has a discretion to exclude them under the Police and Criminal Evidence Act 1984, s 78 (see *R* v *Rasini* (1986) *The Times*, 20 March).

Practical considerations: Evidence adduced under s 27(3)(a) should be confined to the mere fact of possession. Evidence as to the circumstances in which the property was found and as to explanations given by the accused should not be given. However, a statement made by the defendant on an earlier occasion could be given in evidence where it had been suitably edited so that it contained no irrelevant material and merely proved the fact of possession (*R* v *Wood* [1987] 1 WLR 779).

Any evidence under s 27(3)(b) must be confined to the date, place and fact of the conviction. Furthermore, where this provision is to be relied on the prosecution must give at least seven days' notice in writing to the defendant. In practice, this notice will sometimes result in a change of plea.

7.4 Police and Criminal Evidence Act 1984, s 74(3)

The rule in *Hollington* v *Hewthorn* (1943) KB 587 provided that a criminal conviction was not admissible in any subsequent proceedings as evidence of the facts upon which it was based. This rule sometimes produced unjust results.

Example
Maurice is convicted of wounding with intent to cause grievous bodily harm. His victim subsequently dies and Maurice stands trial for murder. Under the rule in *Hollington* v *Hewthorn* the conviction is not admissible as evidence of the fact that Maurice attacked his victim intending grievous bodily harm (a sufficient mens rea for murder).

By the Police and Criminal Evidence Act 1984, s 74(3) this conviction would now be admissible.

The section provides that, where evidence is admissible of the fact that the defendant has committed an offence, if the defendant is proved to have been convicted of the offence then he shall be taken to have committed that offence unless the contrary is proved. Thus in the example of Maurice above he will be taken to have committed the offence of wounding with intent unless he proves the contrary on a balance of probabilities.

Obviously the evidence of commission must be relevant to an issue in the case. It should also be stressed that it is the facts upon which the conviction was based that are important here not the fact of conviction itself.

Evidence is admissible under s 74(3) if it is introduced for some reason other than a 'tendency to show in the accused a disposition to commit the kind of offence with which he is charged'. The evidence must have some other probative value. In cases of similar fact evidence it is the facts upon which the conviction was based that are important. These facts must be proved by admissible evidence. Evidence of the conviction (even with the assistance of the charge sheet, indictment etc) will not give sufficient detail of the facts of the case to justify its reception under the similar facts rule.

Finally it should be noted that even if a conviction is admissible under s 74(3) the court still has a discretion to exclude it under the Police and Criminal Evidence Act 1984, s 78.

Practical considerations: The fact of conviction may be proved by producing a certificate of conviction signed by the clerk to the relevant court and proving that it relates to the defendant (Police and Criminal Evidence Act 1984, s 73).

By s 75(1), the contents of the information, complaint, indictment or charge sheet on which the defendant was convicted are admissible for the purpose of identifying the facts upon which the conviction was based.

7.5 Statutory exclusion of evidence of convictions

Notwithstanding the fact that one of the exceptions to the general rule excluding evidence of previous convictions may apply, on the trial of a person alleged to have committed an offence whilst over the age of 21, no reference can be made to offences committed whilst the defendant was under 14 (Children and Young Persons Act 1963, s 16(2)).

It was seen at **7.1** above that the Rehabilitation of Offenders Act 1974 does not apply to criminal proceedings. Nevertheless spent convictions may only be referred to with leave of the court which will be granted if it is in the interests of justice to do so (see *Practice Direction (Crime: Spent Convictions)* [1975] 1 WLR 1065).

EVIDENCE OF THE PREVIOUS CONVICTIONS OF A NON PARTY

The rule in *Hollington v Hewthorn* noted at **7.4** above prevented the admission of convictions in subsequent criminal proceedings not only of the defendant but also of anyone not a party to the proceedings.

Example
Harry is convicted of theft. Johnny is charged with handling the stolen goods. The conviction of Harry was not admissible to prove at the trial of Johnny that the goods were stolen.

7.6 Police and Criminal Evidence Act, s 74(1)

Section 74(1) states that: 'In any proceedings the fact that a person other than the accused has been convicted of an offence by or before any court in the United Kingdom . . . shall be admissible in evidence for the purpose of proving, where to do so is relevant to any issue in those proceedings, that that person committed that offence, whether or not any other evidence of his having committed that offence is given.'

The effect of this provision is that the conviction of Harry is now admissible at the trial of Johnny as evidence of the facts upon which it is based. Furthermore, by s 74(2) once such a conviction is proved that person 'shall be taken to have committed the offence unless the contrary is proved'. In the above example, the burden would be on Johnny to prove on a balance of probabilities that Harry did not steal the goods.

As in the case of evidence under s 74(3), the facts upon which the conviction was based are relevant rather than the simple fact of the conviction.

Guidance to the courts in the application of s 74(1) was given by the Court of Appeal in *R v Robertson and Golder* (1987) 85 Cr App R 304, in which Lord Lane CJ said that the section should be 'sparingly used' and that there are 'occasions where, although the evidence may be technically admissible, its effect is likely to be so slight that it will be wiser not to adduce it'. His Lordship went on to say that where the evidence is admitted 'the judge should be careful to explain to the jury the effect of the evidence and its limitations'.

Evidence under the section is not restricted to proof of conviction of offences in which the defendant played no part. Conspiracy cases, as *R v Robertson and Golder*, have provided the courts with particular problems in the application of s 74(1). The existence of the conspiracy is clearly relevant in such cases and may be established under s 74(1). A cannot be convicted of conspiring with B unless it is also proved that B conspired with A.

Care has to be taken that by adducing the evidence the implication is not raised that the accused must have been a party to the conspiracy. If B's guilt is established under s 74(1) (and his conviction was based on A having conspired with him) this will leave A with the burden of proving on a balance of probabilities that he is not guilty. This is, of course, a complete reversal of the ordinary rule in criminal cases. In such cases, the judge should exercise his discretion under s 78, or under the common law, to exclude such evidence (see *R v O'Connor* (1987) 85 Cr App R 298 and *R v Curry* [1988] Crim LR 528).

In *R v Lunnon* [1989] 88 Crim LR App R 71 the appellant had been charged jointly with three others with conspiracy to steal. One of the accused pleaded guilty and the judge allowed the prosecution to prove that plea on the trial of the others. He directed the jury to consider, firstly, whether there was a conspiracy and, secondly, who were parties to it. It was made clear to the jury that all the others could be acquitted despite the plea. The Court of Appeal held that the evidence had been relevant and that it had not been unfair to admit it. It would have been otherwise had there been only two conspirators.

The section is not limited in its scope to cases (such as handling and conspiracy) where proof of an offence by someone other than the accused is a pre-requisite to the conviction of the accused. Again, the judge must consider carefully the **purpose** for which the evidence is to be introduced and if it is likely to go to proof of the defendant's guilt he should exercise his exclusionary discretion under s 78. (Police and Criminal Evidence Act 1984, s 5(5)).

In *R* v *Mattison*, (1989) NLJ 20 October it was held that on a charge of gross indecency the guilty plea of the co-defendant, although admissible under s 74(1), should not have been admitted, as it raised a strong inference that M had also committed an act of gross indecency with the co-defendant and so would be likely to go to the issue of M's guilt. Similarly, in *R* v *Kempster* [1989] 1 WLR 1125 the judge should have considered the purpose of introducing evidence of the guilty pleas of co-defendants to offences of burglary and robbery committed at a time when, according to the evidence, K was with them. Had he found that the purpose was to prove the guilt of K, he might have exercised his discretion to exclude the evidence under s 78.

The decisions in these cases may be contrasted with that in *R* v *Bennett* [1988] Crim LR 686. On a charge of theft, evidence was admitted of the guilty plea of the co-accused, a supermarket cashier, who had passed goods to B for less than the marked price. The Court of Appeal was satisfied that the purpose of introducing the evidence was merely to establish that there had been a theft and the issue of whether or not B was a party to the theft had been left fairly with the jury. As Prof Smith observes in his commentary to that case, B was left with the task of providing a reasonable explanation as to how she innocently came to receive £85 worth of goods for £4.99. In practice, if not in theory, she was left with the burden of proving her innocence.

For the purposes of s 74(1) 'issue' includes 'evidential issue' so that, for example, in *R* v *Castle* [1989] Crim LR 567 (following *R* v *Robertson and Golder* (1987) 85 Cr App R 304) it was held that evidence of the guilty plea of a party to a robbery was rightly admitted as being relevant to the reliability of identification evidence given by the victim against the accused. (Having correctly identified one of the parties to the robbery his evidence of identification of the other was more likely to be correct.)

Practical considerations: The provisions of the Police and Criminal Evidence Act 1984, ss 73 and 75 relating to proof of conviction and the admissibility of the charge sheet, etc., apply in the same way as to s 74(3) (see **7.4** above).

Chapter 8

Previous Judgments (and Character) in Civil Cases

As a general rule a party to a civil case is not allowed to adduce evidence of his own good character or of the bad character and convictions of an opponent. Such evidence is not relevant because the characters of the parties are not, generally, in issue.

Example
Peter sues David for damages for personal injuries allegedly caused by David's negligent driving.

In the above case Peter seeks to adduce evidence that:

Peter devotes much of his spare time to charitable work
Peter has no previous convictions
David has previous convictions for:
   Murder
   Speeding (on a quite separate occasion some years earlier)
   Obtaining property by deception

The only issues in the case are whether or not David was negligent and wheher such negligence was the cause of the injury, loss and damage alleged by Peter. None of these items of evidence helps the court to resolve the issues and all are completely irrelevant and therefore inadmissible. (Of course, if a party is to give evidence in the proceedings, evidence as to his character may be relevant to the question of whether or not he is a credible witness. This is considered in Chapter 9.)

In some cases, however, the character of a party may be directly in issue (as in a defamation action) or he may have a conviction which is relevant to the issues to be decided in civil proceedings (as where, in the above example, David has a conviction for careless driving arising out of the same facts) or there may have been other civil proceedings which have involved the same issues.

In such cases the question arises as to what use can be made of the findings in earlier proceedings. Does the decision provide conclusive proof of the matters adjudicated upon? Can the decision, at least, be used as evidence of the matters on which it is founded? These are some of the matters which fall to be considered in the following sections.

8.1 Effect of previous judgment in a case not involving both parties

Unless both parties to the litigation were parties to the earlier proceedings (as to which see **8.2** below) the earlier decision has a very limited effect.

The record of the decision is conclusive as to the fact that on a given date a named court reached a particular decision (eg that the accused was convicted, that the plaintiff recovered judgment etc) but not as to the facts on which that decision was based (eg not that the accused committed the crime, or that the defendant was actually indebted to the plaintiff).

The decision is also conclusive as to any state of affairs which falls to be determined (eg that a marriage be dissolved, that a person be adjudicated bankrupt).

Otherwise, the parties are not bound by the earlier findings and indeed evidence of the judgment is not even admissible to establish a prima facie case. This rule, known as the rule in *Hollington* v *Hewthorn* [1943] KB 587, is now subject to a number of exceptions, principally those under the Civil Evidence Act 1968, ss 11–13.

(a) *Proof of criminal convictions under the Civil Evidence Act 1968, s 11*

In civil proceedings the fact that a person has been convicted of a criminal offence is admissible in evidence for the purpose of proving that he committed the offence, where such proof is relevant to an issue in the civil proceedings. The fact that an employer has been convicted of an offence of breach of statutory duty under the Factories' Acts would now be admissible in evidence in civil proceedings brought by an employee who was injured as a result of such breach of duty. The fact that a motorist had been convicted of careless driving would be admissible in civil proceedings brought by anyone suffering injury as a result of that driving.

On proof of the conviction, the convicted party is taken to have committed the offence until the contrary is proved.

Practical considerations: The provisions of s 11 can be relied upon only if the conviction is pleaded. The party seeking to prove the conviction must plead details of the date, court, offence and the issue in the civil proceedings to which the conviction is alleged to be relevant. If the conviction is pleaded in this way, the party seeking to avoid the effect of the conviction must plead a denial of the fact of conviction, or that the conviction was erroneous, or that it is not relevant to any issue in the civil proceedings. See RSC Ord 18, r 7A (the practice should also be followed in the county court).

The conviction may be proved by certificate of conviction (Criminal Procedure Act 1865, s 6) and, in addition, the contents of the information, charge sheet, complaint or indictment are also admissible.

(*b*) *Proof of adultery and paternity under the Civil Evidence Act 1968, s 12*

If, in matrimonial proceedings, a person is found to have committed adultery then in any other civil proceedings in which that adultery is a relevant issue, the finding is admissible in evidence. By s 12(5) 'matrimonial proceedings' means proceedings in the High Court and county court only.

Section 12 further provides that if a person is adjudged to be the father of a child in affiliation proceedings then in any subsequent civil proceedings in which the fact that he is the father of the child is a relevant issue, the finding is admissible in evidence.

Example
Marjorie petitions for divorce relying on Bill's adultery with Alice. The court find in Marjorie's favour.

If Alice's husband Joe wishes to petition for divorce, relying on her adultery with Bill then s 12 makes the finding of adultery in Marjorie's case admissible in evidence in Joe's action against Alice.

Example
Freda, an unmarried mother, takes affiliation proceedings against Arnold. The court find that Arnold is the putative father of Freda's child.

If Jane, Arnold's wife, wishes to sue him for divorce based on his adultery with Freda, then the finding in the affiliation proceedings is admissible in evidence in the divorce case (s 12(2)(*a*)).

The effect of adducing in evidence the earlier judgment will be that Alice will be taken to have committed adultery and Arnold will be taken to be the father of Freda's child until they prove to the contrary.

A further example will stress the point that the judgments are only admissible by virtue of an express statutory provision.

Example
Hilary takes proceedings in the magistrates' court based on the unreasonable behaviour of her husband, Neil, as evidenced by his adultery with Carol.

The fact that the magistrates' court find that Neil has committed adultery with Carol will not be admissible in any matrimonial proceedings between Carol and her husband, Ted. This is because of *Hollington* v *Hewthorn*. Section 12 does not, as has already been seen, cover matrimonial proceedings in a magistrates' court.

Practical considerations: A party wishing to rely on s 12 *must plead full details of the finding of the court in his petition or pleading*. As with s 11, the opposing party is required to plead the way in which he intends to deal with the allegation (RSC Ord 18, r 7A and Matrimonial Causes Rules 1977, r 10).

A copy of the decree or court order is admissible in evidence in later proceedings *to prove the judgment* (s 12(2)(*b*)).

(*c*) *Proof of criminal convictions in defamation actions under the Civil Evidence Act 1968, s 13*

If a criminal conviction is relevant to an issue in defamation proceedings, then proof of that conviction is conclusive evidence that the person committed the crime.

8.2 Subsequent proceedings involving the same parties

Where both parties were involved in the earlier proceedings the judgment raises an estoppel (*estoppel per rem judicatam*). The party bound by the estoppel is not permitted to deny the judgment nor is he permitted to deny the facts on which it is based. The estoppel also binds privies of the parties in the earlier action (eg ancestor/heir, bankrupt/trustee, vendor/purchaser of land).

The rule derives from the following principles: (*a*) that no-one should be troubled twice by the same cause of action; and (*b*) that the public interest demands finality in litigation.

For such an estoppel to arise, certain conditions must be satisfied:

(1) There must be a final judgment—including a consent or default judgment but not eg where an action has been dismissed for want of prosecution or discontinued.

(2) The judgment must be that of a competent court—which includes not only the superior courts but also the inferior courts and even domestic tribunals.

(3) The action must involve the same parties in the same capacities (*Marginson* v *Blackburn Borough Council* [1939] 2 KB 426; *Randolph* v *Tuck* [1962] 1 QB 175).

Furthermore, the estoppel must be pleaded (RSC Ord 18 r 8), failing which the judgment loses its binding effect, though it retains some value as evidence in the proceedings (*Vooght* v *Winch* (1819) 106 ER 507).

(a) *Cause of action estoppel*

As between the parties to the earlier proceedings the judgment is conclusive as to claims which were determined in the action, or which could have been brought forward as part of the same cause of action or defence (*Henderson* v *Henderson* (1843) 3 Hare 100; *Public Trustee* v *Kenward* [1967] 1 WLR 1062). More recently, the rule in *Henderson* v *Henderson* was applied in *Vervaeke (formerly Messina)* v *Smith* [1983] AC 145 (but cf *Lawlor* v *Gray* [1984] 3 All ER 345).

It has been recognised by the courts that the wider part of this rule can lead to hardship. This is especially so where there has been a default judgment. It was held in *New Brunswick Railway Co* v *British and French Trust Corporation* [1939] AC 1 (per Lord Maugham LC) that '. . . an estoppel based on a default judgment must be very carefully limited. The true principle in such a case would seem to be that the defendant is estopped from setting up in a subsequent action a defence which was necessarily, and with complete precision, decided by the previous judgment'.

(b) *Issue estoppel*

Issues of fact or law which have been litigated in earlier proceedings may not be litigated by the same parties in a subsequent action even though it is founded on a different cause of action. A party is estopped from denying any matter which was in issue in the earlier proceedings and which was resolved against him. The matters which have been determined and which are binding on the parties are ascertained by reference to the pleadings and the judgment in the earlier action.

(c) Matrimonial proceedings

The rules of estoppel per rem judicatam tend to be relaxed in matrimonial cases. Although the parties cannot claim as of right to relitigate an issue which has already been decided, the estoppel binds the parties but not the court: 'the divorce court has the right, and indeed the duty in a proper case, to re-open the issue, or to allow either party to re-open it, despite the objection of the other party (that is what is meant by saying that estoppels do not bind the divorce court)' (*Thompson* v *Thompson* [1957] 2 WLR 138) per Denning LJ.

By statute 'On a petition for divorce it shall be the duty of the court to inquire, so far as it reasonably can, into the facts alleged by the petitioner and into any facts alleged by the respondent'— Matrimonial Causes Act 1973, s 1(3).

Furthermore, a divorce may be granted on the same, or substantially the same, facts as were relied on in earlier proceedings for a decree of judicial separation or in proceedings in the magistrates' court—Matrimonial Causes Act 1973, s 4.

8.3 Similar fact evidence

As to similar fact evidence generally see **7.2** above. Reported cases on similar fact evidence in civil cases are rare. The case usually cited is *Mood Music Publishing* v *De Wolfe Ltd* [1976] 1 Ch 119, in which Lord Denning MR said at 127:

'In civil cases the courts will admit evidence of similar facts if it is logically probative, that is, if it is logically relevant in determining the matter which is in issue: provided that it is not oppressive or unfair to the other side: and also that the other side has fair notice of it and is able to deal with it.'

An example of when the principle is relevant in civil cases is provided by the facts of the case:

Example
The plaintiffs sued the defendants for breach of copyright alleging that they had copied music. The defence was that the similarity between the copyright work and the work complained of was mere coincidence. Evidence was admitted that the defendants had copied other copyright works including those of the plaintiffs.

A further example is provided by the case of *Berger* v *Raymond Sun Ltd* [1984] 1 WLR 625.

Chapter 9

Cross-examination as to Credit

In Chapters 7 and 8 it was established that in both criminal and civil cases, in certain circumstances, evidence of previous findings of a court is admissible. The purpose of introducing such evidence will often be to prove the facts upon which the conviction or judgment was based. This chapter, which applies generally to both civil and criminal cases, deals with undermining the credibility of a witness. One of the ways of doing this is by cross-examining on previous criminal convictions. The essential distinction between this and the rules looked at in previous chapters is that the convictions go only to the credibility of the witness. It will assist in understanding this chapter if it is borne in mind that the term 'witness' includes a party to the case who is giving evidence.

9.1 Witnesses called by other parties

It was established in Chapter 4 that a witness who has given evidence in chief may be cross-examined by the opposing party and that one of the aims of cross-examination is to discredit a witness and thus persuade the court that his evidence is not to be believed. Questions going to the credibility of a witness are allowed in both civil and criminal cases but are subject to the rule that any answer given is final (*R* v *Mendy* (1976) 64 Cr App R 4). This means that the answer given by the witness to the credit question cannot be challenged by calling other evidence on the subject as, if this were allowed, trials would very quickly become distracted from the main issues of the case.

This rule does not apply where the question is relevant not only to credit but also to an issue in the case. An example may be given by reference to the offence of rape.

Example

Amanda complains that she has been raped by Peter. Her evidence is that she did not consent to having intercourse with him, had never had intercourse with him before and had not given any indication that she would like to. Peter's defence is consent and he alleges an intimate sexual relationship with Amanda going back several weeks before the alleged offence.

When Amanda is cross-examined on Peter's allegations, her answers are relevant not only to her credibility as a witness in the case but also go directly to an issue, namely whether she consented or not and her answers will not be final (*R* v *Riley* (1887) 18 QBD 481). However, if the scope of questioning is widened to include Amanda's sexual experience with men other than Peter then that is a question purely as to credit and any answer given will be final (*R* v *Bashir* [1969] 1 WLR 1303). If, however, the scope of questioning is widened to include Amanda's sexual experience with men other than Peter, then such questions may be relevant merely to discredit the complainant's evidence although, depending on the issues raised by the case, the questions may be relevant to establish Peter's belief in consent. The Sexual Offences (Amendment) Act 1976, s 2(1), provides that at a rape trial, evidence of, or questions concerning, the sexual experience of the complainant with men other than the defendant may be put only with leave of the trial judge. Such leave should be given 'if and only if (the judge) is satisfied that it would be unfair to that defendant to refuse to allow the evidence to be adduced or the question to be asked' (s 2(2)). If he is so satisfied leave should be given. Section 2(2) is not discretionary. He must assess the value of the evidence, bearing in mind the issues raised in the case before him. The provision was considered in *R* v *Viola* (1982) 75 Cr App R 125, and again in *R* v *Brown* (1989) 89 Cr App R 97.

The general rule that answers given to questions as to credit are final is subject to a number of exceptions.

(*a*) *To establish bias*

A witness could for example be asked whether she has accepted a bribe to give evidence, whether she is cohabiting with the party on whose behalf she is giving evidence, or whether she has a grudge against a party to the proceedings. If any of these matters are denied in cross-examination, they may be proved by independent evidence.

(b) *To show that the witness has made a previous inconsistent statement*

It is not uncommon for a witness to give evidence that is inconsistent with a verbal or written statement made to someone on an earlier occasion. If so, the witness can be asked about the statement in cross-examination. If he admits making it he should be asked which version is correct. If he admits that his earlier statement is in fact the correct version of events then obviously the court can accept his oral testimony in accordance with the earlier statement as evidence. The court may, of course, decide that in view of what has happened that the witness is not to be believed anyway.

It is worth emphasising the fact that a party to a case who gives evidence is liable to cross-examination on a previous inconsistent statement in the same way as any other witness.

Example
Rowson made a confession to the police which was ruled inadmissible in evidence against him. However on his giving oral evidence inconsistent with the confession a co-defendant was allowed to cross-examine him on the previous statement. (See *R* v *Rowson* (1985) 2 All ER 539.) It should be noted that the prosecution would not be allowed to cross-examine on the statement and the co-defendant was only allowed to do so on the basis that the previous inconsistent statement was relevant to his defence.

If the witness admits making the earlier statement but says that it is incorrect then this brings into question the evidential value of the previous inconsistent statement. The rule differs according to the nature of the case.

In criminal cases the value of the previous inconsistent statement is merely to discredit the evidence of the witness. It cannot be accepted as evidence of the facts stated (*R* v *Golder* [1960] 1 WLR 1169).

In civil cases a previous inconsistent statement is admissible as evidence of the truth of the facts stated therein. This means that on a witness being shown to have made a previous inconsistent statement but denying the truth of it, the judge can decide which version of events to accept (Civil Evidence Act 1968, s 3).

Example
Jim sues Peter for damages for personal injuries sustained when their cars collided. Peter's defence is that Jim was contributorily negligent in giving misleading signals. Jim calls a witness to say that she saw Peter pull out of a side road into the path of Jim's oncoming vehicle which was travelling straight on without signals. In an earlier statement to the police

the witness has said that she saw Jim's car signalling a left hand turn, Peter pulled out and when Jim carried straight on a collision occurred.

If this previous inconsistent statement is introduced into the proceedings then the judge can, if he wishes, accept it as evidence in preference to the oral testimony of the witness.

The witness may, exceptionally, deny having made the statement. If this happens then, by virtue of the Criminal Procedure Act 1865, ss 4, 5 (which apply equally to civil and criminal cases) the statement may be proved by the cross-examining party. On its being proved, the procedure is then the same as in cases where the witness admits having made the statement.

Practical considerations: If the statement is a verbal one then the witness must be given sufficient detail of its circumstances to enable him to identify the occasion referred to before it is proved against him (Criminal Procedure Act 1865, s 4). If a written statement is involved then before it is proved, the witness must be given a copy (Criminal Procedure Act 1865, s 5). In either case proof of the statement will have to come from the person who heard or took it down or is otherwise able to identify the statement as that of the witness.

(c) Criminal convictions

By the Criminal Procedure Act 1865, s 6, which again applies to both civil and criminal cases a witness may be asked whether he has committed a criminal offence. If he denies it, then the criminal convictions may be proved. Although the Act says that any offence may be referred to, there is little point in introducing a conviction unless it affects the witness's credibility. Thus, whilst convictions for dishonesty will usually go to the credibility of a witness, those for road traffic offences, trading on a Sunday and common assault will not. See further *R* v *Sweet-Escott* (1971) 55 Cr App R 316.

In criminal cases there are special rules governing the cross-examination of a defendant on previous convictions—see **9.3** below.

Practical considerations: In relation to bad character and previous convictions there are a number of practical points to consider:

(1) How are the convictions to be proved?
(2) Are there any convictions which cannot be referred to?

In criminal cases the Police and Criminal Evidence Act 1984, s 73(1), provides that a *conviction may be proved* by producing a certificate signed by the clerk to the relevant Crown Court or justices and proving that the person named in the certificate is the witness being cross-examined.

In civil cases proof is again admissible by certificate of conviction in accordance with the Criminal Procedure Act 1865, s 6, and the Prevention of Crimes Act 1871, s 18.

In civil cases the Rehabilitation of Offenders Act 1974, s 4(1), provides that a witness may not be cross-examined on any *conviction which is spent*. In criminal cases spent convictions can be referred to in cross-examination but only with the leave of the court which will be given if the interests of justice require it. (See the Rehabilitation of Offenders Act 1974, s 7 and *Practice Direction (Crime: Spent Convictions)* [1975] 1 WLR 1065).

(d) To show a general reputation for untruthfulness

It is permitted to call evidence to show that a witness has a general reputation for untruthfulness and is therefore not to be believed (*R v Brown* (1867) LR 1 CCR 70).

9.2 A party's own witness

How is a party to a case allowed to treat a witness whom he has called to give evidence but who fails to give the evidence expected of him? It may be that the party to the case would like to discredit the witness by, for example, putting to him the statement that he initially gave before giving evidence. The treatment of such witnesses depends on how they are categorised.

(a) The unfavourable witness

An unfavourable witness is one who fails to prove a fact or facts when he was expected to do so. This may be as a result of the witness being nervous, forgetful or confused. He is not, however, motivated by malice towards the party calling him or by dishonesty and neither is he wilfully refusing to co-operate.

If a witness is unfavourable it is not possible to attack his credit. Thus, it is not permissible to refer to his character and convictions (Criminal Procedure Act 1865, s 3, which applies to both civil and criminal cases), nor is it possible to put to him any earlier statement made by him. However, it is possible to call another witness in an attempt to prove the facts which the unfavourable witness has failed to prove. This is of course largely a matter of common sense. If a party to a case has three witnesses, all prepared to testify to a given fact, it would be absurd if on the first witness failing to give evidence as expected the other two were precluded from giving evidence.

In civil proceedings however, there is another option for a party who has called an unfavourable witness. It may be possible, by virtue of the Civil Evidence Act 1968, s 2(2) to put the witness's written statement (or less usually an oral statement) in evidence after the witness has completed his oral testimony. The court is then entitled to accept that statement as evidence.

Example
Keith is suing his employers for damages following an accident at work. He calls a union official. Arthur, to give evidence of a number of incidents of complaint to the management about the machinery in question. Arthur is very nervous and makes a complete 'hash' of his evidence.

By virtue of s 2(2) with leave of the court, Arthur's statement made to Keith's solicitors may be accepted as evidence. (See further **14.6**.)

Practical considerations: The provisions of the Civil Evidence Act 1968 are subject to rules of court as to giving notice to an opposing party of intention to rely on the Act. These rules are fully discussed in the context of hearsay evidence in Chapter 13. If it is anticipated that a witness may be unfavourable then these rules should be complied with. If, however, the witness turns out to be unfavourable without any prior warning then the court have power in their discretion to allow the statement to be adduced in evidence, notwithstanding the fact that the rules have not been followed. See for example *Morris* v *Stratford-on-Avon RDC* [1973] 1 WLR 1059, the Civil Evidence Act 1968, s 8(3)(*a*), RSC Ord 38, r 29 and CCR Ord 20, r 20.

(*b*) *The hostile witness*

A hostile witness is one who refuses to tell the truth at the instance of the party calling him. He may be acting out of malice or dishonesty. His hostility may take the form of deliberately giving evidence that is at variance with a previous statement or it can take the form of deliberately refusing to answer questions which have been put by the party calling him (*R* v *Thompson* (1977) 64 Cr App R 96).

As in the case of the unfavourable witness the Criminal Procedure Act 1865, s 3, again prohibits attempting to undermine the credibility of the witness by referring to his bad character. However, with leave of the court, any previous statement made by the witness may be put to him. As with previous inconsistent statements made by an opposing witness the evidential status of a statement put to the witness in this way differs according to the nature of the proceedings.

In criminal cases the rule is the same as for inconsistent statements made by opposing witnesses, namely unless the witness actually changes his evidence to accord with his earlier statement all that a previous inconsistent statement can do is discredit a witness. The statement is not itself to be treated as evidence (*R v Golder* [1960] 1 WLR 1169) and the jury should be directed accordingly. The hostility need not arise in evidence in chief but may arise during cross-examination (*R v Norton and Driver* [1987] Crim LR 687).

Example
Annie makes a statement to the police identifying Bill as being at the scene of a robbery. On giving oral evidence Annie says that Bill was not there.

If Annie is ruled hostile, then she may be asked about the earlier statement to the police. If she admits making it but denies that it is true there is no evidence before the court that Bill was present at the scene of the crime. If she denies making the statement it can be proved against her but again unless she changes her evidence to accord with her original police statement there is no evidence before the court that can prove Bill's presence.

In civil cases the Civil Evidence Act 1968, s 3(1), applies to inconsistent statements made by hostile witnesses. The effect of s 3(1) is that on proof of the earlier statement being made by the witness the court can decide, if they wish, to accept it as evidence in the case. Unlike previous statements made by unfavourable witnesses there are no rules of court to comply with.

Practical considerations: If a party calling a witness wishes to treat him as hostile and thus refer him to a previous inconsistent statement, application must be made to the judge or justices for leave to do so. Cross-examination to determine whether or not the witness is hostile should take place in the jury's presence so that they have an opportunity to observe his demeanour and take it into account in assessing his evidence (*R v Darby* (1988) CLR 817).

9.3 Cross-examining the defendant in a criminal trial

It has already been established that the defendant who has given evidence in chief can, just like any other witness, be cross-examined (see **4.1(b)**). However, in cross-examining a defendant the prosecution must take heed of the Criminal Evidence Act 1898, s 1(*f*). This provides that a defendant:

'shall not be asked . . . any question tending to show that he has committed or been convicted of or been charged with any offence other than that wherewith he is then charged, or is of bad character'.

What is the scope of this protection? The section lays down a rule against questions 'tending to show'. This means revealing the convictions to the jury or justices for the first time. For example, if the defendant for some reason decides to reveal his previous convictions to the court whilst giving evidence in chief then the s 1(*f*) protection will not apply and the prosecution can cross-examine on these matters (*Jones* v *DPP* [1962] AC 635).

Example
Fred is charged with robbery. He has a number of convictions for petty theft. As part of his defence he decides to reveal his convictions to the jury and say that although he is a petty villain, robbery is a crime that he would not even contemplate.

The court is now aware of the convictions and the prosecution could cross-examine Fred on the convictions.

In *R* v *Anderson* [1988] 2 All ER 549, the Court of Appeal held that the judge had been right to allow cross-examination of the defendant to establish that she was 'wanted' by the police in connection with another (unspecified) offence. Because of the nature of the defence this did not tend to reveal anything to the jury of which they were not already aware. The defendant was charged with conspiracy to cause explosions and explained her possession of incriminating material, including false identity documents and a large sum of money, by alleging that she was involved in a conspiracy to assist escaped IRA prisoners out of the country. Consequently, the jury was already aware that she must have committed other offences. The purpose of the cross-examination was to show that her explanation was unlikely, as a wanted person would not be chosen to assist escaped prisoners.

In the special circumstances of this case, the cross-examination was not confined to the particular offences already disclosed by the defendant (although the cross-examination stopped short of disclosing the nature of the offence in respect of which the defendant was wanted by the police).

The Criminal Evidence Act, having laid down a basic protection for a defendant, then goes on to give several exceptional circumstances when the protection may be lost and cross-examination on previous convictions allowed. Before looking at these exceptions, it should be noted that s 1(*f*), as set out above, refers not only to convictions but also to charges. The next question therefore is whether, if one of the exceptions set out below applies, a defendant can be cross-examined not only on his convictions but also on any offence of which he has been charged and acquitted. The answer is that in general he cannot. Acquittals are not relevant (see further *Maxwell* v *DPP* [1935] AC 309).

9.4 The exceptions to s 1(*f*) protection

In Chapter 7 two exceptions to the basic s 1(*f*) protection were discussed. These were under s 1(*f*)(i) and the first leg of s 1(*f*)(ii). In both cases the evidence was admissible to help prove guilt. The remaining two exceptions differ in that they are only relevant to the credibility of the defendant as a witness. These exceptions are to be found in the second leg of s 1(*f*)(ii) and in s 1(*f*)(iii).

(a) The second leg of s 1(f)(ii)

This arises where:

'the nature or conduct of the defence is such as to involve imputations on the character of the prosecutor or the witnesses for the prosecution.'

This exception has given rise to much difficulty and case law. In the course of his defence the defendant may make allegations about a prosecution witness which amount to an attack on his character. This may be done in cross-examination of the prosecution witness or when defence evidence is introduced. The purpose in pursuing such a course will in some cases be to try and undermine the credibility of the witness. In other cases the allegations will be an integral part of the defence. Whichever of these two motives lies behind the attack, the result will be that if the defendant does actually give evidence himself then the prosecution may, subject to the discretion of the court, cross-examine the defendant on his previous convictions (see *Selvey* v *DPP* [1970] AC 304). Examples of the circumstances in which the attack on the charac-

ter of the prosecution witness is a necessary part of the defence
may be given by reference to the facts of decided cases.

Example
D was charged with buggery of X. Part of his defence was that X had
offered him money to commit buggery and when he refused to do so X
made up the allegations. (*Selvey* v *DPP*)

Example
D was charged with burglary. His fingerprints were found in the room
of the victim's property and the accused explained this away by an
allegation that he had had a homosexual relationship with the occupant.
(*R* v *Bishop* [1975] QB 274)

In each of these cases cross-examination under s 1(*f*)(ii) was
allowed even though the defendant had to make the allegations
if he was to be able to present his defence adequately.

In many cases it will be only too obvious that the nature and
conduct of the defence has involved attacks on the characters of
prosecution witnesses. However, this is not always the case. In
Selvey v *DPP* it was confirmed that if what is said amounts in
reality to no more than a denial of the charge it should not bring
the accused within s 1(*f*)(ii). Thus, generally, an accusation that
a witness is lying will not invoke s 1(*f*)(ii), being no more than a
denial of the charge. This has caused particular problems in
relation to the accused who is alleged to have made a confession
to the police. If the accused alleges that the confession was
obtained by improper means (see Chapter 12) then clearly
s 1(*f*)(ii) will apply. What of the person who merely denies having
made the statement amounting to a confession? *R* v *Tanner* (1977)
66 Cr App R 56 and *R* v *McGee* (1979) 70 Cr App R 247 suggest
that if police officers are involved, a denial by the accused that
the conversation containing the confession took place is, by inference, an allegation that the officers have fabricated their evidence.
This is sufficient to invoke s 1(*f*)(ii). *R* v *Nelson* (1978) 68 Cr App
R 12 suggests the contrary view, that it is not sufficient to invoke
s 1(*f*)(ii). In *R* v *Britzman* [1983] 1 WLR 350 the Court of Appeal
reviewed the authorities and whilst expressing a preference for
the stricter view put forward in *R* v *Tanner* and *R* v *McGee*, the
court took the opportunity of laying down guidelines for judges
on how to exercise their discretion in cases where s 1(*f*)(ii)
applied. These guidelines are set out under (*b*) below.

If cross-examination is permitted under the second leg of
s 1(*f*)(ii) the question arises as to how much detail should be

elicited from the accused by the prosecution. This has been the subject of judicial interpretation which has decided that the object of cross-examination under this provision is to show the court the type of person who is making allegations about prosecution witnesses (that is, to destroy the credibility of the accused). Accordingly, the courts have permitted cross-examination only as to details of the conviction including date, court, and the barest details of the offence. The plea is sometimes included. This is supported by *R* v *France* [1979] Crim LR 48. However, in *R* v *Duncalf* [1979] 1 WLR 918, the court purported to allow cross-examination under s 1(*f*)(ii) on the facts on which the convictions were based, justifying this approach on the ground that these were sufficiently probative to have been the subject of cross-examination under s 1(*f*)(i). It is a pity that the Court of Appeal missed the opportunity to clarify the point in *R* v *Watts* [1983] 3 All ER 101.

(b) The discretion to disallow cross-examination under s 1(f)(ii)

Even though the conduct of the defence is such as to invoke s 1(f)(ii), the justices or trial judge still have a discretion to disallow cross-examination on previous convictions if it is felt that proof of the convictions would have an adverse affect on the fairness of the proceedings (see **5.5(b)**). Guidelines as to the exercise of this discretion are laid down in *R* v *Britzman* and *R* v *Powell* [1986] 1 All ER 193.

R v *Britzman* gives guidelines to judges as to how to exercise their discretion in cases involving denials of conversations with police officers. Such denials, by implication, involve allegations that the officers have fabricated their evidence and therefore constitute an attack on the characters of the officers thereby invoking s 1(*f*)(ii).

(a) Cross-examination should not be allowed if the defendant makes nothing more than a denial, however emphatically or offensively, of an act or short series of acts amounting to one incident or of what was said in a short interview.

Example
The court referred, by way of illustration, to a defendant in a pickpocket case who denies having said to the police, 'Who grassed on me this time?'

(b) If a long conversation is denied then s 1(*f*)(ii) cross-examination should be allowed, subject to the further points below.
(c) Cross-examination should only be allowed if the jury as a

result of the evidence given will inevitably have to decide whether the allegations have been fabricated.

(d) Allowance should be made for the strain of being in the witness box and particular care should be taken over the defendant who is driven in cross-examination to explain away the evidence by saying it was planted or made up.

(e) There is no need for cross-examination under s 1(*f*)(ii) if the evidence against the defendant is overwhelming anyway.

In *R* v *Powell* the Court of Appeal considered the general discretion to prevent s 1(*f*)(ii) cross-examination. In previous cases such as *R* v *Watts* [1983] 3 All ER 101, cross-examination was disallowed if the nature of the convictions tended to go to guilt rather than credibility. In *R* v *Watts* the defendant was charged with indecent assault and following allegations of impropriety on the part of the police the prosecution were allowed to cross-examine him on his previous convictions for indecent assault on, and unlawful intercourse with, young girls. The Court of Appeal held that the nature of the convictions was such that a jury would be incapable of appreciating that they were relevant only to credibility and were not indicative of guilt. Following *R* v *Watts* arguments were being advanced in practice to the effect that only convictions which clearly revealed a tendency towards dishonesty (eg theft, perjury) could be cross-examined on under s 1(*f*)(ii).

Such arguments proved to be short-lived. In *R* v *Powell* the Court of Appeal refused to interfere with a conviction in a case where the defendant, on a charge of living off the earnings of prostitution, was cross-examined on other convictions, involving prostitution, after alleging that the police had lied on oath. The Court stressed the fact that in *R* v *Watts* the leading case of *Selvey* v *DPP* [1970] AC 304 had not been cited. The effect of *Selvey* was analysed in *R* v *Burke* (1986) 82 Cr App R 156 and adopted in *R* v *Powell*. The following guidelines can be given as to the current attitude of the courts to their s 1(*f*)(ii) discretion:

(1) The judge must weigh the prejudicial effect of the previous convictions against the damage done by the attack on prosecution witnesses and must generally exercise his discretion so as to secure a fair trial.

(2) In the ordinary case the judge may feel that if a deliberate attack is made on a prosecution witness or if there is a real issue about the conduct of an important witness which the jury must decide in order to reach their verdict, the judge

is entitled to let the jury know the previous convictions of the man who is making the attack.

(3) The fact that the previous convictions are not for offences of dishonesty, the fact that they are for offences bearing a close resemblance to the offences charged are matters for the judge to take into consideration when exercising his discretion but they do not oblige him to disallow the proposed cross-examination.

(4) The Court of Appeal will not interfere with the exercise of the discretion by a judge unless he has erred in principle or there is no material on which he could properly have arrived at his decision.

To avoid confusion it should be noted that whilst *R v Britzman* applies to a particular type of case where the second leg of s 1(*f*)(ii) has been invoked, *R v Watts* is a much wider principle covering all cases involving the second leg of s 1(*f*)(ii). For an example of a case in which both principles were applied see *R v Owen* (1986) 83 Cr App R 100.

Practical considerations: In the Crown Court the *application for leave to cross-examine under s 1(f)(ii)* is made to the judge in the absence of the jury. This has the obvious advantage that unless the judge rules in favour of the prosecution the jury will not know about the record of the defendant. The judge, in exercising his discretion will, as has been seen, ask himself two questions:

(1) Has the conduct of the defence been of a nature to invoke s 1(*f*)(ii)?

(2) If yes, should cross-examination be disallowed as a matter of discretion? Convictions can of course be relevant to credibility for a number of reasons. They may speak for themselves if eg they are for theft or perjury. Any conviction can be relevant to credibility if it followed a not guilty plea on the basis that it reveals a reluctance on the part of another court to believe the word of the defendant.

In the magistrates' court the position is more difficult. Justices decide questions of fact and law, the latter with the help of their clerk. Therefore if the prosecution apply for leave to cross-examine under s 1(*f*)(ii) the justices will be aware of the fact that the defendant has previous convictions even if they decide to reject the application. Prosecutors are acutely aware of this and although practice will vary throughout the country, they may have their own method of avoiding the possible prejudice to the defendant that is described above. One method is for the prosecutor, in the absence of the justices, to ask the defence advocate whether or not he concedes that cross-examination under s 1(f)(ii) is inevitable. If the defence advocate indicates that he will be objecting to any application, the clerk is consulted as to the advice that he will give the justices on the position. If he indicates that he would advise in law that the prosecution application is a sound one then the matter will be put to the justices. If the clerk is of a mind to advise the justices that the application is not well-founded then the prosecution may or may not decide to make the application. This will depend on various factors including the overall strength of the evidence against the defendant. It should be stressed that this practice is not standard policy and may even horrify some prosecutors and clerks to the justices! As has been said, practice on this subject varies and at the end of the day if the prosecution do apply for leave to cross-examine under s 1(f)(ii) the ultimate decision rests with the justices.

Section 1(f)(ii) can only apply if the defendant goes into the witness box to give evidence. Therefore if he decides not to give any evidence himself then even though the character of prosecution witnesses has been attacked there is nothing that the prosecution can do to bring in details of previous convictions.

However, that is not the end of the story. There is a danger that the inexperienced will get so wound up in the complexities of this topic that they tend to overlook the ultimate aim in the case. It is not to avoid s 1(f)(ii) but to get an acquittal. Therefore before advising a client not to give evidence himself, very careful thought should be given to the effect that this will have on the weight of evidence before the court (see Chapters 1 and 3).

Example
James is charged with theft. The case is to be tried in the Crown Court. The main evidence against James is an oral confession which he denies making. If James does not go into the witness box and give evidence, he cannot be cross-examined on his previous convictions but he is almost certain to be convicted. The jury will have little evidence to consider in support of the allegation of fabrication.

The point being made is that it will often be an inevitable consequence of the case that the prosecution will be able to invoke s 1(f)(ii). In spite of this the defendant must give evidence. In such cases what can the defence do?

(1) Consider whether or not it can be submitted that the reception of the evidence would have an adverse effect on the fairness of the proceedings. As has been seen from *R* v

Powell if a deliberate attack on a prosecution witness has been made this argument may be doomed to failure.

(2) Consider 'leading the convictions'. This can be a useful practice. During examination in chief the defence advocate can ask the defendant about his previous convictions. This can for example be useful if the defendant has pleaded guilty in the past. He can then explain to the court that although he has been a villain in the past he is pleading not guilty on this occasion because he is genuinely innocent. Needless to say this approach will not be advisable if the client has in the past pleaded not guilty and been convicted! If this approach is to be adopted then the position must be carefully explained to the client and his instructions obtained in writing.

One method of avoiding cross-examination under s 1(*f*)(ii) was for the defendant, rather than give evidence on oath from the witness box, to make an unsworn statement from the dock. There is no doubt that some juries were acquitting defendants on the strength of these statements but the right to make them was taken away by the Criminal Justice Act 1982, s 72.

(c) Section 1(f)(iii)

The final exception to the general rule in s 1(*f*) is contained in s 1(*f*)(iii) which provides that a defendant may be cross-examined on his previous convictions if:

'he has given evidence against any *other person* charged in the same proceedings.'

This covers the situation described in **4.2(d)** where a defendant, in giving evidence in his own defence, implicates another person being tried with him. This of course is evidence against that other person.

The meaning of giving evidence against another has been considered in a number of cases including *Murdoch* v *Taylor* [1965] AC 574, *R* v *Bruce* [1975] 1 WLR 1252 and *R* v *Hatton* (1976) 64 Cr App R 88. In the case of *R* v *Varley* [1982] 2 All ER 519, 522, the Court of Appeal attempted to extract the principles from these earlier cases to give a working guideline as to when s 1(*f*)(iii) will apply:

(1) If one defendant has given evidence against a co-defendant then that co-defendant may cross-examine as to previous

convictions and the trial judge has no discretion to refuse
such an application.

(2) Such 'evidence' against the co-defendant may be given in
chief or it may be brought out in cross-examination.

(3) It must be objectively considered whether the evidence supports the prosecution case in a material respect or undermines the defence of the co-defendant. In either case
s 1(f)(iii) will apply.

(4) If consideration has to be given to the undermining of the
co-defendant's defence care must be taken to see that the
evidence clearly undermines the defence—inconvenience to
or inconsistency with the other's defence is not of itself
sufficient.

(5) A mere denial of participation in a joint venture is not
enough to rank as evidence against a co-defendant. The
denial must lead to the conclusion that if the witness did
not participate in the crime then it must have been the
other defendant who did.

(6) Where one defendant asserts or in due course would assert
one view of the joint venture which is directly contradicted
by the other such contradiction may be evidence against
the co-defendant.

These guidelines were applied in *R* v *Mir, Ahmed and Dalil*
[1989] Crim LR 894 a case in which one of the co-defendants, M,
had given evidence which appeared to amount to a confession of
his own involvement as well as being strong evidence against the
appellant, A. In cross-examination by M's counsel, A claimed to
have acted on M's instructions. It is hard to see how M's defence
could have been undermined in view of his own evidence: nevertheless his counsel was permitted to cross-examine A on a previous conviction. That the judge has no discretion in such cases
was again confirmed in *R* v *Reid* [1989] Crim LR 719. The only
test is that of relevance to the credibility of the co-defendant as
a witness.

Example

Bert and Gerald are jointly charged with robbery. Bert says that he and
Gerald took part and he participated under threats from Gerald amounting to duress. Gerald's defence is that he did not take part in the crime
at all and knows nothing about any alleged threats.

Acting for Bert it should be possible to cross-examine Gerald under s 1(*f*)(iii). Not only is Gerald denying taking part, he is also alleging that Bert's defence of duress is not true.

Example
Alice and Freda are jointly charged with theft of money. The evidence of the prosecution, which is accepted by the defence, is that they were in charge of the office, the money was there in the morning and it was gone by mid-afternoon. Alice and Freda are the only people who had access to the money. Alice denies stealing the money.

Although this is a mere denial of participation it should be noted that on the facts Freda is the only other person who could have done it. Freda should therefore be able to cross-examine Alice under s 1(*f*)(iii).

The object of cross-examining a co-defendant on previous convictions under s 1(*f*)(iii) is to show that he is not to be believed on oath, that is to destroy his credibility (*R* v *Hoggins* [1967] 1 WLR 1223).

Practical considerations: Where the prosecution wish to cross-examine on previous convictions under s 1(*f*)(iii) they must apply for leave to do so. The application is made in the absence of the jury and the trial judge has a discretionary power to refuse the application. Co-defendants wishing to cross-examine under s 1(*f*)(iii) must also apply for leave but in cases where there is sufficient evidence to invoke s 1(*f*)(iii) the court has no discretion to reject the application. In the magistrates' court the problems that were discussed in the context of s 1(*f*)(ii) apply equally to s 1(*f*)(iii).

As there is no discretion to disallow cross-examination by a co-defendant under s 1(*f*)(iii) it is inevitable that there will be cases where undue prejudice will be caused as a result. There will be cases in which a defendant with previous convictions will be convicted if he does nothing to discredit his co-accused, but will have his record put to him if he does, perhaps with devastating consequences for his case. In such cases, it will be possible to avoid the problem if an application for separate trials is successful.

(d) Practical considerations relevant to s 1(f)(i), (ii) and (iii)

In addition to the practical points which have been referred to individually in relation to each part of s 1(*f*) there are three points which are of general application.

The fact that the prosecution allege that a defendant has previous convictions does not necessarily mean that he will be prepared to admit them. If he denies it then the *prosecution must prove the conviction.* This may be done by producing a certificate of conviction signed by the clerk to the relevant court and proving that the person named in the certificate is the defendant (Police and Criminal Evidence Act 1984, s 73).

On the trial of a person alleged to have committed an offence whilst over 21 years of age, no reference can be made to *offences committed whilst the defendant was under 14.* Thus even if one of the exceptions to the general rule excluding evidence of character and convictions applies, no reference can be made to any conviction falling within the Act (Children and Young Persons Act 1963, s 16(2)).

The general effect of the Rehabilitation of Offenders Act 1974 in criminal proceedings was considered at **7.1** above. In particular it was established that if a conviction is spent then it should only be referred to with leave of the judge.

Chapter 10

Opinion Evidence

10.1 General

A witness is generally required to confine himself to a statement of the facts which he has perceived and should not express his opinion drawn from those facts. It is, however, wrong to assume that a witness is never permitted to give his opinion. It is apparent that a distinction must be drawn between admissible and inadmissible evidence of opinion. To draw this distinction it is necessary to consider the reason for excluding opinion evidence. The exclusionary rule is intended to preserve the function of the tribunal of fact.

Example
William witnesses a road accident involving two vehicles driven by Paul and David. William will say he saw that David's vehicle crossed the white line as it rounded the bend and collided with Paul's car.

From these facts and other facts presented to him the judge must decide whether or not David drove negligently. Once the facts have been presented the judge is as capable of forming an opinion as is the witness. It does not help the judge in discharging his function for the witness to go on to say that in his opinion David drove negligently and was to blame for the accident.

In a Crown Court trial it is for the jury to form its opinion on the facts presented to the court. If a witness were permitted to express an opinion then the jury, consciously or otherwise, might allow that to affect its judgment. In the magistrates' court the justices will discharge the same function in their capacity as arbiters of fact and they may be similarly influenced.

149

Example

In a criminal trial for theft a prosecution witness, Walter, gives evidence that he saw Denis take goods from the supermarket shelf and place them in his pocket.

In determining the accused's guilt, the jury or justices must consider whether the elements of the offence have been made out including an appropriation, dishonesty and the intention permanently to deprive. It may be a positive hindrance to them if Walter is permitted to assert that he saw Denis 'steal' the goods.

In these cases, the tribunal of fact is as well equipped as the witness to form an opinion, and there is no difficulty in holding that the opinion evidence should be inadmissible. It is however clear that a simple exclusionary rule would be unworkable and there are many examples of the courts receiving opinion evidence. In some cases, the effect of a simple exclusionary rule would be to deprive the tribunal of fact of access to certain material facts. In a road accident case it may be important for the court to draw conclusions about the speed at which the vehicles were travelling. A witness may be asked to convey his impression of the speed of a vehicle but will be unable to give his answer other than in the form of an opinion (for example 'fast', 'very fast', 'at least 50 mph'). He cannot relate in simple terms the facts from which his inference is drawn and leave it to the judge to form an opinion of the speed of the vehicle. It could be said that the opinion of the witness is admissible because it is inseparable from the facts on which it is based or perhaps because in such circumstances the witness is in a better position than the tribunal of fact to form an opinion.

In other cases, a total exclusionary rule would result in some difficulty for the witness because a simple expression of opinion amounts to a compendious way of narrating a complex set of facts. A witness may, for example, be permitted to assert that the accused was drunk. To exclude this simple expression of opinion would be to insist that the witness recount in detail the various facts on which his conclusion was based, namely that the accused was staggering, slurring his words, and his breath smelled of alcohol. (In *R* v *Davies* [1962] 1 WLR 1111 it was held that a lay witness could give evidence that the accused was drunk but not that he was unfit to drive.) Again, it could perhaps be said that the witness is better placed to form an opinion than is the tribunal of fact.

Other examples of opinion evidence being admitted include

opinion as to road and weather conditions, lighting conditions, age, identity, handwriting, identification of goods. Some of these inclusions may at first appear surprising. A witness may appear to state a fact ('this is Joe's handwriting' or 'this is the man I saw running away from the crime') but in truth the witness is conveying his own opinion. It would be more accurate to say 'I have on earlier occasions seen handwriting which I have known to be Joe's and this writing is in my opinion so similar that it too must be Joe's' or 'the man I saw at the scene of the crime is in my opinion of similar height, build, age, hair colour, facial features and complexion to the accused'. Such evidence is admitted because it is apparent that the witness is better placed than the tribunal to form an opinion, and allowing such evidence does not permit the witness to usurp the function of the tribunal of fact.

In countless matters of art and science a high degree of skill, experience or knowledge may be required before a person is equipped to form any meaningful opinion. In such cases, an expert in that field is better able to form an opinion than the tribunal of fact consisting of laymen. It is upon these principles that the court receives expert evidence in the form of opinions based upon proved or hypothesised facts (see below).

(a) Practical considerations

In cases where the ordinary (non-expert) witness is permitted to give evidence in the form of an opinion, the witness may be tested in cross-examination as to the facts upon which his opinion is based. It may become apparent that his opinion is based on inadmissible facts (for example hearsay) in which case his evidence would have to be disregarded, or upon a very poor observation, or even upon supposition. An example may be found in the cross-examination of a witness who has given evidence as to the speed of a vehicle. The witness may be asked to give estimates of the time and distance and to relate these estimates to other events or objects. 'How far away was the car when you first saw it?' 'About 50 feet.' 'About how many car lengths would that have been?' 'I don't know.' 'About four or five perhaps?' 'No, further than that.' etc.

(b) The Civil Evidence Act 1972, s 3(2)

In civil cases there is express statutory provision permitting the witness to give opinion evidence on any relevant matter 'as a way of conveying relevant facts personally perceived by him' (Civil

Evidence Act 1972, s 3(2)). This provision does not appear to add anything to the common law rules discussed above which will remain applicable in criminal cases.

10.2 Expert evidence

(a) General

An expert witness is called to express his opinion on a subject on which he has special skill, knowledge or experience. The admissibility of expert evidence is subject to different rules in civil and criminal cases and these are treated separately below. In either proceedings it is for the judge or justices to decide whether the proposed witness is qualified to give evidence as an expert. It is not necessary that a witness should have any formal qualifications, nor is it essential that his expertise should have been acquired in the course of his business or employment. The witness should however possess some special skill, knowledge or experience. A solicitor who had acquired some expertise as an amateur over a period of some ten years was allowed to give evidence on comparing examples of handwriting (*R* v *Silverlock* [1894] 2 QB 766).

It would not be possible or even helpful to give an exhaustive list of the matters upon which expert evidence has been received but examples include the following: medical matters, valuations of property, questions of foreign law (see further, in civil cases, the Civil Evidence Act 1972, s 4), matters of science and technology, commercial practices and handwriting. (When it is possible to compare handwriting in court this is a matter for expert evidence. If there is no handwriting with which the disputed document can be compared then non-expert opinion evidence may be admissible (see above).)

Practical considerations: When the expert witness is called, the examination in chief should commence with questions aimed at demonstrating that the witness is suitably qualified to give his opinion on the relevant matters. If the evidence of the expert is to be accepted, then there must be proof by some admissible evidence of the facts on which the opinion of the expert is based. Occasionally, the expert will have perceived these matters for himself and he will be able to give evidence as a witness of fact of the matters upon which his expert opinion is founded. To enable the court to assess the value of opinion evidence it must know the facts upon which the opinion is based and the expert witness should be examined in chief as to these facts. If the facts are not personally perceived by the witness then they must be proved by some other means or the opinion will be of no value (see *R* v *Turner* [1975] QB 834).

Where the witness gives an opinion based on facts proved by others, questions should be put to him in the form of hypotheses. This avoids the need for the expert to presuppose the facts. In this way he can convey his expert opinion without appearing to lend support to evidence of facts which are not within his own knowledge.

In cross-examination of an expert it will be necessary to consider the facts upon which the opinion is based as it may be possible to show that the witness has proceeded on a false premise. If the opinion itself is called into question, then the cross-examiner may hope that the expert can be persuaded to change his mind. It is difficult for an expert to change tack in the course of giving his evidence and he is unlikely to do so unless there is a way in which he can change his opinion without it appearing that he was mistaken. It is probably easier to persuade him to accept alternative views than to admit an error.

An expert is entitled to refer to established works of reference to aid his memory and to support the views which he is expressing. A doctor would be permitted to refer to his medical text books. In this way the expert is seen to be relying not only upon knowledge derived from his own experience but also from the experience of other members of his profession. Similarly, an expert witness in a robbery trial was permitted to refer to certain Home Office statistics (see *R* v *Abadom* [1983] 1 WLR 126). The Court of Appeal held that the evidence of the expert was rightly admitted and that he was rightly allowed to refer to statistical information even though it arose from the work of others. To exclude such references could lead to distortion of the expert's opinion. For an example in a civil case see *H* v *Schering Chemicals Ltd* [1983] 1 WLR 143.

(b) *Admissibility of expert evidence in criminal cases*

It is for the judge or justices to decide questions of admissibility. They will allow an expert to give evidence of opinion on a subject on which he is qualified to give evidence as an expert provided that the subject is not one on which the tribunal of fact is itself capable of forming an opinion without the benefit of expert guidance.

The restriction is illustrated by the case of *R* v *Turner* [1975] QB 834. The accused had killed his girl friend and to a charge of murder he set up a plea of provocation. The killing had taken place when the victim told him that whilst he had been in prison she had been sleeping with two other men and that the child she was carrying was not his. The trial judge refused to admit the evidence of a psychiatrist. It had been argued that the psychiatrist could have given evidence of the effect upon the accused of the confession and also that the behaviour of the accused since the offence was consistent with someone suffering from profound grief. The Court of Appeal held that the evidence was rightly rejected as both these points were well within ordinary human experience. Likewise in *R* v *Reynolds* [1989] Crim LR 220, the Court of Appeal held that a judge had rightly excluded expert evidence on whether D intended to kill or cause serious harm, where neither insanity nor diminished responsiblity were being pleaded. Similarly, on a charge under the Obscene Publications Act 1959, the court would not allow evidence of a psychiatrist on the issue of whether material was or was not obscene. This is something which the tribunal of fact can determine for itself. However where the question was as to the effect of publication on young children the evidence of a child psychiatrist was admissible (*DPP* v *A and BC Chewing Gum Ltd* [1968] 1 QB 159; *R* v *Anderson* [1972] 1 QB 304).

Practical considerations: The Crown Court (Advance Notice of Expert Evidence) Rules 1987 (SI 1987 No 716), which came into force on 15 July 1987, provide for mutual disclosure of expert evidence between the parties to criminal proceedings in the Crown Court. A party must disclose any expert evidence which he is proposing to adduce as soon as practicable after committal. The rules, which are made under the Police and Criminal Evidence Act 1984, s 81, also provide that such evidence will not be admissible, except with leave of the judge, if the correct procedure is not followed. There are no corresponding provisions in the magistrates' court. However, if the other party is taken by surprise there may be an application for an adjournment.

By the Criminal Justice Act 1988 s 30, a written expert's report may be put in evidence as well as calling oral evidence from the author. This applies in both the Crown Court and the magistrates' court. As to using a report in the absence of the maker, see **12.9**.

(c) Admissibility of expert evidence in civil cases

In civil proceedings an expert witness may give his opinion on 'any relevant matter on which he is qualified to give expert evidence' (Civil Evidence Act 1972, s 3(1)).

The provision is rather wider than the common law provision which is applicable in criminal cases and therefore extends the circumstances in which expert evidence will be received in civil cases. The expert will be able to express an opinion on the very matter which the court is asked to determine although under the common law rules the court would have been reluctant to admit such evidence.

Practical considerations: A party wishing to adduce expert evidence at a civil trial can do so only with leave of the court or with the agreement of all other parties unless he complies with RSC Ord 38, r 36 (which also applies in the county court: CCR Ord 20, r 27). This rule requires him to apply to the court for the court to determine whether a direction should be made concerning the disclosure of the evidence to other parties prior to the trial. It is usual for an order to be made that such evidence be disclosed. In personal injury actions in the High Court to which RSC Ord 25, r 8 applies, there is àn automatic direction concerning the disclosure of expert evidence. The scheme of the rules is to encourage the agreement of expert evidence before the trial in appropriate cases. Where this proves possible, the report of the expert witness will be received in evidence without the need for the expert to be called.

The court may limit the number of expert witnesses which a party may call (see RSC Ord 38, r 4) and in cases in which the automatic directions apply the parties are restricted to two medical and one non-medical expert witness (RSC Ord 25, r 8), unless they obtain an order to the contrary.

So far it has been seen that the expert evidence may be given by oral testimony or by an agreed report. In some circumstances the evidence of an expert may also be introduced as a hearsay statement under Pt 1 of the Civil Evidence Act 1968 (see **3.1**) or in the form of an affidavit under RSC Ord 38, r 2. Affidavit evidence may be introduced at the trial only with leave of the court. Such leave would not be granted if the evidence was substantially in dispute. If there is a dispute on the expert evidence then it is far better to call the expert. See further J O'Hare and R N Hill, *Civil Litigation*, 4th ed (Longman 1986), pp 364–7.

Chapter 11

Hearsay Evidence

A consideration of the rule against hearsay involves two distinct problems. The first and most difficult problem facing the practitioner is in deciding what does and what does not amount to hearsay. The second problem is simply whether or not evidence which has been identified as hearsay is nevertheless admissible under an exception to the general rule against hearsay. It is the former of these two problems which will be dealt with here and a consideration of the exceptions to the rule against hearsay follows, in Chapters 12 and 13.

As has already been seen (Chapter 2) the facts which are in dispute in a case must normally be proved by evidence and the most common form which evidence takes is the oral testimony of a witness.

11.1 Oral hearsay

In simple terms the rule against hearsay requires that a witness should not talk about something of which he has no personal knowledge. He should rely upon his own observation and recall of the matters in dispute. If he is not speaking from his own knowledge then his account of the events must be derived from elsewhere. This usually means that he is relying upon something which someone else has said or written which in turn suggests that better evidence is available in the form of oral evidence from the person who originally supplied the information and who could therefore have given original evidence. Furthermore, it is clear that the more often a story has been passed on the more inaccurate it will become. In its simplest form hearsay evidence is evidence which the witness has derived directly from someone who did actually perceive the matters which are in issue.

Example
Suppose that a journalist reports that President X has made a speech in which he stated that he had abolished the state's secret police.

From this report it is possible to conclude that the state's secret police has been abolished. This would be to rely upon a hearsay statement. The journalist has no personal knowledge of that fact. His knowledge is derived from the president's statement. Alternatively, the conclusion could be limited to the fact that President X has made a statement to the effect that he had abolished the state's secret police. This may be relevant, for example, if the journalist was reporting a propaganda campaign. In that case the journalist is not concerned that his readers accept the truth of the President's words, but merely with the fact that the words were spoken. As to this matter the journalist is speaking from his own knowledge and his statement is not hearsay but original.

This example demonstrates that, although reported speech may amount to hearsay, it does not follow that all reported speech is hearsay. If a witness reports a statement made by another person and his purpose in doing so is to persuade the court that what was said was true, then that is hearsay. However, if the statement is reported merely to inform the court of what was said, irrespective of its truth, it is not hearsay but original evidence.

'Evidence of a statement made to a witness by a person who is not himself called as a witness may or may not be hearsay. It is hearsay and inadmissible when the object of the evidence is to establish the truth of what is contained in the statement.' (per Mr De Silva in *Subramaniam* v *Public Prosecutor* [1956] 1 WLR 965 at 970.)

This statement of principle emphasises the importance of the *purpose* for which the evidence is introduced but, as will be seen at **11.2** and **11.3** below, the rule is rather wider in scope than may appear from the reference to 'a person who is not himself called as a witness'.

There are many purposes for which reported speech may be given in evidence. It may prove a threat that was made, or the state of a person's mind at a particular time, or the reason for a particular course of conduct.

Example
A witness is called to give evidence that 'Smith told me that Brown had murdered his rich uncle'.

Does that evidence infringe the rule against hearsay? The question cannot be answered without establishing what it is that the court is invited to infer from the evidence.

Imagine first of all that the evidence is given during the trial of Brown for murder. The evidence would almost certainly be given to prove that Brown was the murderer and in those circumstances the evidence is clearly hearsay. The witness has no personal knowledge of this fact and relies upon information derived from elsewhere.

Suppose instead that the court is asked to infer not that Brown murdered his rich uncle but simply that Smith said that he had done so. This may be the inference that we are asked to draw if Brown sues Smith for defamation (when the last thing that Brown wants is to prove the truth of the words) or if it were necessary to prove the state of Smith's knowledge at a particular time (as where he is charged with some complicity in the crime or even an insurance swindle). The witness heard the words spoken and his evidence is original.

Example
A landlady overhears a conversation in a public bar. Terry is heard to offer some electrical goods to Arthur. In response to a question from Arthur, Terry is heard to say: 'Don't ask silly questions, they fell off the back of a lorry.'

Will the landlady be allowed to give evidence of the conversation she has overheard? Again, it is not possible to say until we know what the court is asked to infer from this evidence. This in turn depends on the facts in issue in the proceedings. The court could be asked to infer that the goods were stolen. That would be hearsay evidence. It is not within the landlady's own knowledge that the goods were stolen. Alternatively, the evidence may be given to prove that Arthur knew or believed the goods to have been stolen. This would be so if the defence conceded that the goods were stolen but denied that Arthur had the necessary mens rea for an offence of handling. The words spoken are relevant to show Arthur's state of mind. The words are then relevant to the proceedings irrespective of their truth and as they were actually heard by the landlady she is giving original evidence.

Example
Livingstone, a motorist, is charged with a number of offences including reckless driving, failing to report an accident, etc. His answer to the charges is that at the relevant time he was not driving the car but was fifteen miles away and he later discovered the vehicle to be stolen. He then reported the matter to the police. There are witnesses to give

evidence as to the manner in which the vehicle was driven. No witness has come forward who can positively identify the accused. A witness is found who is able to say that she heard someone shout, 'Where are you legging it off to Livingstone?' shortly after the collision.

Does this evidence infringe the rule against hearsay? The first step, as always, is to decide what the court is invited to infer from the evidence if it is given. The fact in issue to which the evidence is directed is whether or not the accused was driving the vehicle. It is clearly relevant to the issue that he was in the vicinity at the time of the collision, especially in view of the defence put forward. The conclusion which the court is invited to draw is that Livingstone was indeed in the area. Is this something which is within the personal knowledge of the witness? Clearly, it is not. Her knowledge is derived from the person who actually shouted the words. The evidence is therefore hearsay.

11.2 Written statements

The term 'hearsay' is somewhat inapt as the rules that have just been discussed apply not only to oral statements but also to written ones. There is no difference between the evidence of a witness who says 'X told me . . .' and the evidence of a witness who produces a statement written by X. In both cases the rule requires that X should be called to give oral evidence in court and make himself available for cross-examination. If he cannot attend then his evidence cannot be given by another witness. It should be remembered of course that there may be ways of making X attend (see **4.2(a)**).

Example
A witness to a road accident makes a statement to the police. The witness then disappears and it is sought to introduce in court the statement which the witness made to the police officer.

The police officer may perhaps say 'the Austin Allegro emerged from the minor road causing approaching vehicles to swerve' or 'a witness informed me that he had seen the Austin Allegro emerge . . .' or 'from enquiries made at the scene of the accident I concluded that the Austin Allegro . . .' or finally 'I now produce a statement taken from Mr X who witnessed the accident and whose signature appears at the end of the statement'. In each of these four cases the evidence which the police officer is seeking to adduce is essentially the same. He is trying to give evidence of what happened to lead to the accident. The evidence in each case is hearsay as he is giving evidence of something which is not within his personal knowledge in circumstances where the court are asked to infer from the statement that the driver of the Allegro was to blame for the accident.

It should not be thought that hearsay is to be found only in prepared witness statements.

Example
The defendants, the driver and owners of a motor bus were charged with offences of driving the bus without insurance. There was a policy in force which covered the vehicle only when used for social, domestic and pleasure purposes. The bus had been stopped by the police who had found a list of names and sums of money. Against each name appeared the words 'paid' or 'to come'. On the defendant's appeal against conviction the Divisional Court held that the list provided only hearsay evidence as to the fact that passengers were carried for reward and was consequently inadmissible and the convictions were quashed, there being no other evidence that the vehicle was being used for business purposes. (*Howey* v *Bradley* [1970] RTR 112)

11.3 Inference from conduct

A witness may wish to give evidence not of a statement made by someone else but of some act by that person. In doing so the witness may be inviting the court to draw an inference from such conduct which is in effect equivalent to a statement which might have been made by that other person.

Example
Suppose that the driver of the Austin Allegro in the earlier example puts forward the defence that she took all proper precautions before proceeding into the major road, that at the time she moved off the other vehicle was not in sight and that the driver of the other vehicle must have caused or contributed to the accident by driving too quickly for the road conditions. Suppose further that in support of this defence she says that a pedestrian nearby looked in both directions and then stepped out into the main road.

What is the purpose of introducing this last piece of evidence? What is the inference which the court is invited to draw?

If the inference is nothing more than that the pedestrian looked in both directions and then proceeded to cross the road, then it cannot be said that the evidence infringes the rule against hearsay. What can be said is that the evidence has no bearing on the facts in issue and that the evidence is irrelevant (see **5.3**).

Suppose that the inference which the court is invited to draw is that because the pedestrian looked both ways and then stepped out into the road, the road must have been clear at that moment. It is no more than if the witness had been able to say, 'a pedestrian having looked both ways told me that the road was clear'. The evidence is hearsay. Although the witness must have some personal knowledge of the state of the road, as she had presumably looked for herself, it is not her own personal knowledge on which she is relying in giving evidence of the pedestrian's conduct.

11.4 Conclusion

The above examples and explanation set out to identify the nature of hearsay evidence and to lay down the general rule that such evidence is inadmissible. There is one further aspect to the rule against hearsay, namely whether or not a witness when giving evidence can refer to a statement that he has previously made. Such evidence would, in general, contravene the rule against hearsay and also the separate rule which prohibits the use of self-serving statements. The topic is considered further in Chapter 14. The rule against hearsay may be formulated as follows:

A witness may not give evidence of the statement (whether oral or in writing), or of the conduct, of any person (including himself) for the purpose of proving the truth of any assertion contained in or to be inferred from such statement or conduct.

There are numerous exceptions to the rule against hearsay and these are considered in the two chapters which follow.

Chapter 12

Exceptions to the Rule Against Hearsay in Criminal Cases

In the previous chapter it was sought to identify the nature of hearsay evidence and to lay down the general rule that such evidence is inadmissible. Exceptions to this rule exist both at common law and by statute. The purpose of this chapter is to examine some of the more important of these exceptions.

CONFESSIONS

A confession 'includes any statement wholly or partly adverse to the person who made it . . . whether made in words or otherwise' (Police and Criminal Evidence Act 1984, s 82(1)). Clearly this is wide enough to include, for example, the unguarded statement of a motorist after an accident, 'I'm sorry, I wasn't looking', as well as a written statement under caution by a person in police custody and containing a full description of his part in a robbery. Of course, the confession need not be in words at all. The assertion of a fact may be inferred from conduct.

12.1 How may a confession be made?

A confession may be made at any time and to anybody. If the accused writes a letter to his wife, then any statement in that letter adverse to the interest of the accused would amount to a confession. This would be the case even though the letter was never intended for wider publication. For an example see *Rumping* v *DPP* [1964] AC 814. Similarly, if the accused is overheard talking to himself, any statement he makes is capable of amounting to a confession (*R* v *Simons* (1834) 6 C&P 540).

It has already been seen that the statement amounting to a confession may be made 'in words or otherwise' (Police and Criminal Evidence Act 1984, s 82(1)). Thus it has been held that where a defendant accepted an invitation by the police to re-enact a crime on video (having been told that he was still under caution), the video recording was admissible evidence of the defendant's confessions.

Example
D, on being interviewed by the police, made a full oral confession of murder. He agreed to re-enact the murder on video at the apartment of the victim and did so, providing a commentary. The video was admissible in evidence against D (*Li Shi-Ling* v *The Queen* [1988] 3 WLR 671.)

Although the case is from the Privy Council having originally been tried in Hong Kong there is no reason why the same principle should not be applied under English law.

There are other cases in which the conduct of the accused, including his conduct in remaining silent, may in some circumstances amount to an asssertion which is wholly or partly adverse to his interest.

Example
Parkes was charged with murder. The prosecution evidence was that shortly after the stabbing, the victim's mother Mrs Graham, had asked the accused why he had stabbed her daughter. The accused had made no reply and had drawn a knife and attempted to stab Mrs Graham (*Parkes* v *R* [1976] 1 WLR 1251).

On those facts the Privy Council were of the opinion that the judge had been right in his direction that the reaction of the accused to Mrs Graham's question was something that the jury could take into account. In this case there was clearly something rather more than mere silence in the face of an allegation. However, it is possible that silence alone may amount to a confession. It will be important to examine all the circumstances and to consider whether there may be some other reason for the accused's silence in response to a statement which would normally call for some explanation or denial. See also *R* v *Christie* [1914] AC 545 which shows that the question to be determined is whether the accused can be said, by his words or action, to have accepted the statement as his own.

Where the accused is questioned by the police he has a right to remain silent. This right would be valueless if his silence could be taken to be a confession. He must be reminded of his right to silence by the administering of a caution as soon as the officer has grounds to believe that he has committed an offence and in any event he must be cautioned on arrest. (See section 11.1 of the Code of Practice for the detention, treatment, and questioning of persons by the police issued under the Police and Criminal Evidence Act 1984, s 66.) If the accused chooses to remain silent, this could not normally amount to acceptance of anything put to him. See *Hall* v *R* [1971] 1 WLR 298, though there are conflicting dicta in the case of *R* v *Chandler* [1976] 1 WLR 585. A judge may comment on the failure of the accused to answer questions or to make a statement but he should not invite the jury to draw adverse inferences from the exercise by the accused of his right to silence (*R* v *Gilbert* (1977) 66 Cr App R 237).

Similarly, the accused is not obliged to give evidence at his trial (Criminal Evidence Act 1898, s 1(*a*) and his failure to do so cannot be commented upon by the prosecution (s 1(*b*)). It is not open to the jury to find corroboration of the evidence of any prosecution witness in the fact that the accused declines to give evidence (*R* v *Jackson* [1953] 1 WLR 591). In his summing up, the judge is entitled to comment upon the fact that the accused has not given evidence but should not leave the jury with the impression that absence from the witness box is to be equated with guilt (*R* v *Bathurst* [1968] 2 QB 99). Strong comment would no doubt be made in a case in which the facts which have been established by the prosecution evidence are such as to demand some explanation from the accused. (See also **1.1(*b*)**). It is a matter for the trial judge whether he makes a comment and the judge is not bound to do so (*R* v *Harris* (1987) 84 Cr App R 75).

In *R* v *Smith (RW)* (1985) 81 Cr App R 286 the appellant, who had been charged with robbery, refused to give hair samples which could have been compared with hairs found at the scene of the crime. The Court of Appeal held that the trial judge had been entitled to leave such refusal, and the circumstances of it, to the jury as material which was capable of providing corroboration of the accomplice's evidence. There is provision in the Police and Criminal Evidence Act 1984 (s 55) for the taking of 'intimate samples' (samples of blood, semen or other tissue fluid, urine, saliva or pubic hair, or a swab taken from a person's body orifice). Such samples may not be taken without the consent in writing of the suspect. However, if consent is withheld without good cause, the court is entitled to 'draw such inferences from the refusal as appear proper'. The suspect's refusal may amount to corroboration of other evidence against him.

12.2 Is evidence of the confession admissible?

It should be appreciated that evidence of the confession will amount to hearsay. The prosecution will call a witness to give evidence of a statement made by the accused, or of a statement made by someone else and alleged to have been accepted by the accused as his own. The purpose in giving the evidence is to prove, as the case may be, that the accused was not watching the road, or stole the money, or inflicted the fatal wound. That is to say that the statement is introduced as evidence of the truth of its contents. The prosecution witness is not speaking from his own knowledge and recollection. His evidence is therefore hearsay.

One of the principal objections to hearsay evidence is its tendency to be unreliable. This argument has less force where the hearsay statement is a statement adverse to the interests of the person making it. By the Police and Criminal Evidence Act 1984, s 76(1), a confession made by an accused person 'may be given in evidence against him in so far as it is relevant to any matter in issue in the proceedings'. This provision clearly lays down an exception to the rule against hearsay.

Before the confession is given in evidence the prosecution may be required to prove beyond reasonable doubt that it was not obtained:

'(*a*) by oppression of the person who made it; or
 (*b*) in consequence of anything said or done which was likely, in the circumstances existing at the time, to render unreliable any confession which might be made [by the accused] in consequence thereof' (s 73(2)).

If representations are made to the court to suggest that the confession was or may have been obtained in such a way, then the court must put the prosecution to proof of these matters. The court may, however, of its own motion call upon the prosecution to give such proof.

The test of admissibility of a confession will be examined more fully later in this chapter, but first it is necessary to look at the legal framework within which the police are likely to obtain confessions.

12.3 Police and Criminal Evidence Act 1984, Pts IV–VI

When the court has to consider the propriety of a confession made to the police it will be important to consider the way in which the accused has been treated whilst in police custody. The detention and treatment of suspects and the questioning of suspects (including the manner in which statements should be taken down) are dealt with, in Pts IV and V of the Police and Criminal Evidence Act 1984 and in the codes of practice issued by the Home Secretary under s 66 of the Act.

(a) The codes of practice

The codes of practice lay down strict procedures to be complied with by the police and, together with Pts IV and V of the Act, introduce detailed provisions concerning the records which must be kept during the period of a person's detention at the police station.

The chief officer of police for each police area is responsible for designating those police stations which will be used for the purposes of detention of arrested persons and to appoint one or more custody officers for each such police station (ss 35 and 36).

The custody officer must be of at least the rank of sergeant (s 36(3)). One of the duties of the custody officer is to maintain a custody record which must include details of periods of detention, periods of questioning, the times at which the need for further detention is reviewed, the times at which meals are provided, any complaints made by the suspect concerning his treatment etc. This custody record will be an important document in cases where the propriety of a confession statement is challenged. When a person leaves police custody, or within 12 months thereafter, he or his legal representatives must be supplied with a copy on request. In many areas the police are prepared to disclose the custody record whilst a person is still in custody. It is therefore prudent for the solicitor on arriving at the police station to ask permission to examine the record and to make a note of any entries made up to that time or a note of the refusal as the case may be.

Whilst it is not possible in a work of this nature to examine fully the provisions of the code of practice and of Pts IV and V of the Act, it will be helpful to outline some of the main provisions and then to consider what effect any failure in compliance may have on the admissibility of any evidence which may be obtained from the suspect.

(b) Rights of detained persons

The detention of any person without charge must be authorised by the custody officer (s 37(2)). A person arrested and held in custody is entitled on request to consult privately with a solicitor. The time at which any request is made is to be noted in the custody record and delay in compliance with such a request is permitted only on limited grounds and even then only in the case of a 'serious arrestable offence' and on the authority of an officer of at least the rank of superintendent (s 58(6)). The grounds upon which delay may be justified are that the officer has reasonable grounds for believing that the exercise of the right will result in interference with evidence, interference or physical injury to other persons, the alerting of other suspects or will hinder the recovery of property obtained as a result of the offence (s 58(8)). This decision must be made with reference to the specific solicitor who is seeking access (*R* v *Samuel* [1988] 2 All ER 135).

The detained person has an absolute right to consult with a solicitor after 36 hours in custody and in any event before any court hearing.

The meaning of 'serious arrestable offence' is dealt with in s 116 of the Act and in Sched 5. Some offences are ipso facto serious. These include offences of homicide, certain firearms offences and some sexual offences. In other cases an offence is judged to be serious or otherwise according to the consequences which followed or which were intended or likely to follow. An offence is treated as serious if its consequences are: serious harm to State security or public order; serious interference with the administration of justice; death or serious injury; or substantial financial gain or loss which is serious to the person by whom it is suffered.

The detained person is also entitled to have someone notified of his arrest and place of detention (s 56). Delay is permitted in circumstances identical to those justifying delay in allowing the suspect access to a solicitor.

(c) Maximum periods of detention

The maximum period for which a person may be detained without charge is a period of 24 hours from 'the relevant time' as defined in s 41(2). The relevant time will, in most cases, be the time he is first taken to a police station. In the case of serious arrestable offences an officer of at least the rank of superintendent may authorise this period of detention to be extended to a maximum of 36 hours if the conditions in s 42 are satisfied. Any further period of detention without charge must be authorised by the issue of a warrant or warrants of further detention by a magistrates' court. The period of detention authorised by any such warrant must not exceed 36 hours and the warrant must not expire later than 96 hours after the relevant time (ss 43 and 44). During the period of a person's detention, whether he has been charged or not, reviews of his detention must be carried out periodically in accordance with the provisions of s 40. The first review must take place within six hours after the detention was first author- ised and subsequent reviews must take place at intervals of no more than nine hours. Reviews must be carried out, in the case of a person who has been charged, by the custody officer and in any other case by an officer of at least the rank of inspector who is not directly involved in the investigation. Whenever a review is carried out an opportunity must be given to the suspect, or his solicitor if he is available, to make represen- tations.

(d) Questioning

If the suspect is to be questioned, he should be questioned in an interview room which should be adequately heated, lit, venti- lated and he should not be required to stand (see para 12 of the Code of Practice). During any 24 hour period he must be allowed a continuous period of eight hours rest free from questioning. There should be further breaks for meals at recognised times and approximately every two hours for refreshments. During any 24 hour period he should be provided with at least two light meals and one main meal (para 8 of the Code of Practice).

(e) Records of interviews and taking of statements (s 12 of the Code of Practice)

The interviewing officer must keep a record of each interview, which should include details of when it begins and ends and of any breaks. Normally, the record should be compiled during the interview but otherwise as soon as practicable thereafter. If the suspect is still at the police station when the record is made up he should be given an opportunity to read it. He may sign it as correct or indicate any inaccuracies.

Interviews at the police station in which the police make a written contemporaneous record of what was said are becoming

increasingly rare. The modern trend (which will soon be in operation on a nationwide basis) is for all interviews (except those
relating to purely summary offences) to be tape-recorded. In some
areas, video recording is also being introduced. If an interview is
tape-recorded, two tapes are used. One tape is the master copy,
which is sealed at the end of the interview. The seal may be
broken only if it is necessary to listen to the tape in court. The
other copy of the tape is the working copy, from which a summary
of the interview will be prepared and submitted to the defence
for agreement. If the summary cannot be agreed, a full transcript
of the interview may be produced in court, and if necessary (perhaps because of the way in which something has been said at the
interview) the tape can be played at the trial. Even in areas where
taping does take place contemporaneous notes should be taken
of interviews outside the police station and of any 'preliminary
chats' with the accused that the police may have before commencing an interview.

Where a suspect wishes to make a written statement under
caution he must be allowed to write the statement himself. Before
writing out his statement he will be asked to write out and sign a
statement in the following terms: 'I make this statement of my
own free will. I understand that I need not say anything unless I
wish to do so and that whatever I say may be given in evidence.'

If the suspect wishes his statement to be written down by someone else then a police officer must take down the statement at
the dictation of the suspect. At the beginning of the statement
the suspect will be asked to sign a statement in the following
terms: 'I, . . . wish to make a statement. I want someone to write
down what I say. I understand that I need not say anything unless
I wish to do so and that whatever I say may be given in evidence.'

The suspect should be permitted to read over the statement
taken down on his behalf and to make corrections and alterations.
He will then be asked to sign the following certificate at the end
of the statement: 'I have read the above statement, and I have
been able to correct, alter or add anything I wish. This statement
is true. I have made it of my own free will.'

Examples of statements under caution are given in the case
studies at the back of this book.

The grounds for exclusion of a confession will now be examined
in detail.

12.4 Determining whether the confession is admissible

(*a*) *Oppression*

If it is represented to a court that a confession was or may have been obtained by oppression of the person who made it, then the court must rule the confession inadmissible unless the prosecution can prove beyond reasonable doubt that it was not so obtained (Police and Criminal Evidence Act 1984, s 76(2)(*a*)).

Section 76(8) of the 1984 Act provides that oppression includes 'torture, inhuman or degrading treatment and the use or threat of violence'. The Court of Appeal in *R* v *Fulling* [1987] 2 WLR 923 held that the word 'oppression' was to be given its ordinary dictionary meaning, viz: 'exercise of authority or power in a burdensome, harsh or wrongful manner; unjust or cruel treatment of subjects, inferiors etc; the imposition of unreasonable or unjust burdens' (per Lord Lane CJ, quoting from the Oxford English Dictionary). The Court also stated that it would be difficult to imagine a case of oppression that did not involve deliberate impropriety.

A serious breach of the Codes of Practice or of the 1984 Act may therefore be sufficient to establish oppression but a case is more likely to be made out if a series of breaches or a course of improper conduct can be shown.

Example
D was arrested for handling a ring which had been stolen in the course of an armed robbery. At the end of the interview held with the police, there was no evidence against D and he should have been released without charge at that stage. D was detained further, and some four hours later he was notified that he was now suspected of committing a robbery. D, contrary to Police and Criminal Evidence Act 1984, s 31, was never arrested for the robbery. He was denied access to legal advice. A conversation then took place between D and the police. Although the conversation was noted, D was not given the opportunity to read the note and to alter or add to it. A formal interview was then held. D was again denied access to a solicitor. The confession which D made at the interview was excluded because of oppression, the judge relying on the fact that D's detention from the time when the first interview was ended was unlawful, the fact that the later interview should not therefore have taken place, and the fact that D was never arrested for the robbery. (*R* v *Davison* [1988] Crim LR 442).

(b) Unreliability

The second ground for mandatory exclusion of a confession is s 76(2)(b) of the 1984 Act. If it is represented to a court that a confession was or may have been obtained 'in consequence of anything said or done which was likely, in the circumstances existing at the time, to render unreliable any confession which might be made in consequence thereof', the confession must be ruled inadmissible unless the prosecution can prove beyond reasonable doubt that it was not so obtained.

Thus under s 76(2)(b) it is necessary to consider the actual thing said or done and then to ask whether it was likely to render *any* confession which *might* have been made by the accused unreliable as a result. There is no requirement to consider whether the actual confession made is unreliable.

Whilst the thing said or done will normally come via the police, there is no need for this to be the case. If, for example, a defence solicitor misguidedly put his client under great pressure to confess to a crime this could be the basis of a s 76(2)(b) application to exclude the evidence. It is clear, however, that the accused cannot rely on anything which he himself has said or done; the words or actions must come from someone external to the person making the confession—see R v *Goldenberg* [1988] Crim LR 678.

According to R v *Fulling* [1987] 2 WLR 923 under s 76(2)(b) there is no need for 'suspicion of impropriety' for a confession to be ruled inadmissible.

Example

D was charged with indecent assault and made a confession. He was 42 years of age, but had a mental age of eight. No independent adult was present at the interview. There was no suggestion that the police had deliberately acted improperly, or indeed that they appreciated the condition of D. The Court of Appeal held that failure by the police to summon an independent adult and the mental age of the accused rendered the confession inadmissible under s 76(2)(b) (R v *Everett* (1985) 7 Cr App R 339).

Most applications to exclude a confession under s 76(2)(b) do in fact involve complaints about police conduct, but it is important to appreciate that there must be a causal link between what was said or done and the unreliability of any confession that might have been made.

Example

T was charged with burglary. He was a drug addict and was kept in custody for some 18 hours without any rest. A series of interviews took place, and in the last interview T confessed. The defence alleged that T had wrongfully been denied access to a solicitor. The judge excluded the confession under s 76(2)(b), relying on the fact that T had not been given eight hours' uninterrupted rest as required by the Codes of Practice, and that his solicitor should have been present. The fact that T was a drug addict was a circumstance that was also taken into account. (*R* v *Trussler* (1988) Crim LR 446)

In this case the causal link was established, but if T had been an experienced criminal who was medically fit and who knew his rights, it is possible that a judge could find that the misconduct of the police had no effect on T and any confession made by him was not unreliable.

Example
A was charged with robbery. He was unlawfully denied access to a solicitor and made a confession. He contended that the breach of the Codes meant that his confession should be excluded under s 76(2)(b). Unusually, however, when giving evidence at the trial within a trial, A admitted that he understood that he had a right to remain silent and that he had been cautioned at the correct times. There was nothing to suggest therefore that any confession that he may have made was likely to be unreliable. (*R* v *Alladice* (1988) 87 Cr App R 380)

Even in cases where a causal link cannot be established, the fact that the prosecution have the burden of proving that any confession obtained is not likely to be unreliable can have significant consequences.

Example
D was charged with indecent assault. He was of low intelligence and was interrogated for a number of hours. It was unclear what was said at the interview, as a contemporaneous note was not kept (in breach of the Codes). A psychologist gave evidence that D was ill-equipped to cope with sustained interrogation, and was likely to be confused. The Court of Appeal held that the confession should have been excluded under s 76(2)(b). What was said to D in the interview was crucial. The police had deprived the court of this evidence by failing to take a note. Although there was no direct causal link between the failure to keep a record and unreliability of any confession, it did mean that the prosecution were unable to discharge the burden of proof placed upon them. (*R* v *Delaney* (1989) 88 Crim App R 338).

(c) The discretion to exclude a confession

It has been seen that exclusion of a confession under s 76 of the 1984 Act is mandatory. In addition, there is a discretion to exclude a confession if the admission of the evidence 'would have such an adverse effect on the fairness of the proceedings' that it ought not to be admitted (Police and Criminal Evidence Act 1984, s 78). Section 82(3) of the Act also preserves the common law discretion to exclude evidence, but in practice it is s 78 that is relied upon.

Section 78 is commonly used in relation to confessions where there have been breaches of the Codes of Practice (whether deliberate or inadvertent) which would not necessarily lead to mandatory exclusion under s 76, but which may still lead to an unfair verdict in relation to the accused. It is also true to say that in practice many applications to exclude confessions are 'two-pronged attacks' under both s 76 and s 78. In fact, in some of the reported cases, it is difficult to ascertain under which provision the confession has been excluded.

Whilst breaches of the Codes of Practice are relevant to an application under s 78, it must be understood that not every breach will lead to exclusion. It must be shown that the admission of the confession will have such an adverse effect on the fairness of the proceedings that the evidence ought not to be admitted. As Lord Lane CJ said in *R v Delaney* (1989) 88 Cr App R 338 at 341: 'It is no part of the duty of the court to rule a statement inadmissible simply in order to punish the police for failure to observe the Codes of Practice'.

The concept of unfairness has proved fairly elusive for the courts to tie down, but from the reported cases a pattern has emerged of the most common uses of s 78.

(i) Where D is tricked into confessing

Example

A car had been damaged in an arson attack. At the scene broken glass was found in which petrol and paint thinners had been used. The police had no evidence to associate the accused, M, with the fire and acted merely on suspicion. The officers evidence was that they set out deliberately to make M believe that they had a fingerprint on some of the glass fragments found at the scene, even though no finger print testing had been carried out. The same lie was told to M's solicitor. Thereafter M, on the advice of his solicitor, answered questions and confessed to his involvement. (*R v Mason* [1988] 1 WLR 139)

The Court of Appeal held that the evidence had been wrongly admitted. The deceit practised by the police, (particularly, according to the Court, that practised upon the solicitor) was 'reprehensible conduct' and the admission of the evidence would have an adverse effect on the fairness of the proceedings.

(ii) Where D is denied access to legal advice

Example
D was unlawfully denied access to a solicitor. After a number of interviews he confessed to robbery. D's solicitor said that he would have advised his client to remain silent. There was no indication that D would not have followed the advice of his lawyer or that he could cope equally well on his own. The confession was excluded under s 78. (*R* v *Samuel* [1988] 2 All ER 135).

A different decision may have been made if it had transpired that the presence of a solicitor would have made little difference to D's position as in *R* v *Alladice* (see **12.4(*b*)** above). In such cases, it will frequently be necessary for D's lawyer to give evidence as to what his advice might have been.

The absence of a solicitor may also be relevant under s 78 if, for example, the accused alleges that there was improper conduct during an interview (and perhaps off-tape). The presence of a solicitor could have confirmed or denied this (or realistically perhaps prevented it from happening!). If a solicitor has been unlawfully excluded from the interview then there would seem to be a strong case for exclusion of any confession under s 78.

(iii) Where the police have not kept proper records.

If an interview takes place off-tape, the police are generally required to take a contemporaneous note of what was said and to show the record to the accused. Even in areas where taping is in operation the accused is sometimes questioned before the taped interview, and this provision is still very relevant. A failure to make the correct notes could lead to exclusion of a confession under s 78.

Example
D allegedly made a confession at interviews which were not contemporaneously recorded. D alleged that he only confessed because of certain inducements and promises made to him at the interview. The absence of any proper records made it impossible for the court to find out what was said and not said, and the admission of the confession would have an adverse effect on the fairness of the trial. (*R* v *Canale* (1989) *The Times*, 8 November)

If, however, an interview is not contemporaneously recorded but there is no dispute as to what was said, or why, it would be difficult to show that the admission of a confession would be unfair to the accused.

Whilst the cases discussed above are not an exhaustive list of the types of situation to which s 78 applies, they are certainly the most common. There are other cases (for example *R* v *Fogah* [1989] Crim LR 141 in which a confession made by a juvenile was excluded as there was no appropriate adult present) to which s 78 may apply, but the approach of the courts should be consistent whatever the conduct complained of.

(d) Mentally retarded suspects

Confessions made by mentally retarded or handicapped suspects are subject to exclusion under Police and Criminal Evidence Act 1984 ss 76 and 78 in the usual way. In addition, by s 77 of the Act, if a confession is made by such a person in the absence of an independent adult and in circumstances where the case depends wholly or substantially on the confession, a judge is required to direct a jury on the special need for caution in convicting on the evidence. Failure to give the direction may result in a conviction being quashed on appeal—see *R* v *Lamont* [1989] Crim LR 813.

(e) Practical considerations

If the admissibility of a confession is challenged in the Crown Court, it will be done at a trial within a trial in the absence of the jury. Both the prosecution and defence may call evidence before the judge, although in appropriate cases the issue can be decided from the written witness statements (see *R* v *Keenan* [1989] 3 All ER 598). If the confession is ruled inadmissible then the jury will not hear any evidence of it. Nothing said at the trial within a trial (either in chief or cross-examination) will invoke the Criminal Evidence Act 1898, s 1(*f*)(ii) and the accused will not be liable to cross-examination in front of the jury on his previous criminal convictions (see further **9.4**). If the confession is ruled admissible, then the cogency of the evidence will have to be attacked before the jury (see **12.5** below).

In the magistrates' court, the defence have a choice. They may ask the justices to rule on the admissibility of the confession before the evidence is given, or the point may be taken at the end of the trial (see *R* v *Liverpool Juvenile Court, ex p R* [1988] QB 1). Whenever the ruling is sought, the usual evidential problem will arise, namely that the magistrates will know of the evidence in any event.

12.5 Determining the weight to be attached to the confession

If the evidence of the confession is ruled admissible (or the defence makes no representations that the confession may have been obtained as mentioned in the Police and Criminal Evidence Act 1984, s 76(2)), the witnesses will give their evidence again but now in the presence of the jury. In order to escape the effect of the confession the accused will seek to establish that in view of the circumstances in which it came to be made the confession is such that little (if any) weight is to be attached to it. He will try to do this by cross-examination of the prosecution witnesses and also by giving his own evidence of the circumstances.

Example

The appellant was arrested with others including S and C. According to police evidence the three men were separately interviewed and S and C made detailed admissions of robbery. All three interviews were conducted primarily by the same officer. All three men made complaints that the interviews had never taken place. At the trial of S and C for robbery, the officer's evidence of the admissions was not accepted and both were acquitted. The same officer gave evidence at the trial of the appellant of admissions said to have been made by him during the interviews. In such circumstances the Court of Appeal held that counsel for the appellant should have been permitted to cross-examine the officer about the earlier acquittals when his evidence had been rejected. These matters went directly to the credit of the officer as a witness. (*R v Cooke* (1986) *The Times*, 11 November)

Attempts to discredit prosecution witnesses will often involve casting imputations on the prosecution witnesses in such a way that the protection of the Criminal Evidence Act 1898, s 1(*f*), may be lost. When the accused gives evidence he may then be cross-examined about his previous convictions in so far as these may be relevant to his credit (see **9.4**). Very often this will be unavoidable. Unless the evidence of the confession can be discredited a conviction must surely follow.

It should be borne in mind that there is a distinction between the cases discussed here in which a confession has been made but its propriety is challenged and those cases in which the accused denies having made the confession at all. These latter cases involve quite separate considerations, not being concerned with the admissibility of the evidence of the confession, and the aim will be to convince the jury or justices that the prosecution witnesses have made up the story of the confession.

12.6 Facts discovered as a result of the confession

As a result of information obtained from the accused the police may be able: to recover stolen property; to find where the victim's body has been hidden; to arrest other persons involved in the offence; and to discover other facts.

The fact that the confession is later ruled inadmissible does not prevent these other facts from being given in evidence (Police and Criminal Evidence Act 1984, s 76(4)). However, in these circumstances evidence cannot be given that these matters were discovered as a result of any statement made by the accused (s 76(5)). This latter provision will clearly reduce the damaging effect of these subsequently discovered facts.

Example
Martin is charged with murder. As a result of statements made by him the police are able to recover both the murder weapon and the body. If his confession is ruled inadmissible the jury will hear evidence as to where and when these items were discovered. If his confession is ruled admissible the jury will in addition hear that the accused was able to say exactly where these items could be found.

12.7 The confession as evidence against other persons

A confession, if admissible, is evidence only against the person making it and the Police and Criminal Evidence Act 1984, s 76, does nothing to alter this position: '. . . a confession made by an accused may be given in evidence against him. . . .'

Example
Colin and Chris are jointly charged with burglary. In the course of questioning, Colin makes a full confession which both admits his own part in the crime and implicates Chris.

In this case the confession is admissible in evidence against Colin. The evidence is not admissible against Chris because it is hearsay. The prosecution is introducing an out of court statement (made by Colin) as evidence of facts contained in it (that Chris participated in the crime). If however Colin's confession statement had been brought to Chris's attention previously and Chris had made a confession by accepting the statement as his own then the confession statement would be admissible against both. If Colin gave oral evidence in court, to the same effect, then this would be evidence against his co-accused (4.2(*b*)).

Where one defendant has made a confession implicating a co-defendant it is permissible to edit the confession so as to substitute a letter (eg 'X') for the name of the co-defendant—see, for example, *R* v *Mathias* (1989) CCR 64.

OTHER EXCEPTIONS TO THE GENERAL RULE

12.8 Statements forming part of the res gestae

The facts which constitute the res gestae are those surrounding facts which accompany and explain a fact in issue and facts amounting to a series of facts of which the fact in issue is a part (see **5.3**).

The particular problem under consideration arises where the fact which is relevant as forming part of the res gestae is a statement. If it is relevant that the statement was made irrespective of the truth of anything contained in it, then evidence of the statement will not infringe the rule against hearsay. However, if the court is invited to accept the statement as evidence of some assertion contained in, or to be inferred from it then the evidence would normally be excluded under the rule against hearsay (see Chapter 11).

In *R* v *Andrews* [1987] 2 WLR 413 the House of Lords, applying the earlier decisions of the Privy Council in *Ratten* v *R* [1972] AC 378 and of the Court of Appeal in *R* v *Turnbull* (1984) 80 Cr App R 104, held that evidence had been rightly admitted in the following circumstances:

Example
Two men had entered the victim's flat and attacked him with knives. He went to the flat below to obtain assistance and within minutes two police officers arrived. He named the two attackers (including the defendant). Two months later he died of his injuries.

The statement which was admitted under the res gestae principle was evidence of the truth of any fact narrated in it and therefore its reception was an exception to the rule against hearsay. The principles under which such statements are admissible had been reviewed by Lord Wilberforce in his advice in *Ratten* v *R*. To be admissible as part of the res gestae the statement must have been 'so clearly made in circumstances of spontaneity or involvement in the event that the possibility of concoction can be disregarded' (at p 389: for the facts of this case see **5.3**).

The primary question for the trial judge is: 'can the possibility of concoction or distortion be disregarded?' (per Lord Ackner in *R v Andrews*). The judge must consider the circumstances in which the statement was made to determine whether the event was so unusual or startling or dramatic as to dominate the thoughts of the victim. In such circumstances the possibility of concoction or distortion could be excluded providing that the statement was made in conditions of approximate but not exact contemporaneity. The judge must be satisfied having regard to any special features of the case that there was no possibility of concoction or distortion. The possibility of error goes to weight rather than admissibility and is a matter for the jury.

Lord Ackner emphasised that the res gestae doctrine should not be used as a device to avoid calling the maker of the statement in cases where he is available.

In *Teper v R*, Lord Normand said, at 487, that it was 'essential that the words sought to be proved by hearsay should be, if not absolutely contemporaneous with the action or event, at least so closely associated with it, in time, place and circumstances, that they are part of the thing being done . . . and not merely a reported statement'.

Example
The accused had been charged with setting fire to shop premises. The prosecution adduced the evidence of a police officer who said that he had heard an unidentified person shouting: 'Your place burning and you going away from the fire.' (*Teper v R* [1952] AC 480)

The purpose of introducing the evidence was to show that the accused was in the vicinity and moving away from the scene. The evidence was therefore hearsay. The Privy Council allowed the appeal, holding that the evidence should not have been admitted as part of the res gestae as these words were spoken some way from the premises and half an hour after the fire had been started.

In *Teper* the Privy Council gave approval to the principle established in the earlier case of *R v Bedingfield* (1879) 14 Cox CC 341 that the statement must not be merely narrative of a concluded event. The actual decision on the facts in *R v Bedingfield* has been the subject of a great deal of criticism (see, for example, the advice of Lord Wilberforce in *Ratten v R*). Indeed, the facts of *Bedingfield* provide a good illustration of the circumstances in which a statement should, and probably would, be admissible as part of the res gestae.

Example

The accused was charged with murder. The prosecution tendered evidence that the victim had rushed out of a room and made a statement implicating the accused, apparently something along these lines: 'Oh dear aunt! See what Harry has done to me.' The victim died shortly afterwards. The court held that the evidence was inadmissible being merely narrative of an already concluded event. (*R* v *Bedingfield*)

The House of Lords has now said that this case would not be decided in the same way today (per Lord Ackner in *R* v *Andrews* at 422).

Further illustrations of the principle are provided by the facts of *R* v *Turnbull*:

Example

The victim of a stabbing staggered into a public house. He was removed to hospital but died shortly after admission. When questioned about the incident, both in the bar and in the ambulance on the way to hospital, he was believed to have said that 'Ronnie Tommo' was the person who had carried out the stabbing. Ronald Turnbull and his brother were accused of the murder. The prosecution alleged that these statements by the victim were intended to refer to Ronald Turnbull. The victim had a Scottish accent and had been drinking and this had made it difficult for the witnesses to make out exactly what he had said. (*R* v *Turnbull* (1984) 81 LSG 2142)

And of *R* v *Fowkes* (1856) *The Times*, 8 March:

Example

Fowkes was charged with murder. At the time of the crime the victim was with his son and a police officer. The shot came from a window. The victim's son gave evidence that he had seen the face of the accused (who was known as 'the butcher') at the window and that he had shouted: 'there's Butcher'. The police officer also gave evidence that the boy had spoken these words.

The purpose in introducing the boy's statement was to identify the accused as the murderer and it was therefore hearsay. Nevertheless the evidence was admissible as forming part of the res gestae.

As to the admissibility of statements forming part of the res gestae as an exception to the rule against self-serving statements see **14.1** and **14.2.**

12.9 Written statements and documentary evidence

If a document is introduced in evidence for some purpose other than to prove the truth of its contents, then the question of hearsay does not arise. Allegedly forged documents may be admissible, not to prove that what has been written is true, but simply that they were written by the defendant.

Usually, however, documents introduced by both prosecution and defence will infringe the rule against hearsay and are admissible only if they fall within a recognised exception to the general exclusionary rule which embraces not only prepared witness statements, but such documents as invoices and business records.

There are numerous provisions which enable evidence to be given in written form and which therefore relieve the original witness of the need to attend court, and instead allow his evidence to be introduced in the form of a hearsay statement. The provisions of the Criminal Justice Act 1967, s 9, and of the Magistrates' Courts Act 1980, s 102, were considered in detail in **4.4**. It will be recalled that, under these provisions, a witness statement can be introduced in evidence provided that certain conditions have been complied with, including the requirement that a copy of the statement should have been served on the other party before the hearing and that no objection had been raised to the evidence being introduced in this way. The provisions apply to statements to be used at the trial and at committal proceedings respectively. It will also be recalled that in certain circumstances depositions taken down and statements tendered in evidence at committal proceedings may be used at the trial (Criminal Justice Act 1925, s 13(3)). Similarly, there is provision for the evidence of witnesses who are dangerously ill (Criminal Law Amendment Act 1867, s 6) and in certain circumstances the evidence of children (Children and Young Persons Act 1933, s 42) to be given in the form of depositions. All these categories of written evidence are considered in more detail in **4.4**. These exceptions aside, the admissibility of documentary hearsay was governed by Police and Criminal Evidence Act 1984, s 68, which was repealed when the wider provisions of ss 23 and 24 of the Criminal Justice Act 1988 came into force in April 1989.

(a) Section 23 of the Criminal Justice Act 1988

By s 23 a statement made by a person in a document shall be admissible in criminal proceedings as evidence of any fact of which direct oral evidence by him would be admissible if: (i) the person who made the statement is dead or by reason of his bodily or mental condition unfit to attend as a witness (s 23(2)(a)); or (ii) the person who made the statement is outside the UK and it is

not reasonably practicable to procure his attendance (s 23(2)(*b*));
or (iii) all reasonable steps have been taken to find the person
who made the statement but he cannot be found (s 23(2)(*c*)); or
(iv)(*a*) a statement was made to a police officer or some other
person charged with the duty of investigating offences, and (*b*)
the person who made it does not give oral evidence through fear
or because he is kept out of the way (s 23(3)).

The effect of s 23 is to make first-hand documentary hearsay
admissible, subject to s 23(2) or (3). The statement must not
contain inadmissible opinion evidence, references to bad character
of the defendant or any other matter that could not be given
orally in evidence.

Example 1
David is charged with stealing £18,000 from an office. The money was
deposited in a safe by Tom, a clerk, at the close of business. Tom
recorded the deposit in a ledger.

> Tom (witness as to fact)   Tom's note in ledger
> └───┘

It will be seen from the diagram above that the ledger is first-
hand hearsay and therefore admissible under s 23, provided a
prescribed reason exists for not calling Tom. If Tom is available
to give evidence he can, if necessary, refresh his memory from
the ledger and the question of hearsay evidence does not then
arise (see further **4.1**).

Example 2
David is charged with stealing £18,000 from an office. The money was
deposited in a safe by a clerk, Tom, at close of business. Tom informed
Bill of the deposit. Bill recorded the deposit in a ledger.

> Tom (witness as to fact)   Bill   Bill's note in ledger
> └──────────────────────────────┴────────────────────────┘

The above diagram illustrates that the statement in the ledger
made by Bill is multiple hearsay if adduced to prove the sum
deposited by Tom. This would not be admissible under s 23 (but
see s 24 below). If, however, Tom verified the ledger when Bill
made the entry and is available to give oral evidence, then the
ledger can be used to refresh his memory in the witness box and
the question of hearsay does not arise (see **4.1**).

Example 3
Alice witnesses a robbery and dictates a statement to a police officer.
Alice reads and signs the statement.

Alice (witness as to fact)   Alice's statement

Alice's statement is first hand hearsay and admissible under s 23
provided there is a prescribed reason for not calling her to give
oral evidence. Again, if Alice is available to give oral evidence
then she can refresh her memory in the witness box from the
statement, provided that it was made substantially contemporaneously with the event which was witnessed. The question of hearsay
does not then arise (see **4.1**).

(*i*) Proving a prescribed reason

The admission of a statement under s 23 is dependent not only
on the existence of a prescribed reason for not calling the original
witness, but also on such reason being proved by admissible evidence. Apart from giving courts the power to make such rules
relating to documentary hearsay as appear 'to be necessary or
expedient' (as yet none have been made) the Act is silent as to
how a prescribed reason can be proved. The death of a witness
can presumably be proved by certificate. Medical evidence (either
oral or in the form of a s 9 Criminal Justice Act 1967 statement)
may be necessary to prove incapacity. The fact that a witness is
outside the UK will have to be proved by a person with personal
knowledge (otherwise the rule against hearsay will be infringed).
In *R* v *Bray* (1989) 88 Cr App R 354, the Court of Appeal
considered the question of when it is not reasonably practicable
to secure the attendance of a witness who is outside the UK.
Although the case related to Police and Criminal Evidence Act
1984, s 68, the wording of the relevant prescribed reason was the
same as in the 1988 Act. The Court of Appeal held that whether
it was reasonable to secure the attendance of a witness was not
to be examined at the moment when the trial opened but against
the whole background to the case. Thus a record compiled from
information supplied by a person who went to serve in Korea
seven months before the trial was held to be inadmissible as the
prosecution could not show that anything had been done in the
seven-month period to secure his attendance. At the very least it
would seem to be necessary to produce letters requesting the
attendance of the witness. Similarly, evidence will have to be

given by the person who has attempted to trace the maker of the statement if s 23(2)(*c*) is to be relied upon. If s 23(3) is relied upon, admissible evidence will be required to prove that a witness is absent through fear, or is 'kept out of the way'. In *R* v *O'Laughlin and McLaughlin* (1987) 85 Cr App R 157 the court refused to admit a deposition under Criminal Justice Act 1925, s 13(3) where a witness was allegedly kept out of the way through fear as the only evidence to prove that the witness had been threatened was inadmissible hearsay.

(*ii*) Statements prepared for criminal proceedings

The 1988 Act is wider in effect than the Police and Criminal Evidence Act s 68 (as interpreted by the Court of Appeal) in that prepared witness statements are admissible in evidence under s 23—see *R* v *Cole* (1990) *The Times*, 4 January. The admissibility of such statements are, however, also subject to the provisions of s 26. A statement 'which appears to the court to have been prepared for the purposes of pending or contemplated criminal proceedings or of a criminal investigation' may not be given in evidence without leave of the court. Leave should not be granted unless it is in the interests of justice to do so, and in considering this test the court should have regard to: (*a*) the contents of the statement; (*b*) the risk, having regard in particular as to whether it is likely to be possible to controvert the statement if the person making it does not attend to give oral evidence in the proceedings, that its admission or exclusion will result in unfairness to the accused; and (c) any other circumstances that appear to the court to be relevant.

In assessing the practical significance of s 26 it is instructive to look at previous decisions made relating to similar legislation. In *R* v *Blithing* (1983) 77 Crim App R 86 the Court of Appeal held that an important prosecution witness statement should not have been admitted under Criminal Justice Act 1925, s 13(3), as the defence were deprived of the opportunity to cross-examine the witness further a statement which had been ruled inadmissible on other grounds would not have been admitted in any event as the evidence was extremely important to the prosecution case and the defence would have suffered undue prejudice if the evidence had been admitted as they were not able to challenge it in cross-examination. Such decisions indicated that when the courts came to consider the 1988 Act they would adopt the attitude that the more crucial the statement is to the prosecution case the less likely it is to be admitted. However, in *R* v *Cole*, the Court of Appeal held that a trial judge had not erred in law in admitting the statement of a prosecution witness who had died by having regard to the likelihood of it being possible for the defendant to controvert the statement of the witness by himself giving evidence and by calling the evidence of other witnesses. The trial judge had fully considered the provisions of s 26 and his decision was one which in the opinion of the Court of Appeal the judge had been fully entitled to reach. The court stated that it is necessary for a balance to be struck between the interests of the public in enabling the prosecution case to be properly presented and the interests of a particular defendant in not being put in a disadvantageous position, for example by the death or illness of a witness.

If the prosecution are seeking to rely on s 23(3) for not calling the maker of the statement then prepared witness statements are likely to be admitted in evidence. This will be particularly so if it can be shown that the witness has been 'frightened off' by the accused.

Section 23 also applies, of course, to defence statements. If a statement has been taken from a witness which supports the alibi of an accused and the witness dies before the trial, is the statement likely to be admitted? The crucial test seems to be the prejudice that will be caused to the accused if the statement is excluded. Notice of alibi will have been given to the prosecution if the trial is on indictment and the police may also have interviewed the witness before his death. The court is likely to admit such a statement.

If the statement contains matter which the prosecution have not been given an opportunity to investigate then the position is more difficult. Having regard to the decision in *R* v *Cole*, then the more important the evidence is to the defence the greater the chance of it being admitted.

(iii) Statements not prepared for criminal proceedings

Statements which have not been prepared for the purposes of pending or contemplated criminal proceedings or of a criminal investigation (as in Examples 1 and 2 above) are regulated by s 25. This provides that a court may direct that the statement shall not be admitted having regard in particular to: *(a)* the likelihood of the document being authentic; *(b)* the extent to which the statement appears to supply evidence which would otherwise not be readily available; *(c)* the relevance of the evidence to an issue in the proceedings; and (d) any risk, having regard in particular to whether it is likely to be possible to controvert the statement if the person making it does not attend to give oral evidence in the proceedings that its admission or exclusion would result in unfairness to the accused.

Thus, unlike prepared witness statements, there is a presumption in favour of admitting most other documentary evidence under s 23 and in practice it may be easier to persuade a court to admit such evidence.

(iv) Practical considerations

The general rule relating to documentary evidence is that a party is required to produce the original. By s 27 of the 1988 Act, the court may accept a copy document, whether or not the original is still in existence. Authenticity of a document (or copy) may be established in such manner as the court approves. In relation to original documents, authenticity is normally proved by calling someone with first-hand knowledge of the matter (for example, the person who took a statement) or someone who can identify the signature. Copy documents may require an explanation as to how they came into existence.

There are, as yet, no rules requiring prior disclosure of a document as a condition of admissibility under s 23.

(b) Section 24 Criminal Justice Act 1988

By s 24 'a statement in a document shall be admissible in criminal proceedings as evidence of any fact of which direct oral evidence would be admissible if the following conditions are satisfied:

(a) the document was created or received by a person in the course of a trade, business, profession or other occupation or as the holder of a paid or unpaid office; and

(b) the information contained in the document was supplied by a person (whether or not the maker of the statement) who had or may reasonably be supposed to have had personal knowledge of the matters dealt with'.

By s 24(2) the information in the document may be supplied to the creator of the document indirectly, provided each intermediary received the information in the course of a trade, business, profession or other occupation or as the holder of a paid or unpaid office.

The broad effect of s 24 is to make first-hand and certain multiple documentary hearsay in the form of business records admissible in evidence. The effect of the section may however extend beyond what would normally be regarded as a business record.

In Examples 1 and 2 above, the ledger would, on the face of it, be admissible under s 24. In both cases, the document is created in the course of a business. In Example 3, the statement of Alice would again seem to be admissible under s 24 as it has been received by a person as the holder of a paid office (ie the police officer).

Example 4
Bert witnesses a road traffic accident between a car and a van. The van stops after the accident but the car does not. Bert gives the registration number of the car to the van driver who makes a note of it. Bert does not sign or verify the note.

Bert (witness as to fact)   Van driver   Van driver's note

The van driver cannot give oral evidence of what Bert told him as this would be hearsay evidence, and there is no recognised exception to the exclusionary rule which would cover such a case. The note made by the van driver could be admissible under s 24. Arguably, the note has been created by the van driver in the course of his trade and therefore comes within s 24. If the van driver had instead been the driver of a private vehicle, however, the note could not be admitted under s 24 and as multiple hearsay would not come within the provisions of s 23 either.

It has been seen that statements falling within s 23 are only admissible if there is a prescribed reason for not calling the original maker of the statement contained in the document. If, however, the statement is to be admitted under s 24 a prescribed reason is required only if the document containing the statement was prepared for the purposes of pending or contemplated criminal proceedings or of a criminal investigation. The prescribed reasons are the same as for s 23, but with one addition. A s 24 statement can be admitted if the person who made the statement cannot reasonably be expected (having regard to the time which has elapsed since he made the statement and to all the circumstances) to have any recollection of the matters dealt with in the statement.

The provisions of ss 25 and 26 of the Act apply to s 24 statements in the same way as to s 23 statements. Notwithstanding the fact that certain s 24 statements may be admitted without a prescribed reason for not calling the original witness, this is not likely to be interpreted by the courts as encouraging trial by statement.

The provisions relating to originality and authenticity discussed in relation to s 23 statements apply in the same way to documents which are to be adduced under s 24. Again, there are no rules requiring prior disclosure of a document as a condition of admissibility.

(c) Supplementary provisions to ss 23 and 24

If a statement is admitted in evidence without the maker being called the prosecution or defence, as the case may be, will be at a disadvantage in that they will not be able to cross-examine the maker. Schedule 2 to the Criminal Justice Act 1988 goes some way to compensating for this disadvantage by providing that any evidence which, if the person making the statement had been called as a witness, would have been admissible as relevant to his credibility as a witness, shall be admissible for that purpose in the proceedings. Further, evidence may, with leave of the court, be given of any matter which, if that person had been called as a witness, could have been put to him in cross-examination as relevant to his credibility as a witness, but of which evidence could not have been adduced by the cross-examining party. Also, evidence tending to prove that the person, whether before or after making the statement, made some other statement which is inconsistent with it, shall be admissible for the purpose of showing that he has contradicted himself.

The amount of weight to be given to any document admitted under ss 23 or 24 will of course be a matter for the magistrates or jury to determine, but Schedule 2 provides that, in estimating the weight, if any, to be attached to such a statement, regard shall be had to all the circumstances from which any inference can reasonably be drawn as to its accuracy or otherwise.

(d) Statements taken abroad

If a witness (defence or prosecution) is outside the jurisdiction in a place outside the UK an application can be made to a justice of the peace or judge for an order that a letter of request be issued to a court or tribunal or appropriate authority in the foreign territory requesting it to assist in obtaining for the purposes of the criminal proceedings evidence specified in the letter. The prosecution can make such an application if criminal proceedings have been instituted or are likely to be instituted if evidence is obtained for the purpose, whereas the defence can make an application only if proceedings have already been instituted. (Criminal Justice Act 1988, s 29).

Any statement obtained in response to the letters of request will of course have been prepared for use in pending or contemplated criminal proceedings, but s 26 of the Act (whereby leave of the court is necessary to admit the document) does not apply. The s 25 discretion to exclude the evidence does, however, apply, and by s 29(6) the court shall have regard to whether it was possible to challenge the statement by questioning the person who made it and to whether the local law allowed the parties to the criminal proceedings to be legally represented when the evidence was being taken.

(e) Expert reports

By Criminal Justice Act 1988, s 30, an expert's report is admissible as evidence in criminal proceedings whether or not the person making it attends to give oral evidence in those proceedings.

The main purpose of this provision was to enable magistrates or a jury to have the expert's report in front of them in addition to listening to oral evidence from the author.

However, by s 30(2) it is also possible, with leave of the court, to put the report in as evidence without calling the maker to give oral evidence. In deciding whether or not to admit the report the court should have regard to:

  (i) the contents of the report;
 (ii) the reasons why it is proposed that the person making the report shall not give evidence;
(iii) any risk, having regard in particular to whether it is likely to be possible to controvert statements in the report if the person making it does not attend to give oral evidence in the proceedings, that its admission or exclusion will result in unfairness to the accused or, if there is more than one, to any of them;
 (iv) to any other circumstances that appear to the court to be relevant.

(f) Computer records

A statement made in a document on a computer is admissible only if it comes within the provisions of ss 23 or 24 of the Criminal Justice Act 1988 (or any other of the exceptions to the rule against hearsay which have been discussed above). Even if the computer record is admissible, it is also subject to Police and Criminal Evidence Act 1984, s 69. This provides that a statement in a document produced by a computer is inadmissible as evidence of the facts contained in it unless it is shown:

(i) that there are no reasonable grounds for believing it to be inaccurate because of improper use of the computer;

(ii) that at all material times the computer was operating properly or if not the production of the document and the accuracy of its contents are unaffected;

(iii) that rules of court are complied with.

A party wishing to introduce a document produced by a computer may give in evidence a certificate which identifies the document and describes how it was produced, gives particulars of the equipment used to produce the document, deals with the matters mentioned above, and which is signed by someone who occupies a responsible position in relation to the operation of the computer. The court may, however, require oral evidence as to these matters. It is an offence to make a statement in such a certificate knowing it to be false or not believing in its truth (see Police and Criminal Evidence Act 1984, Schedule 3, Pt II).

Rules of court may be made requiring information to be given concerning any statement which it is proposed to introduce under s 69.

12.10 Statements made by persons now deceased

(a) Dying declarations in homicide cases

A statement made by the victim of an offence of murder or manslaughter and concerning the circumstances of the offence is admissible in evidence as an exception to the rule against hearsay provided that the statement was made at a time when the maker was under a settled and hopeless expectation of death. It is not sufficient that the victim is in a dying condition at the time of the statement. It must be shown that he realised that death was imminent. This is clear from a number of cases including *R* v *Berry* (1986) Crim LR 394. A statement taken from a victim contained a declaration that the statement was made 'with the fear of death before me and with no hope of my recovery'. At the request of the victim, this sentence was amended so that it read: 'with no hope at present of my recovery'. The amendment showed that she had not abandoned hope of recovery. The statement was not therefore admissible as a dying declaration.

In the case of *R* v *Bedingfield* (see **12.8** above) the victim had not had time to consider her impending death and her statement was not admissible as a dying declaration.

(*b*) Declarations against interest

A statement which is against the pecuniary or proprietary interests of the person making it will be admissible as evidence of the facts contained in it provided that:

(1) The maker has since died.

(2) He knew the statement was against his interest.

(*c*) Declarations in the course of duty

A statement made by a person in the course of a duty to report or record his acts is admissible provided that:

(1) He has since died.

(2) The statement was contemporaneous with the act reported or recorded.

(3) He had no reason to misrepresent the facts.

This exception covers oral as well as written declarations and to that limited extent may occasionally have some relevance even following the enactment of the Criminal Justice Act 1988.

Chapter 13

Exceptions to the Rule Against Hearsay in Civil Cases

By virtue of the Civil Evidence Act 1968, s 1(1), hearsay evidence is admissible in civil cases by virtue of the provisions of Part I of the Act, or of any other statutory provision or by agreement but not otherwise. This chapter examines the 1968 Act in some detail and then briefly considers other statutory exceptions to the basic exclusionary rule.

13.1 First-hand hearsay—Civil Evidence Act 1968, s 2

Before looking at the provisions of s 2 it is necessary to understand the difference between first-hand and multiple hearsay.

Example
Johnny witnesses a road accident in which Peter runs down Colin. Johnny gives a statement to Colin's solicitor. Colin sues Peter and at the trial wishes to adduce in evidence Johnny's written statement.

Original witness	Hearsay 1
Johnny	Written statement of Johnny

The diagram above illustrates that Colin would be adducing first-hand hearsay as the statement is once removed from the witness who could have given original evidence of what he perceived.

Example
On the same basic facts Johnny, instead of making a statement to a solicitor tells Gertie what he saw. As Johnny is now dead Colin wishes to call Gertie to relate to the court what Johnny told her.

This is again first-hand hearsay as the statement relied upon is once removed from the person who could have given original evidence of what he perceived.

Example
Gemma witnesses a road accident. She tells a policeman what happened. The policeman makes a note of what was said. At the trial of the civil action for damages the plaintiff wishes to rely on what Gemma saw as evidence of negligence. Gemma cannot be found and the policeman who took the statement is dead. The only way of adducing the evidence is through the policeman's notebook.

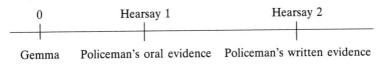

The diagram shows that this would be multiple hearsay evidence as the statement is twice removed from the witness who could have given original evidence of what she perceived.

Example
On the same basic facts Gemma, instead of making a statement to a policeman, tells Lucy what she saw and Lucy in turn tells Olive.

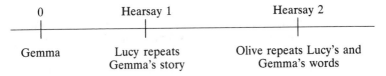

If the plaintiff called Olive to give evidence she would be giving multiple hearsay as her evidence is twice removed from Gemma, the original witness.

The importance of being able to distinguish first-hand from multiple hearsay is that s 2 makes all first-hand hearsay evidence of fact and (by virtue of the Civil Evidence Act 1972, s 1) opinion admissible, subject to the following conditions:

(a) The evidence is such that the original maker of the statement could have given.

Example

Dick sees a lorry go past him at great speed. Two miles down the road he sees that the lorry has had an accident. He says to Katie 'It was obviously caused by that lorry going too quickly'. Although if Katie tells the court what Dick said to her it would only be first-hand hearsay, the evidence is not admissible under s 2. The reason is that Dick could not have given the evidence himself as it is inadmissible opinion (see **10.1**).

(b) Either, one of the reasons specified in the Civil Evidence Act 1968, s 8, for not calling the original maker of the statement exists or the opposing party does not object. The specified reasons are that the original maker of the statement is dead or beyond the seas or unfit by reason of his bodily or mental condition to attend court as a witness or cannot with reasonable diligence be identified or found or cannot reasonably be expected to have any recollection of the matters relevant to the accuracy of the statement having regard to the time which has elapsed since it was made. In *Rover International Ltd* v *Cannon Film Sales Ltd* (1987) *The Times*, 30 March some indication was given of the meaning of the vague expression 'beyond the seas'. It was held that the Channel Islands were beyond the seas in the sense that they 'were beyond the realm of the Crown in the right of the United Kingdom' and that therefore a statement made in Guernsey could be admitted without calling the maker.

(c) The rules of court relating to hearsay evidence are complied with.

(a) *Practical considerations*

The rules of court (RSC Ord 38, rr 20–34 and CCR Ord 20, rr 14–26) relating to hearsay evidence in the High Court and the county court are very detailed. All that can be attempted in a work of this size is to give a broad outline of the essentials. Further discussion can be found in J O'Hare and R N Hill, *Civil Litigation*, 4th ed (Longman 1986. p 356).

A party wishing to rely on first-hand hearsay is required to serve on all other parties to the action notice of his intention to do so. In the High Court this should be done within 21 days after setting down for trial and in the county court at least 14 days before the trial. The notice should include a copy of the statement or a summary of the evidence to be given and any relevant s 8 reason for not calling the original maker of the statement to give evidence. Examples of such notices are given in case study C at the back of this book.

Any party to an action who is served with a notice may (within 21 days in the High Court and seven days in the county court) serve a counter-notice requiring the original maker of the statement to attend court as a witness. This has the effect, normally, of rendering the hearsay evidence inadmissible (but see **13.1(*d*)** below). However if there is a s 8 reason for not calling the original maker of the statement, the right to serve a counter-notice is limited to disputing the validity of the s 8 reason. This point will then be determined by a Master or Registrar before the trial date.

The case of Colin and Peter referred to earlier will illustrate how the rules work in practice.

Example
The first situation was a written statement made to a solicitor with no s 8 reason.

Colin must serve notice on Peter attaching a copy of Johnny's statement. As there is no s 8 reason Peter can serve a counter-notice requiring Johnny to attend the trial. If a counter-notice is not served then the hearsay evidence will be admissible.

Example
The second possibility was a verbal statement made to Gertie with Johnny having died.

Colin must serve on Peter a notice including a summary of the evidence that Gertie will give. It should also contain the s 8 reason for not calling Johnny (that he is dead). This means that unless Peter wishes to dispute the s 8 reason the hearsay evidence is admissible.

If the hearsay evidence relied upon is a written statement of opinion by an expert (for example a medical report) then RSC Ord 38, r 41 and CCR Ord 20, r 28 state that where an application is made to the court for a direction on disclosure of expert evidence (as to which see **10.2(c)**) the court may direct that the notice counter-notice procedure shall apply with such modifications as the court sees fit. In a High Court personal injury action automatic directions apply and it would appear that a party wishing to rely on expert hearsay should simply serve notice in the usual way.

The final point on the rules of court is that if a party is served with a Civil Evidence Act notice in respect of a statement made in previous legal proceedings a counter-notice should not be served. Instead an application should be made to the court for directions as to whether, and if so, on what conditions, the evidence may be adduced. The reason for this is that a party may seek to put in merely an extract from a previous statement or it may be that in the previous proceedings the witness was discredited. (See generally RSC Ord 38, r 28 and CCR Ord 20 r 8(3)).

(b) *The weight to be attached to a hearsay statement admitted under s 2*

There is a danger when considering hearsay evidence in civil cases that in mastering the rules it is easy to forget the overall objectives in a case, namely to win. The point to be made is that it is of little use adducing hearsay evidence if the court is going to discount it as it is opposed by impressive oral testimony from a witness.

Example
Larry breaks a leg in a road accident. He sues for damages in the High Court. He obtains a medical report which predicts that in a few years he will be severely disabled by arthritis. This report cannot be agreed as it is in direct conflict with the defendant's report which says that the risk of arthritis is minimal. The plaintiff's doctor dies before the trial and the question arises as to what action the plaintiff should take. The report is admissible as first-hand hearsay under s 2 and the plaintiff could serve notice with a s 8 reason that the doctor who made the original statement is dead. However, it is also necessary to consider whose evidence is likely to be more impressive. The plaintiff will be relying on a piece of paper. However impressive the argument in the report, will it be more persuasive than the sworn testimony of the defendant's consultant which will have been tested by cross-examination? Whilst it is possible that the doctor giving oral evidence will fail to impress, the chances are that the judge will be of a mind to accept the oral testimony of the witness in court rather than the written word of a man who isn't. Therefore the better solution is probably to find another consultant if at all possible.

It is always necessary when faced with hearsay evidence to ask whether there is a better solution to the problem than putting in the evidence under s 2. If oral testimony can be found then normally it is to be preferred.

If there is no alternative to adducing hearsay evidence then the Civil Evidence Act, s 6 gives guidelines as to the weight that should be attached to it. Two factors specifically mentioned are whether or not the statement was made contemporaneously with the events being referred to and whether the maker of the original statement had any incentive to lie. Apart from these two factors the Act says that all other circumstances should be taken into account. It is suggested that the following points should be borne in mind:

(1) The evidence is not sworn and is untested by cross-examination.

(2) If the hearsay evidence is the only independent evidence before the court then it is likely to carry far more weight than if it is opposed by the sworn testimony of impressive witnesses.

(c) Attacking the credibility of the maker of the statement

If a party to an action is able to adduce hearsay evidence under the provisions of s 2 then his opponent may be at a disadvantage in that he will not be able to cross-examine the original maker of the statement. The Civil Evidence Act 1968, s 7, goes some way towards remedying this by providing that any evidence which could have been used for the purpose of attacking the credibility of the witness had he been called to give evidence is admissible if a hearsay statement is admitted under s 2. Thus for example previous convictions could be introduced. There is further provision in s 7 for any previous inconsistent statement made by a witness whose evidence is adduced under s 2 to be proved. As with any other previous inconsistent statement in civil cases the trial judge may, if he wishes, accept the prior statement as evidence of the facts stated in preference to the hearsay evidence adduced under s 2.

Practical considerations: If s 7 is to be relied upon then RSC Ord 38, r 30 and CCR Ord 20, r 21 must be complied with. These rules provide that if a notice of intention to adduce hearsay evidence has been served on a party and there is no s 8 reason given then evidence admissible under s 7 can be adduced only if a counter-notice is served requiring the original witness to attend the trial. This of course will probably mean that the witness can then be cross-examined in person anyway but the object of the rule is to prevent a party to a case from deliberately agreeing to a statement going in under s 2 to enable an attack on the witness's credibility to be made in his absence.

Example
Freddie, the plaintiff to an action, serves the defendant William with a notice of intention to adduce hearsay evidence of a statement made by Harry. William has details of previous convictions for Harry and feels that it would be to his advantage to introduce them in the absence of Harry, thus depriving him of an opportunity to defend his character. This is not possible. William must serve a counter-notice requiring the attendance of Harry at the trial. If he does not do so then he cannot adduce evidence of the previous convictions.

A party intending to adduce a previous inconsistent statement under s 7 must give notice of his intention to do so (RSC Ord 38, r 31 and CCR Ord 20, r 22).

(d) The court's discretion

If the rules of court are not complied with or if there is no s 8 reason in existence there is still a discretionary power vested in the court to admit hearsay evidence (see RSC Ord 38, r 29 and CCR Ord 20, r 20). Obviously the court will want to know the reason for non-compliance with the rules and if this information is withheld the hearsay evidence should not be admitted (*Ford* v. *Lewis* [1971] 1 WLR 623). An example of the court admitting a statement when the rules were not complied with is *Morris* v *Stratford-on-Avon RDC* [1973] 1 WLR 1059. The rules also specifically provide that the court may exercise its inclusionary discretion and allow a statement to be given in evidence if a refusal to do so might oblige a party to call an opponent (or his servant or agent) to give evidence (See *Greenaway* v *Homelea Fittings (London)* [1985] 1 WLR 234).

13.2 Multiple hearsay—Civil Evidence Act 1968, s 4 (as extended by CEA 1972, s 1)

Section 4 provides that documentary hearsay evidence of fact and opinion is admissible subject to the following conditions:
  (1) The evidence is such that the original maker of the statement could have given. (This has already been explained when considering s 2.)
  (2) The document

(i) is or forms part of a record. (In *H* v *Schering Chemicals Limited* [1983] 1 WLR 143 at 146 Bingham J said: 'The intention of that section was, I believe, to admit in evidence records which a historian would regard as original or primary sources, that is, documents which either give effect to a transaction itself or which contain a contemporaneous register of information supplied by those with direct knowledge of the facts.' There is no definition of the term 'record' in the Act. Common examples include a police officer's notebook and ledgers kept for business purposes. Each case must be judged on its facts. In *Knight* v *David* [1971] 1 WLR 1671, for example, a tithe map and survey were held admissible under the Act. In *Re D* (*a minor*) [1986] Fam Law 263, the interview notes made by a solicitor following a conversation with a client were held not to be a record under s 4.)

(ii) is compiled by a person acting under a duty.

(iii) is compiled from information supplied either directly to the compiler of the record by a person having personal knowledge of the matters referred to or through any number of intermediaries provided each is acting under a duty to pass on information.

(3) The rules of court are complied with.

The significance of s 4 therefore is that whereas s 2 admits both oral and documentary first-hand hearsay s 4 goes further and admits any degree of hearsay provided it is in the form demanded by the Act.

Example

Hops Brewery sue Imbibing Wine Company for non-payment of the price of 2000 crates of wine. The defendants claim to have received only 1000 crates. They wish to adduce in evidence the ledger of the receipts department clerk to prove that only 1000 crates were received. The system of work at the Wine Company is that a delivery man takes the wine and checks it. His job is to inform the delivery clerk who has to send a written memo to the receipts clerk who records the information in a formal ledger.

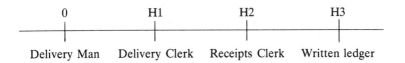

0	H1	H2	H3
Delivery Man	Delivery Clerk	Receipts Clerk	Written ledger

The ledger is of course multiple hearsay but falls within the scope of s 4. The receipts clerk is acting under a duty to compile records and although the person having personal knowledge of the quantity delivered (the delivery man) did not supply the information directly it came through an intermediary (the clerk) who was acting under a duty to pass on information.

A further example of the workings of s 4 is the case of Gemma, referred to in **13.1** above.

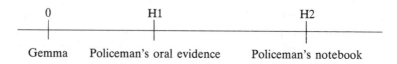

In the first example she told a policeman what she saw and he made a note of it in his notebook. The notebook is multiple hearsay and again is covered by s 4. The policeman is acting under a duty to compile records and the record is compiled from information supplied directly by someone having personal knowledge of the matters recorded.

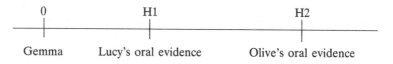

Compare this to the position in the second example. Instead of telling a policeman what she saw, Gemma told Lucy who told Olive. Olive's evidence would be multiple hearsay but it would not be admissible under s 4 (or indeed any other provision). The hearsay is not in a document and we need therefore look no further.

(a) Practical considerations

As with s 2 the rules of court prescribe a notice/counter-notice procedure and s 8 of the Act also applies. The notice must include details of the compiler of the record, the supplier of the information and any intermediary. A copy of the record relied upon must be attached and if there is a s 8 reason for not calling the supplier of the information then it should be stated. A s 8 reason again precludes the service of a counter-notice unless it is for the purpose of disputing the validity of the reason given.

Example

In the *Hops Brewery* v *Imbibing Wine Company* example given above the defendants must serve notice on the plaintiffs. A copy of the ledger must be attached and full details of the two clerks and the delivery man given. Assume that there is no s 8 reason. If the defendants serve a counter-notice the person who supplied the information (the delivery man) must be called as a witness. If no counter-notice is served then the record is admissible. It is worth remembering at this point that the record must be authenticated (see **4.7**).

Example

In the first case of Gemma given above a notice must be served on the defendants attaching a copy of the relevant entry in the policeman's notebook. Full particulars of Gemma and the policeman should be given including the s 8 reason for not calling Gemma (she cannot with reasonable diligence be found). This means that the notebook is admissible unless the defendant wishes to dispute the s 8 reason.

The procedure for s 4 statements is however further complicated by the requirement that s 8 reasons must also be given, if applicable, for any other person referred to in the notice. Thus in Gemma's case the policeman who compiled the record will be mentioned in the notice and as he is dead there is a s 8 reason for not calling him which must be stated. If there were no s 8 reason the defendant could serve a counter-notice requiring the attendance of the policeman as a condition of admissibility of the record (see RSC Ord 38/26/4).

(*b*) *Other matters relating to s 4*

The provisions of the Civil Evidence Act, ss 6, 7, RSC Ord 38, r 29 and CCR Ord 20, r 20, considered in **13.1**(*b*), (*c*) and (*d*), apply equally to evidence adduced under s 4. To understand the provisions in this context remember that any references under s 2 to the original maker of the statement should be read under s 4 as the supplier of the information.

13.3 Computer records—Civil Evidence Act 1968, s 5

A statement contained in a document produced by a computer (defined in s 5(6) as any device for storing and processing information and therefore including such machines as word processors) is admissible in civil proceedings subject to the following conditions:

    (1) The statement contains facts of which direct oral evidence would be admissible. It is worth pointing out here that in

contrast to s 2 and s 4 there is no requirement that anyone should have personal knowledge of the matters referred to in the statement.

(2) The document was produced by the computer whilst it was being used regularly to store or process information for activities carried on over that period.

(3) Over the period in question information of the kind in the document to be adduced in evidence was regularly supplied to the computer.

(4) The computer was operating properly.

(5) The information contained in the statement reproduces or is derived from information supplied to the computer in the course of the relevant activities.

(6) Rules of court are complied with.

(a) Practical considerations

RSC Ord 38, r 24 and CCR Ord 20, r 16 provide that a party wishing to adduce in evidence a statement under s 5 must serve notice of his desire to do so on all other parties. A copy of the document should be attached and the notice should specify persons who occupied a responsible position in relation to management of the relevant activities, supply of the relevant information and operation of the computer respectively. The notice should also specify whether or not it is alleged that the computer was working properly. If there is a s 8 reason for not calling any person named in the notice to give evidence then it should be stated. If there is a s 8 reason stated in the notice then a counter-notice may be served. The effect of this is that the record will be admissible only if the person the subject of the counter-notice attends court to give evidence.

In practice it would seem that s 5 is little relied upon. Most computerised records are admitted by agreement.

(b) Other matters relating to s 5

Everything said in the context of s 2 statements relating to the weight to be attached to a hearsay statement and the discretion of the court to admit evidence even though the rules of court have not been complied with applies equally to evidence adduced under the provisions of s 5.

13.4 Informal admissions—Civil Evidence Act 1968, s 9

An informal admission is a statement made by a party to a case (or by one having an identity of interest with him) out of court and which is against that party's own interests. They are not to be confused with formal admissions which were looked at in **2.1**. Formal admissions can be made in certain specified ways and once made cannot usually be withdrawn. Informal admissions, however, can be made orally, in writing and exceptionally by actions. They can be explained away by the party making the admission.

Example
Eric is driving along and decides to turn on his car radio. As he is looking at the radio he runs into the back of Sheila's stationary car. Eric runs over to Sheila and says 'Sorry, I was looking for Radio 1'. This is an informal admission and is admissible as an exception to the hearsay rule by virtue of s 9. At the trial Eric could of course deny ever speaking the words or try to convince the court that he was not speaking about the accident.

Examples of cases where a party may be affected by an informal admission made by a party having an identity of interest with him are one joint owner of property making admissions affecting the others, a predecessor in title making an admission relating to land which may affect successors and in some situations an admission made by an employee which affects an employer (as to which see *Kirkstall Brewery Co* v *Furness Railway Co* (1874) LR 9 QB 468 and *Burr* v *Ware RDC* [1939] 2 All ER 688).

Practical considerations: Unlike hearsay evidence adduced under ss 2–5 of the Act there are no formal rules of practice and procedure to follow. The advantage of this (quite apart from being a boon to the unwary!) is that it is possible to take an opponent by complete surprise at the trial of an action.

13.5 Public documents—Civil Evidence Act 1968, s 9

Public documents were considered in some detail in **4.6** and **4.7**. It is sufficient here to point out that a public document adduced in evidence may offend against the hearsay rule, in which case it is only admissible because s 9 creates an exception, or if the document does not fall within that exception possibly through a specific statutory provision.

13.6 Other provisions of Civil Evidence Act 1968, s 9

Other exceptions to the rule against hearsay in s 9 include statements establishing reputation or family tradition (which may be used for example in pedigree proceedings).

13.7 Documentary hearsay in the magistrates' court—Evidence Act 1938, ss 1, 2

Magistrates' courts are still awaiting a statutory instrument bringing into effect the provisions of the Civil Evidence Act 1968. Until such time as the Act comes into force, magistrates' courts in civil cases (for example affiliation proceedings) are governed by the narrower provisions of the Evidence Act 1938. Briefly the 1938 Act admits first-hand documentary hearsay statements provided that the statement was made by a person interested at a time when proceedings were pending or anticipated, involving a dispute as to any fact which the statement might tend to establish. There is a further condition relating to the availability of the original maker of the statement which is similar to the Civil Evidence Act 1968, s 8.

Multiple documentary hearsay is also admissible provided that it is contained in a record compiled from information supplied by someone having personal knowledge of the matters recorded. This is subject to the same two conditions as mentioned previously relating to interest in the proceedings and availability of the original maker. Unlike the Civil Evidence Act 1968 there are no rules relating to service of notices etc.

Other exceptions to the hearsay rule contained in the Civil Evidence Act 1968 are governed by common law rules in the magistrates' court. As the 1968 Act codified a number of existing common law provisions, there is little difference in the magistrates' court.

13.8 Affidavits

Affidavits were examined in **4.6** and **4.7**. It is sufficient here to say that an affidavit is admissible in evidence only because of a specific exception to the rule against hearsay.

13.9 Depositions

In **4.4** and **4.5** it was seen that depositions are used in civil proceedings for a number of reasons, each being covered by a separate statutory provision. These are all exceptions to the rule against hearsay.

13.10 Bankers' books—Bankers' Books Evidence Act 1879

Bankers' books were looked at in **4.4** and **4.5**. The only reason for mentioning them again is to remind the reader that they offend the rule against hearsay and are only admissible because of specific statutory provision.

13.11 Witness statements under RSC Ord 38, r 2A

RSC Ord 38, r 2A, previously restricted in its scope, now extends to all divisions of the High Court including the Queen's Bench Division. (Since February 1990 there has been a similar rule in operation in the county court.) It provides that the court may direct at any stage of the proceedings that a party serve on the other parties written statements of the oral evidence which that party intends to lead on any issues of fact to be decided at the trial (r 2A(2)).

The Vice-Chancellor issued a Practice Direction on 23 January 1989 which deals with the directions to be made on the hearing of the summons for directions. An order will normally be made for the exchange of all oral evidence which any party intends to lead at the trial, specifying the day on which such exchange is to take place.

The rules further provide that the court may direct that the statement of a witness should stand as his evidence in chief or as part of such evidence (r 2A(5)(*b*)). It will, of course, be necessary for the witness to be present for cross-examination and if it is not proposed to call the witness the usual notice procedure under Civil Evidence Act 1968 would have to be followed (see **13.1**).

Unless the court otherwise orders, a party may not lead evidence from the witness the substance of which was not included in the statement served in accordance with any direction given under Ord 38, r 2A(2).

13.12 Hearsay and the Children Act 1989

By the Children Act 1989 s 96 (3)–(7) the Lord Chancellor is empowered to make orders which override the rule against hearsay in civil cases involving children. The children (Admissibility of Hearsay Evidence) Order 1990 came into force on 10 March 1990 with the following effect:

(1) In civil proceedings before the High Court or a county court evidence given in connection with the upbringing, maintenance or welfare of a child is admissible notwithstanding the fact that it may be hearsay. Such issues in connection with a child arise under a number of jurisdictions including the Guardianship of Minors Act 1971, the Guardianship Act 1973, the Matrimonial Causes Act 1973, the Children Act 1975, the Adoption Act 1976 and the Family Law Reform Act 1987.

(2) In civil proceedings before a juvenile court the hearsay rule will not apply to the following statements adduced as evidence in connection with the upbringing, maintenance or welfare of a child:

— statements made by children;

— statements made by a person concerned with or having control of a child, that he has assaulted, neglected or illtreated the child;

— statements in guardian ad litem and social enquiry reports.

It should be noted that the Order does not extend to domestic proceedings in the Magistrates' Court.

Chapter 14

Self-made Evidence

A witness may seek to support the evidence which he gives in court by introducing a statement which he made on an earlier occasion which is broadly consistent with his testimony.

Example
Sally is arrested outside a supermarket and is subsequently charged with theft. She goes home and tells her husband what happened and explains that although she had paid for most of the goods in her bag she must have inadvertently placed a few items in her own shopping bag instead of the store's basket.

When giving her evidence Sally may tell a similar story to the court to that told to her husband and she may feel that it would help her to establish her defence that she did not act dishonestly if she were to introduce evidence of that earlier conversation. Neither she nor her husband would be allowed to give such evidence (see *R v Roberts* [1942] 1 All ER 187).

There are two separate rules which generally preclude self-made evidence (or self-corroboration). It is necessary to examine the purpose in seeking to introduce the evidence. In the above example Sally or her husband may ask the court to believe that the previous consistent statement was true and to accept it as evidence that she lacked the dishonest intent alleged. If this is the purpose of the evidence then it is inadmissible because it is hearsay evidence. This is the final aspect of the rule against hearsay referred to in **11.4**. Alternatively the purpose in introducing the evidence may be to ask the court to believe that her testimony is more likely to be true because it accords with an earlier consistent statement. In this case the evidence is excluded under the separate rule against self-made evidence. The evidence has no evidential value. Furthermore, to admit such evidence would make it a very straightforward matter for the unscrupulous to manufacture evidence.

The rule against self-made evidence is subject to a number of important exceptions.

EXCEPTIONS RELEVANT TO BOTH CRIMINAL AND CIVIL PROCEEDINGS

14.1 Rebutting a suggestion of recent fabrication

In both civil and criminal cases a witness may adduce evidence of a statement made on an earlier occasion for the purpose of rebutting a suggestion that his testimony is a recent invention. In such cases it is considered to be relevant to the issue of the witness's credit to show that his testimony accords with an earlier statement made either contemporaneously with the event or at a sufficiently early time to be inconsistent with the suggestion of recent fabrication (see *R* v *Oyesiku* (1972) 56 Cr App R 240).

Example

Ron is charged with burglary, having been picked out at an identity parade. He protests his innocence and claims that at the material time he was not in the vicinity. He cannot remember where he was. At his trial in the magistrates' court, Ron calls a witness who says that he and Ron were drinking together at the time of the crime in a pub several miles away. The prosecutor puts the suggestion to the witness that he has made the story up, after visiting Ron in a remand centre two weeks ago, in order to provide his friend with an alibi.

In such a case the witness would be permitted to prove an earlier statement to the same effect as his evidence in chief and made to Ron's solicitor some eight weeks ago.

In a criminal case the effect of introducing the earlier statement is merely to show consistency on the part of the witness. The earlier statement is not evidence of its contents. In the above example the earlier statement is not evidence that the witness was with Ron on the night in question, it is merely evidence to rebut the suggestion that the witness has recently concocted his story to try to help his friend. The explanation is simply that although the evidence is admissible as an exception to the rule against self-made evidence, it is not admissible as an exception to the rule against hearsay.

In a civil case the effect of introducing the previous consistent statement is governed by the Civil Evidence Act 1968, s 3(1)(*b*).

In contrast to the position in criminal cases this provides that the previous statement, if admissible to prove the consistency of the witness's account, is also admissible as evidence of the facts stated.

14.2 Statements forming part of the res gestae

It has already been seen that where the fact in issue is a part of a series of facts then evidence of those other facts may be admissible (see for example *O'Leary* v *R* (1946) 73 CLR 556 at **5.3**). It has also been established that evidence of surrounding circumstances may be admissible to explain a fact in issue. Evidence of these surrounding circumstances will often consist of or include evidence of a statement.

A witness may wish to reinforce his testimony with the proof of a statement he made as part of the res gestae. Again it is necessary to consider the quite distinct questions of admissibility and evidential value.

Example
Roberts shot and killed his girlfriend, Nina with a rifle. His defence to a charge of murder was that the discharge of the rifle was accidental. In support of his defence he sought to adduce evidence that after his arrest and whilst in custody he had told his father that his defence would be accident. (*R* v *Roberts* [1942] 1 All ER 187)

On appeal it was held that the evidence was rightly excluded as self-made evidence but the appellant was allowed to call two witnesses to give evidence of what he (the appellant) had said contemporaneously with or within a minute of the shooting. 'It has always been regarded as admissible that a person should be allowed to give in evidence any statement accompanying an act so that it may explain the act' (per Humphreys J at 191).

In a criminal case a statement admitted as part of the res gestae is admissible as evidence of the facts stated (*Ratten* v *R* [1972] AC 378; *R* v *Andrews* [1987] 2 WLR 413). The doctrine therefore provides an exception both to the rule against self-serving statements and to the rule against hearsay.

The test of admissibility of a statement is whether 'the statement was so clearly made in circumstances of spontaneity or involvement in the event that the possibility of concoction can be disregarded' (see *Ratten* v *R* and see further Chapter 12).

In civil cases a statement admissible as part of the res gestae is not evidence of the facts stated. The Civil Evidence Act 1968, s 1(1), provides that hearsay evidence is admissible only by virtue of that Act, or other statutory provision, or by agreement. Some common law exceptions are preserved by s 9 of the Act but no mention is made of statements admissible as forming part of the res gestae. Accordingly where a statement is admissible under this principle its evidential value lies solely in its tendency to show consistency on the part of the witness.

It may however be possible to introduce the statement under s 2(2) or s 4(2) (see **14.6** below).

EXCEPTIONS RELEVANT ONLY IN CRIMINAL CASES

14.3 Statements concerning previous identification

It has long been considered undesirable that a witness should be asked to identify the accused for the first time when the accused is in the dock. The Code of Practice for the identification of suspects prescribes identification parades, group identification or confrontation as being acceptable to a court.

When the witness is questioned in court about his identification of the accused he will support his testimony by reference to the prescribed method used and any statement made at that time. Furthermore it is usual for a police officer to give evidence of what happened at the identity parade. The practice of the courts is to receive such evidence as an exception to the rule against self-serving statements.

It seems that such evidence is admissible only to show the consistency of the witness and is not itself evidence of identification. (But see *R* v *Osbourne* [1973] QB 678).

14.4 Previous exculpatory statements

If the accused makes a statement to the police which is against his own interest it may be admissible as a confession, as an exception to the rule against hearsay (see Chapter 12). The statement may, however, be of a wholly or partly self-serving nature. Such statements are considered below.

(a) Wholly exculpatory statements

In *R* v *Tooke* (1989) *The Times*, 25 October, the Court of Appeal laid down the following guidelines as to the admission of wholly self-serving statements made by an accused to the police:

(1) A self-serving statement is admissible to show the attitude of the accused at the time that he made it. It is not admissible to prove the truth of the matters stated.

(2) This principle is not limited to a statement made on first encounter with the police. The longer the time that had elapsed after the first encounter the less weight which would be attached to the denial. It was for the judge to direct the jury on this point.

(3) There might be a rare occasion when an accused produced a carefully worded written statement to the police with a view to it being made part of the evidence in a case. The trial judge would plainly exclude such a statement as being of no probative value.

(4) In deciding whether to admit a statement a judge should consider the spontaneity, relevance and the extent to which the statement added weight to other testimony which had been given in the case.

Example
Following a search of Fred's premises the police recover certain items of stolen jewellery. When quizzed about his possession of these items, Fred tells the police that he purchased them in good faith from a man in a public house.

Evidence of Fred's explanation is likely to be admitted to show his reaction when faced with incriminating facts and also, if Fred gives evidence in his own defence, to show consistency of story. The interview is not admissible to prove the truth of the matters stated however. The significance of this is that if Fred does not give evidence in the witness box, unless he calls evidence from another source, there will be nothing before the court to prove Fred's explanation for possession of the jewellery.

Example
D is charged with rape. He has two interviews with the police and refuses to answer questions. He then consults a solicitor and at a third interview again refuses to answer questions. D later makes a written statement in the presence of his solicitor. (*R* v *Newsome* (1980) 71 Cr App R 325).

The court refused to admit this statement as it was made so long after the first interview and in such circumstances as to render it of little or no probative value.

(b) Statements containing incriminating and exculpatory material

Where evidence is given of a mixed statement, containing both incriminatory and exculpatory material, the jury should be told that 'both the incriminatory part and the excuses or explanations must be considered by them in deciding where the truth lies' (per Lord Widgery CJ in *R* v *Duncan* (1981) 73 Cr App R 359 at 365).

Example
D is charged with s 20 Offences Against the Person Act 1861 assault. Whilst being interviewed he admits hitting the victim and that he was angry when he did so. He goes on to claim that he was acting in self-defence. At the close of the prosecution case D's solicitor submits that there is no case to answer on the basis that the prosecution have failed to adduce any evidence to disprove the defence (see *R* v *Hamand* (1986) 82 Cr App. R 65).

The court wrongly ruled against the submission on the basis that there was no admissible evidence of self-defence before the court. As the statement was a mixed statement the whole of the contents were admissible to prove the truth of the matters stated.

14.5 Statements amounting to complaints in sexual cases

It was held as long ago as 1896 that evidence may be given of the fact that the victim of a sexual offence made a complaint shortly after the offence and that the terms of such complaint may also be proved. The complaint was not evidence of the facts stated but only of the consistency and also, in cases where consent was in issue (for example rape) as being inconsistent with consent (see *R* v *Lillyman* [1896] 2 QB 167). The decision concerned sexual offences against women and girls but the principle has been extended to include charges of sexual offences against males (*R* v *Camelleri* (1922) 16 Cr App R 162; *R* v *Wannell* (1922) 17 Cr App R 53). If the complaint is to be admissible it must have been made as soon after the acts complained of as could reasonably be expected. A further requirement is that the complaint should have been spontaneous and not elicited by leading questions or intimidation. A distinction must be drawn between on the one hand questions such as 'what is the matter?' and on the other hand, questions such as 'did (the accused) assault you?' or 'did he do this and that to you?' (see *R* v *Osborne* [1905] 1 KB 551).

If the victim does not give evidence and consent is not in issue there is no reason to admit the evidence.

Example

Wallwork was charged with incest with his five year old daughter. Although called as a witness the girl was unable to give evidence. Her grandmother gave evidence of the terms of a complaint which the girl had made and in which the accused was named. (*R* v *Wallwork* (1958) 42 Cr App R 153)

The Court of Appeal held that evidence of the complaint was inadmissible as the girl had not given evidence and consent was not in issue.

As to corroboration of the evidence of the complainant see **3.1(*b*)**.

EXCEPTIONS RELEVANT ONLY IN CIVIL CASES

The extent to which a previous self-serving statement may be admissible to rebut a suggestion of recent invention or as part of the res gestae has been considered (above). In civil cases there are statutory provisions enabling the previous consistent statement of a witness to be proved as evidence of the facts stated and as evidence of the consistency of the witness's testimony.

14.6 The Civil Evidence Act 1968

The admissibility of hearsay statements in civil proceedings is dealt with in Chapter 13. The present concern is the extent to which it is permissible to seek to prove a fact by the testimony of a witness and then to reinforce his testimony with evidence of a statement he has made on an earlier occasion.

Example

Paul's car is in collision with a car driven by Derek. Paul brings an action in negligence. Derek's defence includes an allegation of contributory negligence and he counterclaims for his own loss, alleging negligence on the part of Paul. Derek calls a witness, Wilma, who says that Paul's car slowed down and the left indicator was flashing. Derek then pulled out of the minor road into Paul's path.

Derek may call Wilma to give evidence in person, clearly the preferable course of action. Alternatively he may seek to rely upon a statement made by Wilma to Derek's solicitor. If the rules as to notice were complied with and Paul did not serve a counter-notice requiring the attendance of the witness, then the statement may be proved under s 2 of the 1968 Act as a first-hand hearsay statement (see Chapter 13). Derek would not normally be permitted to *both* call the witness *and* prove the earlier statement. The judge does however have a discretion in this matter. See s 2(2) of the 1968 Act and the comments below.

(a) Civil Evidence Act 1968, s 2(2)

The court does have a discretion to allow an earlier statement to be proved in appropriate cases. If the witness gave the evidence expected of him then there could be no purpose in proving his earlier statement and leave would not be granted under s 2(2) to do so. If the witness does not give evidence in accordance with his earlier statement then there may be reason to allow the statement to be proved. This is a matter for the court's discretion and would depend upon the reasons for the failure of the witness to come up to proof.

Example
A lorry driver is involved in an accident and some time afterwards makes a full statement to his employer's insurance company. At the trial five years later he gives very confused evidence. (*Morris* v *Stratford-on-Avon RDC* [1973] 1 WLR 1059)

On these facts it was held that the judge had rightly allowed the earlier statement to be proved.

A party wishing to introduce a statement in this way would give the usual notice of intention to rely upon hearsay evidence. In the case of *Morris* v *Stratford-on-Avon RDC* the evidence was admitted even in the absence of such notice because the party calling the witness had no reason to suppose that his evidence would be so confused.

Practical considerations: In a case where there is a specified reason (under RSC Ord 38, r 25 which also applies in the county court (CCR Ord 20, r 16)) for not calling the witness it is possible to introduce the evidence as a hearsay statement as of right. This may on occasions be a preferable course of action to calling the witness and having to rely upon the court's discretion under s 2(2). See further **13.1**.

In a case where leave is given to prove the earlier statement of a witness under s 2(2) such evidence should not normally be given until the end of the examination in chief of the witness who made the statement.

Two exceptions to this general rule are provided by the subsection. The first exception is where, before the witness is called, the court allows another witness to give evidence of the making of the statement. The second exception applies where the witness gives evidence of his earlier statement during his examination in chief on the ground that the intelligibility of his evidence would otherwise be adversely affected. A third exception is provided by RSC Ord 38, r 43. If the witness is an expert witness and he has previously made a report which has been disclosed to other parties then his report may be put in evidence at the commencement of his examination in chief or at such time as the court may direct.

(b) Civil Evidence Act 1968, s 4(2)

If the earlier statement of a witness cannot be proved as a first-hand hearsay statement under s 2 then it may be possible to prove the matters contained in his statement under s 4. As to the conditions of admissibility of a statement under s 4 see Chapter 13.

Example
The fact in issue is how many suits of a particular description were delivered to a retailer. An employee, Ernest checked the goods on delivery and reported to a clerk, Charles, who made a note in his records that twenty items had been received.

If Ernest gives hesitating evidence as to the number of suits received then, with leave of the court, the note made by Charles in his record book may be given in evidence (s 4(2)). Again the evidence should not be given until the conclusion of Ernest's examination in chief. The exceptions to this rule mentioned in relation to s 2(2) do not apply to evidence admitted under s 4(2). It should be noted that in the example above, it would equally be possible for Charles to prove Ernest's statement under s 2(2).

Part III

Case Studies

Case Study A

Summary

Albert Hipster is charged with driving without due care and attention. The allegation against him is that he was not keeping a proper look out when driving his Ford Fiesta along Exchester Road at 9.10 am on 7 December, and as a result was forced to brake hard on a slippery road. He skidded across the road into the path of an oncoming vehicle and there was a collision. It will be seen from the evidence that at first sight the defence case is not a very hopeful one but the study is designed to illustrate the sort of action that a relative novice may have to conduct. As the idea of the case study is to illustrate points of evidence that may arise the number of evidential points included may not be representative of a typical case of this nature.

The prosecution have served on the defence all of their witness statements and the reader is therefore presented with a complete defence file.

Prosecution statements

EXCHESTER CONSTABULARY

STATEMENT OF: Joe Pills

AGE OF WITNESS: Over 21

OCCUPATION OF WITNESS: Dentist

ADDRESS: 1 Molar Way, Cutherbertstown.

This statement consisting of one page signed by me is true to the best of my knowledge and belief and I make it knowing that if it is tendered in evidence I shall be liable to prosecution if I have wilfully stated in it anything which I know to be false or do not believe to be true.

Dated the 7th December

Signed.......................

On the morning of 7 December I was driving my MG Metro registration number A 567 BCD along the Exchester Road in the direction of Exchester. It was about 9 am and I was on my way to work at my surgery. There had been a fall of snow during the night but this had turned to slush on the road making it quite slippery. Shortly after I had passed the 'Romping Donkey' public house I saw a red Ford Fiesta come skidding across the road towards me. I tried to swerve out of its way but did not have time to do so and the car crashed into the rear offside of my vehicle. I have no idea why the car skidded across the road as it did.

Signature ....

Taken by ....

EXCHESTER CONSTABULARY

STATEMENT OF: Ivan Fogg

AGE OF WITNESS: Over 21

OCCUPATION OF WITNESS: Unemployed

ADDRESS: 875 Exchester Road, Exchester.

This statement consisting of one page signed by me is true to the best of my knowledge and belief and I make it knowing that if it is tendered in evidence I shall be liable to prosecution if I have wilfully stated in it anything which I know to be false or do not believe to be true.

Dated the 7th December

Signed......................

At about 9 am I was standing at the bus stop on the Exchester Road just before the 'Romping Donkey' public house. I was waiting to catch a bus to Cutherbertstown to go to an interview about a job. I saw a red Ford Fiesta go past me and I thought to myself that he was shifting a bit for the conditions as it had snowed during the night and the road was very wet. There is a pelican crossing about 100 yards up from the bus stop and when the Fiesta was about 50 yards away from it I saw its brake lights go on and it skidded across the road and went into the path of an oncoming car. The car, which I think was a Metro, had no chance of avoiding the Fiesta and crashed into it.

The crash was obviously caused by the driver of the Fiesta going too quickly for the conditions. I suspect that he was not looking where he was going either as he braked very hard when he saw the pelican crossing turn to red.

Signature ....

Taken by ....

EXCHESTER CONSTABULARY

STATEMENT OF: Alan Bore

AGE OF WITNESS: Over 21

OCCUPATION OF WITNESS: Barman

ADDRESS: 6 Lumsden Walk, Exchester.

This statement consisting of one page signed by me is true to the best of my knowledge and belief and I make it knowing that if it is tendered in evidence I shall be liable to prosecution if I have wilfully stated in it anything which I know to be false or do not believe to be true.

Dated the 7th December

Signed.....................

Every morning at around five past nine I walk around the corner from my home to the newsagents which is on Exchester Road. I walked down Exchester Road on the 7th December and had just passed the 'Romping Donkey' pub which is on the opposite side of the road when I witnessed an accident. What happened was that there are some traffic lights by the pub which are there to regulate a crossing point for pedestrians. I saw the lights turn red. On the side of the road where I was walking a car had just gone through the lights before they changed to red. It was a Metro I think. I then heard a screeching noise and saw a red Fiesta come sliding across the road into the path of the Metro. The two cars collided although the force of the impact was not that great as neither the Metro nor the Fiesta seemed to be going at any great speed.

It seemed to me that the Fiesta driver braked too hard and too soon for the traffic lights and this caused him to lose control of his car. He probably was not looking where he was going. I say that, as after the crash I spoke to a woman who had been on the other side of the road and she said that she had noticed the driver of the Fiesta looking out of his side window as though he were trying to find the address of a house or a shop.

There had been a heavy fall of snow that morning and the roads were very wet.

Signature ....

Taken by ....

EXCHLSTER CONSTABULARY

STATEMENT OF: Ray Nab

AGE OF WITNESS: Over 21

OCCUPATION OF WITNESS: PC 2345 Exchester Constabulary

ADDRESS: Police Station, Exchester.

This statement consisting of one page signed by me is true to the best of my knowledge and belief and I make it knowing that if it is tendered in evidence I shall be liable to prosecution if I have wilfully stated anything which I know to be false or do not believe to be true.

Dated the 7th December

Signed ....

On the morning of 7 December I was on traffic patrol on the Exchester Road when I noticed what appeared to be an accident. It was about 9.15 am at the time. I pulled up and saw two damaged vehicles at the side of the road. One was a red Ford Fiesta registration number QWR 222Y and the other an Austin Metro registration number A567 BCD.

I made some enquiries and ascertained that the Fiesta had skidded onto the wrong side of the road and collided with the Metro. I therefore spoke to a person whom I now know to be Mr Albert Hipster and asked him if he was the driver of the Fiesta. He confirmed that he was and I told him that I would be reporting the facts and that he may be prosecuted as a result. I cautioned him and asked him whether he had anything to say. He replied: 'I am sorry, but I momentarily took my eyes off the road and then hit the brakes. I went into a skid and ended up across the road and hit the Metro.' Hipster declined to make a written statement under caution. I checked his driving documents which were in order and then took various measurements and I produce a plan illustrating the position of the vehicles after the accident.

Signature ....

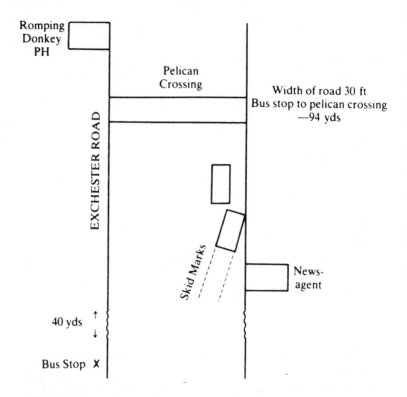

Defence statements

Albert Hipster of 38 Hatstand Street, Exchester will say:

I am a married man with six children, employed by Earmark Publishing Ltd as a representative. On Monday 7 December I was on my way to Trimbletown for a meeting. I was a bit late as there had been a heavy fall of snow during the night and I couldn't get the car going. I was travelling along the Exchester Road out of Exchester at about 9 am and the traffic was fairly heavy. I was travelling at about 25 mph. The road was wet and in places covered in slush.

I was approaching a stretch of road that I know well. It was the long bit of road that leads to the 'Romping Donkey' pub. I know it well as I often drink there. I was about 50 yards away from the pub when out of the corner of my eye I saw a boy throw something at the car. There was then a thud and instinctively I hit the brakes. I did this without thinking. It was a natural reaction to something hitting the windscreen. I realise now that the little devil had thrown a snowball at the car but at the time it could have been anything. As a result of braking sharply I felt the car go into a skid. I tried to regain control but ended up sliding across the road into the path of another car. On the slippery road there was nothing that I could do to avoid a collision.

I looked for the lad who threw the snowball but he had run away. There were quite a few witnesses about but I could not find anyone who saw the snowball thrown at the car. One woman came up to me before the police arrived and was quite abusive. She told me that I caused the accident by not looking where I was going and then having to brake hard for the lights. This is rubbish. I braked because of the shock of something hitting the windscreen. I wish to plead not guilty to the charge. I did nothing wrong.

I have previous convictions for speeding two years ago, reckless driving three years ago and assault seven years ago.

I have the following observations to make on the prosecution statements:

Joe Pills
No comment.

Ivan Fogg
This is rubbish. I was not travelling very quickly at all. I was within the speed limit. I did not even see the lights turn to red because of the snowball. I would not have braked that hard for the lights 50 yards away.

Alan Bore
I have no comment on the first paragraph. The second paragraph is rubbish. As I have said already I would not brake that hard for the lights. As for looking for a house or shop I had no need to. I was on my way to work not shopping. Where is the woman anyway?

PC Nab
He has got it all wrong. When I told him what happened I was a bit shaken up but I definitely told him that I hit the brakes because of a snowball being thrown at the car. He asked me who threw it and when I told him that I didn't know he just stared at me and wrote something down. I didn't want to be arrested at that time so I did not pursue the matter any further.

Signed......................

Dated ....

General comments on the case

The prosecution have to prove that the accused Hipster failed to exercise the degree of care and attention that a reasonable and prudent driver would have exercised in the circumstances.

They have the legal burden of proof in the case. The evidence available suggests that they will be able to satisfy the evidential burden which will then move to the accused. Assuming that no evidence of the snowball is forthcoming from the prosecution witnesses he will have to adduce some evidence of it before the justices can take it into account in deciding whether the prosecution have satisfied the legal burden of proof and proved careless driving beyond all reasonable doubt. [**1.1.(a)** *and* **1.1.(b)**]

Points of evidence arising

Statement of Joe Pills

This evidence does not conflict with Hipster's story and therefore could be accepted in written form under the Criminal Justice Act 1967, s 9. [**4.4(a)**]

However, although there are no evidential points as such to object to, it will be useful to see Pills give evidence and it may be possible to elicit something that helps the defence. In crossexamination be careful not to ask speculative questions such as what speed Hipster was travelling at. The answer may not be that which is hoped for. Only ask such a question if the answer is fairly certain from the general tenor of the evidence. [**4.1(b)**]

Statement of Ivan Fogg

This should not be accepted in written form under Criminal Justice Act 1967, s 9 [**4.4(a)**]

In the first paragraph phrases such as 'shifting a bit for the conditions and had no chance of avoiding' are unlikely to be objected to though technically opinion evidence. [**10.1**]

The second paragraph of the evidence is inadmissible opinion. Ask the prosecution to make sure that the evidence is not given in chief. [**10.1**]

The witness must be cross-examined on the defendant's explanation. Ask him to agree that to brake that hard so far before the lights suggests that something out of the ordinary happened. [**4.1(b)**]

The evidence of high speed is not easy to deal with. The witness could become very emphatic about this and underline the fact for the justices. It is probably best to point out that there are no other allegations of high speed and that he could have misjudged the matter. The witness Bore will contradict this evidence anyway.

The allegation of excessive speed is the only damaging evidence that this witness will give and therefore, a final point to crossexamine on is that this witness claims that the Metro hit the Fiesta whereas other stories say that the Fiesta collided with the Metro.

The unreliability of the evidence as to speed can possibly be illustrated by reference to this.

Statement of Alan Bore

This should not be accepted as written evidence under Criminal Justice Act 1967, s 9 [**4.4(a)**]

The second paragraph of the evidence is inadmissible. The first two sentences are inadmissible opinion. The remainder is inadmissible hearsay. [**10.1** *and* **11.1**]

This witness may be able to help the defence. He states that the defendant was not travelling at any great speed. It may therefore be useful to confirm that braking hard 50 yards from the traffic lights was an unusual thing to do. [**4.1(b)**]

Statement of PC Nab

This should not be accepted as written evidence under the provisions of the Criminal Justice Act 1967, s 9. [**4.4(a)**]

The first paragraph is unobjectionable. The first line of the second paragraph is technically hearsay. However as there is no dispute on the fact reported and it will be proved by other witnesses there is no need to object. [**11.1**]

The crucial point about the evidence of the police officer is that he gives evidence of what amounts to a confession by Hipster, [*Chapter 12*] who of course is denying using the words attributed to him. How should this be dealt with? The police officer will no doubt want to refer to his notebook. Before he does so check the words recorded as being spoken by Hipster. [**4.1(b)**] How soon after the event did the officer record them? The best approach seems to be to suggest a mistake. Justices are not going to be impressed by a suggestion that a policeman will fabricate evidence to get a conviction on a fairly minor driving offence. In any event this should not be a case in which the client is liable to cross-examination on his previous convictions. [**9.4**]

The policeman must be asked about the snowball explanation allegedly given to him by the client. If he seems unsure about this then further questions can be asked about his not investigating the claim at the time. [**4.4(a)**] If however, as is more likely, he denies any knowledge of such explanation nothing further can be done.

Statement of Hipster

When giving evidence in chief Hipster may inform the court of the explanation that he gave to the policeman at the time of the accident [**14.4(a)**] This being an exception to the rule against self-made evidence.

He should not refer to the conversation with the woman mentioned in the third paragraph of the statement.

Evidence of his previous convictions will not be admissible [**7.1** *and* **9.4**] but obviously the client should not be put forward as having a good driving record.

Conclusion

This case hinges on whether the justices think that Hipster braked because he was not paying attention and was surprised by the traffic lights or whether he braked because of the shock of a missile hitting the windscreen of his car (although even then they could find that this was not a reasonable thing to do). When the inadmissible evidence is removed from the statements of Fogg and Bore they appear much less damaging, particularly as they contradict each other in parts. The crucial evidence is that of PC Nab. If he can be persuaded that he is mistaken in the words attributed to Hipster then there may be a chance of an acquittal.

Case Study B

Summary

Harry Wimp is charged with robbery of a post office. His co-accused are Nathaniel Stub and Graham Fodder. Stub intends to plead guilty at the trial of the case and give prosecution evidence against Wimp who denies all knowledge of the incident. Fodder will also plead guilty but has not made a statement to the police and has made it quite clear that he is not prepared to give prosecution evidence or testify on behalf of Wimp. This case study is designed to illustrate some major evidential points of hearsay, confessions and corroboration. As robbery is an indictable offence the trial will be in the Crown Court before judge and jury. The defence have been served with copies of the prosecution witness statements and the reader is therefore presented with a complete defence file in respect of Wimp. There would of course be other papers relating to the other two defendants.

Prosecution statements

STATEMENT OF: Albert Spats

ADDRESS: Needletown Post Office, Needletown

AGE: Over 21

OCCUPATION: Sub Postmaster

The statement consisting of one page signed by me is true to the best of my knowledge and belief and I make it knowing that if it is tend-ered in evidence I shall be liable to prosecution if I have wilfully stated in it anything which I know to be false or do not believe to be true.

Dated 29th June

Signed......................

I am the sub postmaster at the Needletown post office. At around 11.15 today the 29 June, I was serving in the post office when two men burst in. They were both dressed in black and had stockings or tights on their faces. One was very tall probably six feet six inches or so and the other was very stockily built with a large paunch. Other than that I cannot give a better description. As the men came in I saw that the tall one had a shotgun and at that moment it went off. There was a lot of screaming and the shorter man demanded the cash. He seemed to have a Welsh accent. The tall man did not speak. I handed the money and other items over and the men turned to leave. As they did so the smaller man produced a gun and fired a shot. I waited a few moments and called the police.

The following items were taken, namely £875 in money orders and giros, £73 in stamps and £2,300 cash.

I would not be able to recognise the men again.

Extracts from further statements made by the same witness:
Further to my statement of 29 June I confirm that the money orders, giros and stamps shown to me today by PC Fox are among the items missing after the raid. There is still some £2,300 in cash missing.

Dated 1st July

Signed......................

STATEMENT OF: Felix Crow

ADDRESS: 5 Trop Terrace, Needletown

AGE: Over 21

OCCUPATION: Unemployed

This statement consisting of one page signed by me is true to the best of my knowledge and belief and I make it knowing that if it is tendered in evidence I shall be liable to prosecution if I have wilfully stated in it anything which I know to be false or do not believe to be true.

Dated 29th June

Signed......................

I was in the post office today at around 11.00. I was in the queue waiting to cash my giro. Suddenly all hell let loose. Two men with masks on burst in firing guns or rifles and robbed the place. It all happened so quickly but I do remember that one of them was tall and the other was quite fat. I think that the fat one had an Irish accent. As the men left the fat one let off another shot.

I would not be able to recognise the men again.

Signature ....

Taken by ....

STATEMENT: Nathaniel Stub

ADDRESS: 89 Crayfish Avenue, Wrongtown

AGE: Over 21

OCCUPATION: Unemployed

I, Nathaniel Stub, wish to make a statement. I want someone to write down what I say. I understand that I need not say anything unless I wish to do so and that what I say may be given in evidence.

Signed......................

On 14 June I was drinking in the 'Rabid Dog' public house in Wrongtown. It was about 14.00. I was alone. I was approached by Harry Wimp. I have known Harry for a number of years and I think we first met in prison. I have never been close friends with him but then again I have nothing against him. He offered to buy me a drink and I accepted. The pub was pretty crowded and he suggested that we move to a quiet corner. Harry then told me that he was putting one together and asked me if I was interested. At first I said no as Harry is not a very clever villain and his standard of thieving is knocking off a few videos from the local shops. However he was persistent and told me that he was planning to move up a league and do a post office. He said that he had a good driver and wanted someone who could handle a shooter. I asked him who the driver was but he would not say. He told me that it was a job worth doing and offered me a 40 per cent share of the take. I told him that I would think about it and let him know later that week.

I was in fact very short of cash and needed some fast bread so I telephoned Harry and told him that I was in. He said that he would arrange the shooters and contact me again when the date and place were definite. He said that he would not tell me any more for security reasons.

On the afternoon of 28 June Harry called me again. He said that the job was next day. I went to meet him at a derelict warehouse in the centre of Wrongtown where he ran through the plan and showed me the shooters. He had a sawn-off shotgun and some sort of handgun. I was to take the shotgun and go into the Needletown post office with Harry. All he wanted me to do was put the frighteners on the people in the shop and deal with any trouble if the going got rough.

I met up with Harry and the driver who I still don't know at 10.00 next day. We arrived at the post office at 11.15. The car parked around the corner and we went in. We had stockings on our heads. As arranged, when we went in I let off a blast of the shotgun through the roof and Harry demanded the money. It was put into two canvas bags and I took one, Harry the other. As we turned to leave Harry produced a pistol from his pocket and fired a warning shot in the air. We got out alright and made it to the car. The idea was to get back to the warehouse. However after a short while the police were on our trail and Harry dived out of the car taking the money and shotgun with him. I stayed in the car and we were intercepted by another patrol car.

I had no part in planning the job. That was all down to Harry.

Signed......................

I have read the above statement, and I have been able to correct, alter or add anything I wish. This statement is true. I have made it of my own free will.

Signed......................

This statement was taken by me on the 1st day of July at Wrongtown police station commencing at 11.13 am and finishing at 11.48 am.

Signed......................

[Note—the above statement was taken after Stub had confessed on a tape recorded interview which is not reproduced.]

STATEMENT OF: Derek Trouble

ADDRESS: The Police Station, Wrongtown

AGE: Over 21

OCCUPATION: Detective Inspector

This statement consisting of one page signed by me is true to the best of my knowledge and belief and I make it knowing that if it is tendered in evidence I shall be liable to prosecution if I have wilfully stated in it anything which I know to be false or do not believe to be true.

Dated

Signed......................

On the morning of 1 July I went to 446 Council Houses, Wrongtown together with DC Ferret. I wanted to interview Harold Wimp in connection with a robbery that had taken place at Needletown, a couple of days earlier. I also had a warrant to search the premises. I arrived at approximately 8.20. I knocked on the door and there seemed to be a commotion inside the house with a lot of banging and bumping. I therefore forced the door as I was afraid that Wimp was trying to escape. I found Wimp in the hallway, half dressed. I identified myself to him and informed him that I intended to make a search of the house, informing him that I was authorised by warrant to do so. He did not make any reply.

I searched the downstairs part of the house but found nothing of interest. DC Ferret had similar results upstairs and then went outside to the garage and coal shed. A few minutes later he came back in with a canvas bag and a sawn off shotgun. I asked DC Ferret to empty the bag and he did so to reveal a bundle of giro cheques and money orders. At this point Wimp cried out. 'You bastards, you never leave off do you!' I asked Wimp for an explanation for the articles found in the coalshed and he replied that 'the bloody coalman must have delivered them by mistake'. I then formally cautioned Wimp and told him that he was under arrest on suspicion of armed robbery. I then conveyed him to the Wrongtown Police Station. On the way he was swearing and shouting about a fit up. On arrival at the police station I handed Wimp over to the custody officer and told him that I would speak to him later. It was about 9.15.

At about 12.15 I saw Wimp in his cell together with DC Ferret. I was waiting to interview Wimp on tape, but no equipment was available at that time. I decided to hold a preliminary interview off-tape. I informed him that he was still under caution and told him that I had reason to believe that he was involved in a robbery on 29 June at Needletown Post Office. Wimp replied: 'Rubbish! You know that sort of thing is out of my league.' I asked him how he explained the shotgun at the house and the money orders that had been identified as belonging to the post office in question. Wimp answered: 'Some bastard has fitted me up good and proper. It's a plant.' I asked him who would go to the trouble to do that and Wimp said: 'How do I know?' I then told him that his fellow robber had identified him as being involved in the crime. He replied: 'What fellow robber? I have told you that there was no robbery on my part.' I then confronted Wimp with a copy of the statement made under caution by the accused Stub. Wimp replied 'Looks like you've got me nicely tied up then doesn't it?' I asked him whether he was admitting the offence. He replied 'I suppose so'. A contemporaneous note of this interview was not made as DC Ferret and I decided that it was better to proceed with the interview quickly. We made up the interview record several hours later and showed it to Wimp, who refused to sign it. I was then informed that tape recording facilities were available. I, in the presence of DC Ferret interviewed Wimp on tape. A summary of the interview, at which Wimp remained silent, is produced and marked TR1.

NB DC Ferret has made a statement confirming everything said by Trouble. He also tells how he searched the coal shed at Wimp's house and found the shotgun and post office goods. For the sake of brevity this statement is not reproduced in full.

[Note— the record of tape recorded interview is not reproduced as Wimp refused to answer any questions. The police officers did put to Wimp the fact that he had allegedly made a confession in his cell but Wimp did not reply.]

STATEMENT: Thomas Clerk
ADDRESS: Police Station, Wrongtown
AGE: Over 21
OCCUPATION: Police Sergeant

This statement consisting of one page signed by me is true to the best of my knowledge and belief and I make it knowing that if it is tendered in evidence I shall be liable to prosecution if I have wilfully stated in it anything which I know to be false or do not believe to be true.

Dated

Signed......................

On the morning of 1st July I was on duty at the Wrongtown police station. I was on the shift running from 6.00 to 14.00 and I was the designated custody officer for the day.

At 9.25 DI Trouble arrived at the station accompanied by DC Ferret and a suspect, Wimp. I was asked to arrange for the detention of Wimp pending further enquiries. I informed Wimp that he was being detained on suspicion of robbery and asked him if he wanted to inform anyone of his arrest. He made no reply. I then handed to Wimp a written notice of his right to inform someone of his arrest and to consult with a solicitor. I asked him whether he wished to contact anyone and he said that he did not. Wimp then signed a waiver of his right to legal advice. I produced the custody record showing the signature. At 9.55 Wimp was taken to the cells.

At 10.15 I spoke to DI Trouble about the detention of Wimp and the possibility of charging him. I was told that certain stolen goods and a shotgun had been found in possession of Wimp. His detention was necessary as a fellow suspect was shortly to give a statement incriminating Wimp, no satisfactory explanation had been offered for the goods found and a substantial amount of money was outstanding. I considered that these were adequate grounds for detention and noted them in the custody record.

At 11.00 I made arrangements for Wimp to be offered refreshment and he refused. I duly noted this in the custody record.

At 12.30 Wimp was taken from his cell to a room for a tape recorded interview. At 13.20 Wimp was handed over to me to be formally charged with robbery. Wimp made no reply. I decided that the case was not suitable for bail and Wimp was returned to a cell at 13.40.

Signature ....

Defence statement

<u>Harold Wimp of 446 Council Houses, Wrongtown will say</u>:

I am charged with robbery at a post office at Needletown on 29 June and I plead not guilty. At the time of the robbery I was drinking in a club in Wrongtown.

The first thing that I knew about the robbery was when I received a visit from two detectives early on the morning of 1 July. There was a knock on the door and I was in bed with the wife. I was asleep and it took me a few minutes to realise what was going on. By the time I got down into the hall the two coppers had kicked the door down and were in the hallway themselves. I began to protest but one of them said something about a robbery and searching the place. I was amazed but knew from experience that it was no use trying to stop them. Anyway I had nothing to hide.

Nothing was found until one of them went outside. I should have gone with him really. He came back with a sawn-off shotgun and a bag full of papers that he said came from a post office that had been robbed the day before or thereabouts. I could not believe it and my first thought was that the coppers had planted the stuff there themselves before they turned my place over. I knew better than to allege that though. That would be an invitation to a hiding. I therefore said the first thing that came into my head and they arrested me on suspicion of robbery.

I was taken to the police station and by this time I was pretty scared. I have been to the police station on many occasions before but never for anything as serious as robbery. I knew there was a real chance that they would come down heavy on me.

I was taken to see a uniformed copper sitting at a desk. All the time I was trying to work out who had fitted me up. I therefore did not listen to a word he said to me. I probably did sign something but I do not know what. All I wanted was time to think. I got this when I was taken to a cell.

I was left in a cell for a few hours. I was not given anything to eat or drink. No one came near me until a bobby took me up to an interview room. There I was seen by the two detectives who picked me up that morning. They told me their names and cautioned me. It turned out in the interview that a guy called Nathaniel Stub had been picked up for a robbery. Some other geezer had got away with the money and Stub had told the police I had set the whole thing up. Stub is a right nasty piece of work. I first came across him in prison when he knifed my cell mate. I gave evidence against him on that one and he has had it in for me ever since. We have met once or twice in pubs and nearly come to blows. I was worked over one night last year and I have always suspected that it was his doing. Now it looked as though he had been given the opportunity to drop me right in it. I refused to answer any questions. They kept on at me about having already confessed to them in my cell. I didn't understand this as they never came near my cell. I decided that it was a trick to get me to talk. I remained silent. I was eventually taken back to my cell, having been charged with robbery and refused bail.

I am a married man with four kids. I have not had a job for eight years and live on the social. I have the following previous convictions but have never been mixed up in anything to do with shooters or violence. I am 30 years of age.

1973	Theft of Mars Bar	Absolute discharge
1975	Criminal damage to telephone kiosk	Fined £10
1976	Theft of purse	Fined £50
1978	Handling stolen radio	Probation
1980	Theft	6 months imprisonment suspended for one year.
1981	Burglary of house	6 months imprisonment and suspended sentence activated. Consecutive.
1984	Theft of trousers	Community service
1984	Drunk	Fined £10
1987	Burglary of houses	12 months imprisonment

I have the following comments to make on the prosecution evidence:

Albert Spats
Stub is very tall and he admits that he was the man with the shotgun. I am not fat. Quite the opposite in fact. I am not Welsh. I have a Birmingham accent which cannot be easily confused with a Welsh one. I have never used a gun in my life. If seems funny that they should recover the money orders and other rubbish from my house yet the money was not there. Why split it up?

Felix Crow
Again I can only say that the description does not fit. I am not fat. An Irish accent is nothing like a Birmingham accent.

Nathaniel Stub
This man has set me up. It is interesting to note that the statement was made to the police some two days after the arrest. By this time he'd had the chance to dump the stuff at my place. The motive was revenge for the incident in prison which I have referred to earlier.

The first allegation is that I tried to arrange the job in the pub on 14 June. This is the major hole in the story. At the time described by Stub, I was at an interview for a job. I was at a firm in Wandleside being interviewed by an uncle of my wife. He will confirm that I arrived at 13.30 and left at 14.30. Wandleside is about a full hour's drive from Wrongtown and I could not have been at the meeting as alleged. The account of what I am supposed to have said is just pure invention. Robbery is way out of my league. I do not know one end of a gun from another.

I did not know the name of the driver I am supposed to have arranged. I now know his name of course but it means nothing to me. I should think he was recruited by Stub or the geezer who I am taking the rap for.

I cannot make any comment on the remainder of the statement other than to say that it is all news to me—I was drinking in the pub at Wandleside when they did the post office. It is a deliberate frame up.

Derek Trouble

The account of how he arrived at the house is correct except I was not trying to escape. I was merely trying to get up and get downstairs. I thought it was the milkman who wanted paying. The remainder of the account up to my arrival at the police station is correct. I have already explained why I gave that stupid explanation about the coalman.

The account of the tape recorded interview is correct but the incident in the cells when I'm supposed to have confessed simply did not happen. I did not see anyone in the cells and was not shown an interview record.

Thomas Clerk

On arrival at the police station I was not given any piece of paper. He makes no mention of anyone visiting me in the cells before the tape recorded interview.

Signed......................

Dated ....

Sam Suds will say:

I have known Harry Wimp for a number of years. He is married to my niece. At the beginning of June, Harry asked me about a job. I run an insurance brokers and finance company. I asked him to come for an interview at my office in Wandleside on June 14 at 13.30. We had a good chat and Harry left at 14.30. He decided not to take the job because he thought that he was too soft for debt collection.

Signed......................

Dated ....

Sara Deb will say:

I am the owner of 'Debs' a little club/wine bar in the centre of Wrongtown. Harry Wimp is a regular customer. I can confirm that Harry was in the club on the morning of 29 June from 11 onwards. I remember

because it was my birthday and he bought me a drink. He left at about
14.30.

Signed......................

Dated ....

General comments on the case against Harry Wimp

The prosecution have the legal burden of proving all of the
elements of the offence of robbery. [**1.1(a)** and (**b**)] On the evidence revealed by the statements there is no doubt that the men
in the post office are guilty of robbery. The case is simply based
on whether or not Wimp was one of the men involved or whether,
as he alleges, he is the victim of a plot to frame him.

The prosecution evidence against Wimp can be summarised as
follows:

(1) An accomplice says that Wimp took part.
(2) Some of the stolen goods were found on Wimp's premises.
(3) Wimp has allegedly made a confession.

There is no doubt that the prosecution will be able to satisfy
their evidential burden, thereby allowing the case to be decided
by the jury. The evidential burden will then pass to the defendant
and given the nature of his defence he will have to adduce some
evidence if he hopes to be acquitted.

Points of evidence arising

Statement of Albert Spats

This statement could be accepted in written form. [**4.4(a)**] Spats
gives evidence of the robbery but does not identify Wimp. However it is arguable that the witness should be asked to attend as
in cross-examination it may be possible to highlight the different
physical characteristics of Wimp and the man described. The
accent is more difficult to deal with as people are easily mistaken
and it may be better to leave this point alone.

Statement of Felix Crow

The comments relating to Spats apply equally to this witness.

Statement of Nathaniel Stub

As he is giving evidence for the prosecution he is an accomplice
for evidential purposes [**3.1(b)**]. This means that the judge should

give a full corroboration warning. If the jury believe the evidence of Stub and are therefore looking for corroboration they can find it in the evidence of the stolen goods (if they reject the explanation of the defendant) or in the confession (if they accept it as true).

Although Stub is allowed to give prosecution evidence having pleaded guilty [4.2(d)] the confession that he made to the police is not admissible against Wimp as it is hearsay. Stub has to give oral evidence. [Chapters 11 and 12].

Wimp will be suggesting in cross-examination that Stub has fabricated the evidence because of a grudge. This will be sufficient to allow the judge in his discretion to permit the prosecution to cross-examine Wimp on his previous convictions when he gives evidence. [9.4] In any event, part of his defence is the grudge that Stub had against him and in cross-examining Stub reference may have to be made to the incident in prison which will of course disclose that Wimp has served a prison sentence.

All of the evidence of Stub will have to be challenged and it must be put to him that he played some sort of role in planting the goods at Wimp's house. (Harry's case is that on Stub being arrested he decided to give Wimp's name to protect his true accomplices. There would have to be an opportunity for the plant following Stub's arrest.) [4.1(b)]

Any previous convictions suggesting that Stub is not a credible witness can also be cross-examined on as Wimp's own convictions will come out anyway. [9.4]

Derek Trouble

It would be easy to get involved in arguments about the method of entry into Wimp's house. [5.5] This is not really a relevant issue however. Indeed it would be better to object to Trouble informing the jury of his opinion that Wimp was trying to escape. This is not relevant and may be unfair to Wimp [10.1 and 5.2].

The important evidence introduced by the officer is that the stolen goods were found in the coal shed and that Wimp confessed. As the goods were found by DC Ferret it is hearsay evidence if Trouble relates to the court how they were found. Even though Ferret will be giving evidence on this point, objection should be raised to Trouble also mentioning it so as to avoid giving a misleading impression to the jury that the officers' evidence supports each other on the matter. The important thing about the goods being found is that the doctrine of recent possession will apply and an explanation will be necessary from Wimp. [**2.6(*b*)**]

As to the confession, Wimp is denying that the interview ever took place. The lack of a contemporaneous note is a clear breach of the Codes of Practice and as Wimp is challenging the evidence of the officers the trial judge may well accede to an application to exclude the evidence under Police and Criminal Evidence Act 1984, s 78. This application will be made in the absence of the jury. If evidence of the alleged confession is admitted then it will be necessary to put allegations of fabrication to the officer in front of the jury.

This again will lead to an application to cross-examine on Wimp's previous convictions when he gives evidence but it will not matter given the general nature of the defence.

Statement of DC Ferret

As for Trouble.

Statement of Sergeant Clerk

He should be cross-examined primarily on the fact that he makes no mention of Trouble and Ferret going to the cells to see Wimp.

Conclusion

One general point is worth mentioning for the sake of clarity. Although the defendant is denying being at the scene of the crime this is not the type of case to which a *Turnbull* warning is appropriate because there is no identification evidence against Wimp. [**3.9**]

As far as the defence case is concerned it hinges on the acceptance by the court of an alibi as to the conspiracy to commit the offence and a second alibi concerning the time of the offence and evidence will have to be adduced if they are to be taken into account when the jury decide whether or not the prosecution have satisfied the legal burden of proof.

In view of the fact that the previous convictions of Wimp are inevitably going to come out during the trial, consider approaching the case on the basis of Wimp admitting to the court that he has been a petty villain in the past but armed robbery is something that he would never do.

Case Study C

Summary

James Krug is the plaintiff in a High Court action in which he is seeking damages for personal injury and loss sustained as a result of the alleged negligent driving of the defendant, Paul Trend. The case is defended and there is a counterclaim. The pleadings are set out below and the reader is asked to assume that a defence to the counterclaim has been served. The other documents set out include extracts from the police report, medical reports and witness statements. At this stage of a defended action many solicitors will instruct counsel to advise on evidence and this case study will illustrate some of the points likely to arise.

Documents

[Document 1]

IN THE HIGH COURT OF JUSTICE   No. OF ACTION 1989 K 1234

QUEEN'S BENCH DIVISION

BLANKTOWN DISTRICT REGISTRY

BETWEEN

JAMES KRUG Plaintiff

and

PAUL TREND Defendant

STATEMENT OF CLAIM

1 At all material times the plaintiff was the owner and driver of a Morris Marina Estate motor car registration number ABC 234T and the defendant was the owner and driver of a Triumph Spitfire motor car registration number XXC 486H.

239

2 On or around the 23rd day of February 1989 the defendant so negligently controlled his said motor car at a point near the Bluebell public house, Dripstown Road, Blanktown that it came into collision with the plaintiff's said motor car.

Particulars of negligence

(a) Driving at a speed which was excessive in the circumstances.
(b) Failing to keep a proper lookout.
(c) Driving on the wrong side of the road.
(d) Failing to observe or heed the plaintiff's said vehicle.
(e) Losing control of his said vehicle.
(f) Failing to apply his brakes in time or at all or so to steer or control his motor car so as to avoid striking the plaintiff's said vehicle.

3 By reason of the matters aforesaid the defendant was convicted on the 14 March 1989 by the Blanktown Magistrates' Court of the offence of driving the said motor car on a road at a speed exceeding the statutory limit contrary to s 71. The said conviction is relevant to the issue of negligence and the plaintiff intends to rely thereon as evidence in this action.

4 By reason of the said collision the plaintiff who is aged 38 has suffered injury, loss and damage.

Particulars of injuries

Sub capital fracture of the neck of the left femur necessitating fixation by Pugh nail plate. The plaintiff was in hospital as an inpatient for 15 weeks and has since been attending as an outpatient.

Particulars of special damage

Loss of earnings from 24 February to 26 August at the net rate of £110 per week (and continuing)		£2860.00
Less statutory sick pay received	£781.50	
Less tax rebate	£84.00	
Less credit pursuant to Administration of Justice Act 1982 for living expenses saved whilst hospitalised	£200.00	£1065.50
		£1794.50
Value of motor vehicle damaged beyond repair		£1050.00
Travelling expenses to and from hospital at £2 per week (and continuing)		£22.00
		£2866.50

And the plaintiff claims damages and interest pursuant to Supreme Court Act 1981, s 35A at such rate and for such period as the court thinks just.

B LEARNED

Served

By...........................

[Document 2]

IN THE HIGH COURT OF JUSTICE   No. OF ACTION 1989 K 1234

QUEEN'S BENCH DIVISION

BLANKTOWN DISTRICT REGISTRY

BETWEEN

JAMES KRUG Plaintiff

and

PAUL TREND Defendant

Defence

1 The defendant admits that on the date and at the place mentioned in the statement of claim a collision occurred between a motor car driven by the plaintiff and a motor car driven by the defendant.

2 The defendant denies that he was guilty of the alleged or any negligence or that the said collision was caused as alleged in the statement of claim.

3 Further or in the alternative the said collision was caused wholly or in part by the negligence of the plaintiff.

Particulars of plaintiff's negligence

(a) Driving at a speed which was excessive in the circumstances.
(b) Failing to keep any or proper lookout or to observe or heed the defendant's said motor car.
(c) Driving on the wrong side of the road.
(d) Losing control of his said motor car.
(e) Failing to steer his said motor car so as to avoid striking the defendant's said vehicle.

4 No admission is made as to any of the alleged injuries, loss or damage.

5 The defendant admits that he was convicted as set out in paragraph 3 of the statement of claim but says that the said conviction is irrelevant in that it does not relate to the incident pleaded in paragraph 1 of the statement of claim.

Counterclaim

6 The defendant repeats paragraphs 1 and 3 hereof.

7 By reason of the said collision the defendant has suffered loss and damage.

Particulars of special damage

Value of motor car damaged beyond repair   £700.00
Damage to trousers   £ 20.00

And the defendant counterclaims damages against the plaintiff and interest thereon pursuant to Supreme Court Act 1981, s 35A at such rate and for such period as the court thinks fit.

A COUNSEL

Served

By............................

[Document 3]

Sketch plan showing position of vehicles after accident

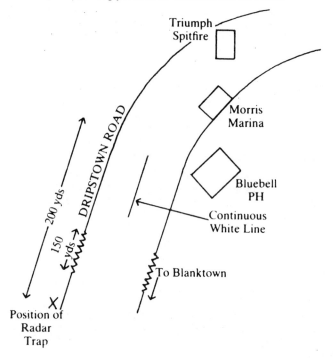

Extracts from police report

The police report confirms the details given by the plaintiff and his witnesses concerning injuries, road and weather conditions. Attached to the report there is a sketch plan and witness statements. The report also confirms that Trend was convicted of speeding by the Blankshire Magistrates and fined £80.

[Document 4]

Extract of statement of PC Dixon attached to police report

On 23rd February, I was on radar gun patrol duty on the Dripstown Road. I was positioned on a fast stretch of road just before the Bluebell public house and about 200 yards away from a right hand bend in the road. At about 3 pm I saw a green Triumph Spitfire approaching travelling towards Dripstown. I checked the speed on the gun which read out at 65 mph. The road had a 40 mph speed limit and I therefore radioed through to the motor cycle officer positioned half a mile down the road to intercept the vehicle. I did not watch the vehicle as it went into the bend but I heard a crash. On arriving at the scene I discovered that the vehicle had collided with another car out of my sight. I measured the distance from my position to the scene of the accident and found it to be 248 yards.

NB This witness has died since making the statement.

[Document 5]

Extract from statement of Bert Thumb attached to police report

I was a passenger in the Morris Marina driven by Jimmy Krug. As we went into a bend on the Dripstown Road not far from Blanktown I said to Jimmy that he was clocking on a bit and had best slow down as it was a nasty bend and was sharper than people thought. Next thing I remember was a crash.

[Document 6]

Extract from medical report of Mr Herman Bone

Mr James Krug was admitted to the casualty department of the Dripstcwn Infirmary on 23 February 1989. It was found that he was suffering from a fracture of the left femur and an operation was performed to insert a Pugh nail plate . . .

   Mr Krug is making a good recovery but is not yet fit to resume his full pre-accident activities in relation to his job as a driver. I anticipate that he will eventually make a full recovery and an absence from work of approximately 45 weeks would be justifiable . . .

[Document 7]

Statement of Bert Thumb (to Krug's solicitor)

On the afternoon of 23rd February 1989 I was a passenger in the front seat of a Morris Marina motor car driven by my mate Jimmy Krug. We were on our way to see a couple of women in Blanktown. I would say that we were travelling at about 40 mph although I cannot give a precise speed. We were not far from Blanktown when the accident happened. We drove into a fairly sharp bend. We were definitely on our side of the road. I remember saying to Jimmy that a green car approaching was clocking on a bit and then I saw that it seemed to be on the wrong side of the road and was going to hit us. It seemed to lose control as a result of the speed that it was doing. Jimmy tried to avoid the car by turning across the road away from it but there was a sickening crash. I felt dazed. I remember being taken to hospital where I was found to be suffering from mild concussion and cuts and bruises to the head.

Whilst at the hospital I made a statement to the police. It came out all wrong because of the confused state I was in. It looks as though I am saying that Jimmy took the bend too fast when in fact I was commenting to him on the speed of the green car which hit us.

[Document 8]

Statement of Tory Laing (made to Krug's solicitor)

On the afternoon of 23rd February I was walking home from the Bluebell pub. I had been there for my lunch and had drunk about five pints. I was not drunk as I am used to it. I walk home along the main Dripstown Road in the direction of Dripstown. As I was walking around the bend in the road I saw an accident happen. Two cars collided. As far as I could see a green sports car came around the bend on the wrong side of the road and collided with a Morris Marina which was coming in the opposite direction. It was obviously the fault of the driver of the green car. I happen to know him by sight. He is always driving that car around the area like a nutter and has been in court for driving offences before.

I did not wait for the police to arrive as I have had the odd spot of bother with them in the past over buying things that they claim belonged to someone else. I gave my name and address to the driver of the Marina and explained to him why I was doing a runner. He seemed a bit dazed but said it was OK.

NB Whilst this witness was being interviewed by the solicitor acting for

Krug, he appeared extremely inarticulate. He had great difficulty in getting his words out and seemed very nervous.

[Document 9]

Extract from statement of James Krug (made to his solicitor)

On 23rd February 1989 at around 3 pm I was on my way to Blanktown. I was driving my Morris Marina Estate and I had a front seat passenger, Bert Thumb, a mate of mine. We were on our way to see some women. I was driving at a steady 40 mph. The road was dry and the weather and visibility good.

As you get near to Blanktown there is quite a nasty left hand bend. It is just before the Bluebell public house. As I drove into the bend I saw a green sports car approaching at a great speed. I suddenly realised that it was on my side of the road and seemed out of control. I turned towards the crown of the road to try to avoid a collision but the other car seemed to do the same as we collided. My leg was trapped in the car and I had to be released by firemen. The leg was broken quite badly and I had two operations. I have been off work for some five months now and do not know when I will be able to return. I am losing £110 per week from my job as a driver with Rods the Builders. My car was a write-off and as I have only got third party insurance I have not received a penny for it.

The accident was definitely caused by the other driver coming around the bend too fast and on the wrong side of the road. Just before the crash my passenger shouted out something about the speed of the green car. I can't remember what he said exactly though.

I have two criminal convictions. One was for assault five years ago and the other for speeding and driving without insurance three years ago.

General comments on the plaintiff's case

The facts in issue in this case can be ascertained from the pleadings. There is not a dispute that a collision occurred. Therefore no formal evidence is required to prove it.

The plaintiff has the burden of proving negligence and the defendant has a similar burden in respect of his counterclaim.

Points of evidence arising

Statement of PC Dixon

This man together with the speeding conviction provide evidence in support of the allegation of excessive speed. There is of course no direct evidence that the defendant was exceeeding the limit at the time of the accident. The plaintiff will rely on the presumption of continuance. [2.6(a)] This will also deal with the claim of the defendant that the conviction of the offence of speeding is not relevant.

The witness has died and therefore the only way in which his evidence can be introduced is by way of a written statement which will contravene the rule against hearsay. [Chapter 11] A notice of intention to adduce hearsay evidence should be served on the defendant. [13.1(a)] An example of the likely form of the notice is set out at the end of the case study.

Statements of Bert Thumb

The statement given in document 7 indicates that the oral evidence of this witness can be used to prove that the defendant was driving too fast and lost control of his car, ending up on the wrong side of the road. There are however a number of problems to deal with.

Bert will undoubtedly be cross-examined on the prior inconsistent statement made to the police (document 5). [9.1(b)] It will be for the trial judge to decide which version of events to accept. In view of the injury suffered by Bert it may be wise to obtain some medical evidence to substantiate his claim of being confused.

Bert's reference to what he said at the time of the accident to Jimmy about the speed of the green car contravenes the rule against self-made evidence. [Chapter 14]

Statement of Tony Laing

This man appears to be the only independent witness available to the plaintiff and his evidence appears to be crucial as, if believed, he will prove the major fact in issue, namely who was driving on the wrong side of the road. However, the following points are inadmissible and should not be referred to when Tony gives oral evidence:

(1) Tony's opinion as to blame. [10.1]
(2) Reference to the driving record of the defendant. [Chapter 8]

There is a reference to Tony's criminal convictions in the statement. They appear to be for offences involving dishonesty and therefore if the defence find out about them they can cross-examine on them to undermine the credibility of the witness. [9.1.(c)]

The final problem is the note underneath the statement of the witness. The plaintiff should consider serving a Civil Evidence

Act notice on the defence attaching a copy of the statement suitably edited to take into account the matters referred to above. The advantage of this will be that if the witness fails to come up to proof (as seems likely) the trial judge may well give leave for the written statement to be read out. [*14.6(a)*] An example of the likely notice and counter-notice are given at the end of the case study.

Statement of James Krug

He will of course give evidence of the speed of the defendant and the fact that the defendant was on the wrong side of the road.

He will not be allowed to comment on the fault of the other party as this is inadmissible opinion. [**10.1**]

He will not be allowed to refer to his passenger shouting out about speed as this contravenes the rule against hearsay (as it is civil case statements forming part of the res gestae are not admissible to prove the truth of their contents). [**11.1** and **14.2**]

The previous convictions of the plaintiff are not relevant to an issue in the case nor to credibility and are not therefore admissible. [*Chapters 8 and 9*]

Report of Herman Bone

Quite apart from liability there are also the issues of injury and loss to be proved. The injury will be proved by oral evidence from the plaintiff and medical evidence. The report from Mr Bone is privileged [**6.3(b)**] but normally if the report is to be relied upon at the trial the plaintiff is required to effectively waive his privilege and disclose a copy to the defendant. If the report can be agreed then it is admissible in its written form.

However if the report is not agreed then the evidential problems are greater. The report is of course based to a large extent on opinion. This is admissible if the witness is an expert [**10.2(c)**] As Mr Bone is presumably a consultant at the hospital, this should not be a problem. However, it will be necessary for Mr Bone to give oral evidence as if his written report is presented this will contravene the rule against hearsay. [**11.2**]

Damages

There are several aspects to proving the damage suffered by the plaintiff. Dealing first with the claim for loss of earnings there should not be any evidential problem as these are normally agreed. However if a figure is not agreed in good time before the trial then the following points of evidence and procedure should be borne in mind. If letters are produced to prove the relevant figures then these may contravene the rule against hearsay. **[11.2]** Therefore serve either a Civil Evidence Act notice or a notice to admit facts on the defendant [*Chapter 13*]. If a Civil Evidence Act notice is served bear in mind the requirement that any documentary evidence may have to be proved to be authentic. **[4.7]**

The only problem is likely to relate to the figure for the car. If it can be agreed that the car is a write off and that it is worth £1,050 then no evidential problem arises. However if either of these matters is in issue then any written report produced in court will contravene the rule against hearsay **[11.1]**. Again a notice to admit facts or a Civil Evidence Act notice should be served and as a last resort the engineer who prepared the report writing off and valuing the vehicle will have to be called. He will of course be giving opinion evidence but as long as he qualifies as an expert there will not be any problem **[10.2(c)]**.

Example of Civil Evidence Act notice for PC Dixon

IN THE HIGH COURT OF JUSTICE   No. OF ACTION 1989 K 1234

QUEEN'S BENCH DIVISION

BLANKTOWN DISTRICT REGISTRY

BETWEEN

JAMES KRUG Plaintiff

and

PAUL TREND Defendant

Notice of intention to adduce hearsay evidence

TAKE NOTICE that at the trial of this action the Plaintiff intends to give in evidence the statement made in the following document, namely, the statement of PC Dixon dated 23 February 1989 a copy of which is annexed hereto.

AND FURTHER TAKE NOTICE that the particulars relating to the said statement are:

(1) It was made by PC Algernon Dixon
(2) It was made to PC Dick Copper
(3) The statement was made on 23 February at 6 pm at Blanktown police station.
(4) It was made in the following circumstances namely by PC Dixon in the course of his normal duties as a police officer.

AND FURTHER TAKE NOTICE that the said PC Dixon cannot be called as a witness because he is dead.

Example of Civil Evidence Act notice for Tony Laing

IN THE HIGH COURT OF JUSTICE   NO. OF ACTION 1989 K 1234

QUEEN'S BENCH DIVISION

BLANKTOWN DISTRICT REGISTRY

BETWEEN

JAMES KRUG Plaintiff

and

PAUL TREND Defendant

Notice of intention to adduce hearsay evidence

TAKE NOTICE that at the trial of this action the Plaintiff intends to give in evidence that the statement made in the following document, namely, the statement of Tony Laing dated 2 June 1989 a copy of which is annexed hereto.

AND further take notice that the particulars relating to the said statement are:

(1) It was made by Tony Laing.
(2) It was made to Piers Lease the Plaintiff's solicitor.
(3) The statement was made on 2 June 1989 at 4 pm at 1 Chargem Chambers, Blanktown.
(4) It was made in the following circumstances namely that the Plaintiff's solicitor was given the name and address of the witness by the Plaintiff who also arranged for the witness to attend the offices of the solicitor to make a statement.

Example of counter-notice to be served on the Plaintiff's solicitors

In The High Court of Justice   No. of Action 1989 K 1234
Queen's Bench Division
Blanktown District Registry
Between

James Krug Plaintiff

and

Paul Trend Defendant

Counter-notice requiring person to be called as a witness

TAKE NOTICE that the Defendant requires you to call as a witness at the trial of this action, Tony Laing, particulars of whom are contained in your notice dated. . . .

To the plaintiff

Part IV

EVIDENCE IN THE POLICE STATION

Evidence in the Police Station

General

[In this section references to 'PACE' are to the Police and Criminal Evidence Act 1984 and references to 'the Code' are to the Codes of Practice issued under PACE, s 66.]

The implementation of the Police and Criminal Evidence Act 1984 has resulted in suspects detained by the police gaining access to legal advice in far greater numbers than was once the case. Solicitors may be called to the police station as participants in a twenty-four hour duty solicitor scheme or (as a 'named' solicitor) on the direct instructions of a client. Whatever the circumstances there is no doubt that advice must be given to the suspect whilst working under a great deal of pressure. The solicitor is in a hostile environment, sometimes during the early hours of the morning and may be dependent on the police for information about the evidence available against the suspect. It is easier to offer the best possible advice to a client if the solicitor has a clear view in his mind of the evidential implications of the various options available. This section of the book is intended to provide a summary of the most important points to bear in mind. It is largely self-contained in that with one or two necessary exceptions there are no cross-references to other parts of the book.

The Right to be Present

(1) To advise a client

A person who has been arrested and is in police custody is entitled to consult a solicitor privately at any time (PACE, s 58).

Suspects should be given a written notice to this effect by the custody officer who is also required to confirm the right orally. Access to legal advice can be delayed for no more than thirty-six hours from the time when detention of the suspect was first authorised (PACE, s 58(8) and Code C Annex B). The delay must be authorised by a superintendent who has reasonable grounds for believing that access to a solicitor will:

(a) lead to interference with, or harm to evidence connected with, a serious arrestable offence, or interference with or physical harm to other persons; or

(b) lead to the alerting of other persons suspected of having committed such an offence but not yet arrested for it; or

(c) hinder the recovery of any property obtained as a result of such an offence.

A decision to delay access must be taken with reference to the specific solicitor concerned. This makes it very difficult for the police to keep a suspect away from legal advice; even if there are reasonable grounds for believing that access to a specific solicitor *will* lead to one of the s 58 consequences there will almost certainly be another solicitor in respect of whom the same will not apply. See *R* v *Samuel* [1988] 2 All ER 135.

A serious arrestable offence is defined in PACE, s 116 and Sched 5. Some arrestable offences are always within the definition (eg murder, rape) whereas others (eg theft, robbery) may or may not be according to the circumstances of the case.

(2) During interrogation

A person who has asked for legal advice may not be interviewed or continue to be interviewed until he has received it (Code C 6.3). The exceptions to this provision are:

(a) if Code C Annex B applies (see above); or

(b) if a superintendent has reasonable grounds to believe that:

(i) delay will involve immediate risk of harm to persons or serious loss of, or damage to property; or

(ii) a solicitor has agreed to attend but waiting for his arrival would cause unreasonable delay to the process of investigation; or

(iii) a nominated solicitor cannot or will not attend and the suspect has declined to ask for another; or

(iv) the suspect has agreed in writing to the commencement of the interview.

If the suspect has consulted a solicitor and that solicitor is available at the time of the interview then he must be allowed to be present at the interview (Code C 6.5).

(3) At an identification parade

A suspect must be given a reasonable opportunity to have a solicitor or friend present at a parade and a written notice to this effect must be given to the suspect (Code D Annex A).

THE EVIDENTIAL IMPLICATIONS

(1) The suspect who is denied access to legal advice

Wrongful denial of access to a solicitor will only take on any great evidential significance if the suspect makes a confession.

A confession includes any statement wholly or partly adverse to the person who makes it and whether made in words or otherwise (PACE, s 82(1)). A confession made by an accused person is admissible in evidence against him unless it is excluded under PACE, s 76(2). This provides that where the prosecution proposes to give in evidence a confession made by an accused person, if it is represented to the court that the confession was or may have been obtained: (i) by oppression of the person who made it; or (ii) in consequence of anything said or done which was likely, in the circumstances existing at the time, to render unreliable any confession which might be made by him in consequence thereof, the court shall not allow the confession to be given in evidence against him except insofar as the prosecution proves to the court beyond reasonable doubt that the confession was not obtained as aforesaid.

According to *R v Fulling* [1987] 2 WLR 923, oppression is to be given its ordinary dictionary meaning (eg the exercise of authority or power in a burdensome, harsh or wrongful manner). The court further stated that such oppression will usually entail some impropriety on the part of the interrogator. Thus breaches of the Codes of Practice, whilst not automatically rendering a confession inadmissible, will be a relevant consideration in deciding whether there has been oppression (PACE, s 67(11)).

To render a confession unreliable the court will have to find something which has been said or done which means that there is a risk of an untrue confession having been made as a result. Breaches of the Codes of Practice will again be a relevant consideration.

The court also has a discretion under PACE, s 78 to exclude evidence if it appears that having regard to all of the circumstances, including the circumstances in which the evidence was obtained, its admission would have an adverse effect on the fairness of the proceedings. Thus if breaches of the Codes of Practice are not sufficient to show oppression or unreliability, they could still be relevant to an application under s 78.

In the light of these provisions it is important for a solicitor at the police station to remember that he is, potentially, a witness at a future trial. On being denied access to the suspect it is therefore important that the solicitor makes a detailed contemporaneous note of the reasons given by the police and of any arguments put forward to challenge the decision. If the solicitor is then called to give evidence at the criminal trial, he will be able to use the note to refresh his memory in the witness box (see *Attorney-General's Reference No 3 of 1979* (1979) 69 Cr App R 411).

(2) Advising a client who has confessed

If access to a client is initially denied, wrongfully or otherwise, he may have confessed to the police by the time that he has the benefit of legal advice. A similar position may occur if the client initially indicated that he did not want legal advice and subsequently changed his mind. What points should be borne in mind by a solicitor at the police station in these circumstances?

Problems only really arise if the client indicates that he only confessed because of improper conduct by the police. The law relating to the admissibility of confessions set out at (1) above should again be referred to. Detailed instructions as to the alleged improprieties should be taken. The solicitor should consider making an immediate complaint to the custody officer at the police station. This will be useful if the prosecution make allegations that the suspect has dreamed up his story at leisure whilst on remand awaiting trial. If the investigating officers are available, the solicitor should inform them that the suspect wishes to make a further statement denying his guilt and explaining why he confessed. Needless to say the police will not be overly keen to comply with this request. If they do not agree, the solicitor should again make a note of the time of request and the reason for refusal. At the very least this may help to reduce the weight to be attached to the confession. If the police agree to a further statement, then if the confession is admitted in evidence it would seem that the later statement should also be put to the jury or magistrates (see (4) below).

(3) Advising a client who is prepared to admit his guilt

A suspect who is prepared to admit that he has committed the offence under investigation has two options open to him. He can confess to the police or remain silent. The effect of silence is examined in detail at (4) below, but this may be the best course of action if the solicitor has ascertained from the police that the evidence against the suspect is weak or non-existent. Silence should also be considered if the police are not prepared to reveal the evidence available to them. From an ethical point of view, if the suspect indicates his guilt to his solicitor and then pleads not guilty, that solicitor should only agree to conduct the case on the basis of a submission of no case to answer. If the client wishes to give evidence in his own defence he should instruct new solicitors.

If the evidence against the suspect is strong then it can be pointed out that a confession may be advantageous from the point of view of mitigation. This is particularly so if stolen property is recovered as a result or other people are arrested. A solicitor should however be alive to the possibility of a suspect later alleging that he was pressurised by his own legal adviser into confessing. If a decision is reached with a suspect that he is prepared to make a confession statement then the circumstances in which that decision was arrived at should be carefully recorded and if possible instructions should be confirmed in writing.

(4) Advising a client who wishes to deny his guilt

There are four options open to to a suspect who denies that he has committed the offence under investigation:
—to refuse to answer questions;
—to agree to an interview on the basis that he will answer only certain questions;
—to agree to an interview without conditions;
—to make a statement.

The implications of each course of action will now be examined in turn.

(a) Silence

On arrest a suspect must be told that 'you do not have to say anything unless you wish to do so, but what you say may be given in evidence' (Code C 10.3). That caution must be repeated before questioning begins.

The suspect is effectively told that he has a right to silence. It seems to be clear from *R* v *Gilbert* (1977) 66 Cr App R 237 that a judge cannot comment adversely on the failure of a suspect to answer police questions. Furthermore in *R* v *Martin* (1983) *The Times*, 1 July, it was held that evidence of an interview in which the defendant refused to answer questions put to him or simply gave the answer 'no' was inadmissible as being of no probative value. In *W* v *Boothby* (1986) *The Times*, 4 July, a Divisional Court held that magistrates had wrongly allowed the prosecution to cross-examine a defendant as to why, after, caution, he had refused to answer police questioning.

Legal considerations aside however, it is possible that magistrates will view with some suspicion a defendant who gives an explanation for his conduct at the trial, having failed to do so when being questioned by the police. The bench will possibly infer the absence of explanation from the fact that they have not heard any evidence from the prosecution of an interview with the defendant. This could lead to the inference that the defence has been constructed at leisure after charge.

Example
Wally is charged with theft. He refuses to answer police questions. His defence at the trial is that he believed the property to be abandoned. The defence may have carried more weight if a statement to this effect had been made to the police.

There is probably less danger of this happening where the trial is by jury. Many jurors will be less familiar than magistrates with the criminal process and therefore will not be disposed to query the absence of evidence of an interview between the defendant and the police.

The decision as to whether to remain silent will rarely be an easy one. It will depend upon a number of factors:
>   (i) Have the police revealed the evidence available against the suspect?

If not then silence may be the best course of action.

Example
Fred is accused of indecently assaulting a stepchild. He tells his solicitor that he is used to indulging in innocent 'horseplay' with the child whilst she is in the bath and before she goes to bed. The police refuse to give any details of the precise allegations that the child is making.

As the child is the alleged victim of a sexual offence the judge must give a full warning to the jury of the dangers of convicting on her uncorroborated evidence (see further **3.1** in the main text). If Fred agrees to be interviewed he may inadvertently provide corroboration of the child's story.

    (ii) The state of mind of the suspect.
If he is tired or confused then it may be wise to be silent rather than to be pressurised into giving an account for his behaviour or movements that turns out to be false.

    (iii) Whether it is thought that an explanation will avoid prosecution.
    (iv) Whether it is thought that an explanation will add cogency to the defence.

In conclusion it should be pointed out that the mere fact that the suspect refuses to answer questions does not prevent the police from asking them (Code C 1B). However, prolonged questioning on this basis may help to show oppressive conduct by the police.

(*b*) *Selective silence*

If a client is unable to give a clear account of his movements or a clear explanation for his behaviour, extreme caution should be exercised before advising him to answer police questions. If the suspect is selective in answering questions it would seem from *R* v *Mann* (1972) 56 Cr App R 750, that evidence of the whole dialogue is admissible. Needless to say evidence presented in this way may look very bad to a jury or magistrates.

(*c*) *Interview*

A number of problems can arise if the suspect agrees to answer questions put by the police. Assuming that he does not actually break down and confess his guilt, will evidence of the interview be admissible? If so, to what effect?

If the interview consists solely of the suspect denying his involvement in the offence then evidence of the interview is admissible merely to show consistency of story with the testimony given at the trial (see *R* v *Pearce* (1979) 69 Cr App R 365).

Alternatively the interview may have resulted in a 'mixed' statement. This means that the suspect has made some statement against his interests but has also made denials or put forward explanations. It is clear from such cases as *R* v *Duncan* (1981) 73 Cr App R 359 that evidence of the whole of the interview is admissible to enable the jury to decide where the truth lies. This rule of evidence can on occasions, prove to be signficant.

Example
D is charged with assault contrary to the Offences against the Person Act 1861, s 20. Whilst being interviewed he admits hitting the victim and that he was angry when he did so. He goes on to claim that he was acting in self-defence. At the close of the prosecution case D's solicitor submits no case to answer on the basis that the prosecution have failed to adduce any evidence to disprove the defence (see *R* v *Hamand* (1986) 82 Cr App R 65).

If, as happened in this case, the judge rules that there is no admissible evidence of self-defence before the court, there are grounds for appeal. The statement provided to the police, which will have been given in evidence, is a mixed statement and provides evidence of self-defence for consideration by the court. Whilst in most cases the defendant will go on to give evidence at the trial the statement is significant in cases similar to *R* v *Hamand* and in those where for various reasons it is decided that it would be unwise for the defendant to go into the witness box.

(d) Statement

Offering to make a written statement to the police as opposed to taking part in an interview may have the advantage of the solicitor being able to advise and assist in its preparation. In many cases the evidential status of such a statement will be the same as evidence of an interview (see 4(c) above) However, the Court of Appeal have been prepared to uphold the decisions of some judges to refuse to admit in evidence a statement that has obviously been carefully prepared on legal advice (see *R* v *Pearce* (1979) 69 Cr App R 325 and *R* v *Newsome* (1980) 71 Cr App R 325).

(5) Attending an interview

A solicitor attends an interview to advise his client whether to answer questions, to object to improper questioning or behaviour and to record relevant matters arising. The main point to bear in mind from an evidential point of view is that if the suspect confesses in the presence of his solicitor it will make it all the more difficult to challenge its admissibility. The solicitor should therefore carefully consider the propriety of questions and the behaviour of the investigating officers and object if necessary. The police may only require a solicitor to leave an interview if his conduct is such that the investigating officer is unable properly to put questions to the suspect. It is not misconduct to seek to challenge an improper question or the manner in which it is put or to seek a pause to give the client further legal advice (Code C 6D).

During an interview which is not tape-recorded the police will keep contemporaneous notes and the suspect and the solicitor may be invited to sign them. Opinion is divided as to the desirability of doing so. Some solicitors take the view that they are not present to assist the police whilst others will sign the notes if they agree with the contents. The evidential significance of the signing of an interview record (by the suspect or the solicitor) is that it becomes an exhibit in the case for consideration by the jury (see *R* v *Todd* (1980) 72 Cr App R 299).

(6) Identification parades

If the police wish to hold an identification parade, a suspect may require advice from his solicitor as to whether he should take part. There is no obligation to participate in a parade (Code D 2.7). However a refusal may result in the police arranging for a confrontation which can be held without the consent of the suspect (Code D 2.5). A confrontation simply involves a witness being taken before the suspect and being asked 'Is this the person?'

If a parade is held, the solicitor attending must be aware of the requirements of the Code of Practice. In particular check the segregation of witnesses, the appearance of participants as against that of the suspect, the number of people in the line-up (eight required plus the suspect) and if possible the description given by the identifying witness to the police. If the initial description is nothing like the suspect what is the point of holding a parade? If any of the provisions of the code are not complied with the solicitor should object and ensure that the objections are recorded. If the parade is held in the face of objections it may be possible to have evidence of it excluded under PACE, s 78 (see *R* v *Beveridge* (1987) *The Times*, 20 January).

If a suspect is identified at a parade and maintains that the witness is mistaken, the guidelines laid down in *R* v *Turnbull* (1977) 65 Cr App R 242 will apply at the trial. It does not necessarily follow that the suspect will be convicted. This will depend upon the quality of the identification at the scene of the crime and in some cases on the presence or absence of supporting evidence (see further **3.7** of the main text).

(7) Samples

Intimate body samples may only be taken from a suspect if he consents and a superintendent has authorised it. The authorisation must be on prescribed grounds. The superintendent must have reasonable grounds.

—for suspecting the involvement of the person from whom the sample is to be taken in a serious arrestable offence; and

—for believing that the sample would tend to confirm or disprove his involvement (PACE, s 62).

An intimate body sample is defined by PACE, s 65 as a sample of blood, semen or any other tissue fluid, urine, saliva, pubic hair or a swab taken from a person's body orifice.

If consent is refused without good cause, in any proceedings against the suspect for an offence, the court may draw such inferences from the refusal as appear proper and may treat such refusal as or capable of amounting to corroboration.

Example
Roger is suspected of raping Hilda. He refuses to give a sample of semen. In the subsequent trial, the judge must give a full corroboration warning to the jury in respect of Hilda's evidence (see further **3.1** in the main text). If the jury are looking for corroboration then Roger's refusal to give a sample can provide it.

Non-intimate samples (eg hair other than pubic hair) may only be taken with the consent of the suspect unless a superintendent authorises it on prescribed grounds. These grounds are the same as those upon which authority for an intimate sample can be given. There is no provision in PACE as to corroboration if the suspect refuses to give a sample (which he is at liberty to do if the superintendent does not give authority). However, the pre-PACE case of *R* v *Smith* (1985) 81 Cr App R 286, suggests that such refusal is capable of amounting to corroboration.

Index